D0952451

The BEST PEOPLE

*Trump's Cabinet and the
Siege on Washington*

ALEXANDER NAZARYAN

hachette
BOOKS

NEW YORK   BOSTON

Hachette Books
Hachette Book Group
1290 Avenue of the Americas
New York, NY 10104
hachettebookgroup.com
twitter.com/hachettebooks

First Edition: June 2019

Hachette Books is a division of Hachette Book Group, Inc.

The Hachette Books name and logo are trademarks of Hachette Book Group, Inc.

The publisher is not responsible for websites (or their content) that are not owned by the
publisher.

The Hachette Speakers Bureau provides a wide range of authors for speaking events. To
find out more, go to www.hachettespeakersbureau.com or call (866) 376-6591.

Library of Congress Cataloging-in-Publication Data has been applied for.
Library of Congress Control Number: 2019930810

ISBNs: 978-0-316-42143-0 (hardcover), 978-0-316-42142-3 (ebook)

Printed in the United States of America

LSC-C

10 9 8 7 6 5 4 3 2 1

To Donald J. Trump,
for infuriating Americans
to the point of caring
for America once again.

You know, you don't sleep quite so well anymore when you know some of the people going to Washington.
—Lucian W. Pye, political scientist at the Massachusetts Institute of Technology, on the John F. Kennedy administration

Why should I mourn
The vanished power of the usual reign?
—T. S. Eliot, "Ash Wednesday"

CONTENTS

PROLOGUE: "GET THE HELL OUT OF HERE NOW"

The White House
February 19, 2019

He loved the job. He was very clear about that. He said it enough times that I started to entertain the notion that he was halfway serious. Certainly, that would be news to the pundits who said he'd rather be golfing in South Florida than trying to tame North Korea. And to the Democrats who figured that impeachment would be a favor, since he seemed as thrilled by his presidency as they were. It was not so, he said. "Those are just the haters and losers," explained President Donald J. Trump with that special Queens charm of his, when we met in the Oval Office to discuss the first two years of his administration. "I love it. I enjoy it."

But he didn't have to do it, see? He'd had options, had them still. "They offered me everything to not run and to do *The Apprentice*," he said later, referencing the television program that was at least partly responsible for the fact that Trump was now sitting where John F. Kennedy and Ronald Reagan once sat. "If you check the ratings on *The Apprentice*," he said some time after that, "through the roof. Big hit."

He was indignant, though this too bore a touch of his New York shtick, the elaborate act that was Trump. Not that the indignation was feigned. He didn't need to explain himself to this journalist he didn't know, for a book he would never read. "I'd be doing it right now," he said of *The Apprentice*, "but I like this better."

To show how much he loved the job, and to supply evidence of the many accomplishments that love had yielded, Trump summoned his executive assistant Madeleine Westerhout, asking her to bring him a list of his administration's achievements. "In the first two years, this administration has done more than any other administration in the history of our country," Trump said with typical immodesty as he sat beneath a portrait of Abraham Lincoln.

Westerhout came into the Oval Office—where I was sitting with Trump, press secretary Sarah Huckabee Sanders and senior adviser Kellyanne Conway—setting some papers on the edge of the Resolute Desk, whose surface was otherwise almost complete bare. Trump examined the papers, then showed them to me. The glossy sheets were filled with what was obviously an East Asian script. Trump explained that this was a letter from North Korean leader Kim Jong Un, with whom the president was about to hold a second summit in Vietnam.

"That's actually dated," the president said of the letter. "It's pretty amazing."

This wasn't the right evidence, but for him it was evidence all the same, in this case that he would make peace where others would stumble ineptly into nuclear cataclysm. "You would have been at war. If I didn't get elected, you'd be at war right now with North Korea," he told me. "If 'Crooked Hillary' were President right now, you'd be fighting. She would be sleeping and you would be fighting a war. She'd be upstairs sleeping, resting, to gain her strength for a two-hour day."

He still called her that, *Crooked Hillary.* The election was now more than two years ago and still he called her that. Because the election was not really over for him, would never be over. It was the victory beyond all victories, a triumph not only over Clinton but something much grander than that, as far as he and his supporters were concerned. The forces aligned against him on the morning of November 8, 2016, were no weaker as we sat talking in the Oval Office on February 19, 2019.

If anything, they were stronger, precisely because he *was* in the Oval Office, despite predictions that he would not last a single full year as president.

Finally, the correct list was brought, three thick pages of bullet points titled "TRUMP ADMINISTRATION ACCOMPLISHMENTS." Those accomplishments included the creation of 5.3 million jobs and other broadly auspicious economic indicators. Some of those indicators had started trending upward during the Obama presidency, but that was neither here nor there (certainly, it wasn't on the list). There were other claims on the list, like the one about declining drug prices in 2018, that have been adjudicated to be untrue. Others, like withdrawal from the "job-killing" Paris climate accords and cancelling the "illegal" Clean Power Plan, may have been accomplishments to Trump's base. To many others, these were terrible mistakes.

He also boasted about opening the Arctic National Wildlife Refuge oil drilling, which he did by attaching a rider to the 2017 tax bill and in effect sneaking the measure through Congress. "Nobody could get it," Trump boasted. "I got it." And he did so despite "the environmental problems" being much worse than they had been in the past. *Wait a fucking second:* Had the president just admitted, however inadvertently, that global warming was real? It certainly seemed that way: one small step for mankind, one giant step for Donald Trump.

Trump knew that I was interested in his cabinet, in the men and women he had hired to execute his agenda. I had quite a bit of skepticism about that agenda, though there were parts of Trump's program—reviving manufacturing, improving infrastructure—that would have benefited all Americans, were he only able to make them reality. So far, they remained campaign promises, the stuff of political fiction.

Trump's cabinet had instead undertaken a program that vacillated between maliciousness and self-interest. Sometimes this was done with license from Trump, sometimes without. In either case, it often ran counter to the populism that had elevated Trump above his Republican competitors and then, in the general election, over Clinton.

For the best people, there was another list. The president consulted it. He liked what he saw.

Secretary of State Mike Pompeo: "has been fantastic."

Transportation Secretary Elaine Chao: "has been great."

Labor Secretary Alex Acosta: "has been great."

Housing and Urban Development Secretary Ben Carson: "has done a very good job."

Health and Human Services Secretary Alex Azar: "fantastic."

Energy Secretary Rick Perry: "has been great."

Agriculture Secretary Sonny Perdue: "he's been great."

Attorney General William Barr: "will be…really outstanding."

White House chief of staff Mick Mulvaney: "People are liking him a lot. I think he's doing a good job. I'm very happy with him."

Trump did allow that there been "some clinkers," by which he presumably meant people like Environmental Protection Agency administrator Scott Pruitt and HHS head Tom Price, both of whom left the administration in disgrace, as did several other of their colleagues.

"But that's okay," he said of hiring men and women who turned out to be less than they seemed and less than he'd hoped. "Who doesn't?" True enough. But there's a difference between a clinker and a thief, a man who is no good at his job and a man who sets out to do that job poorly. The total number of investigations into unethical or improper conduct by members of the Trump cabinet easily tops fifty. Clinkers don't usually require so much scrutiny.

"It's very difficult for people," Trump said, as if feeling the need to apologize for some of the people who work or once worked for him (not that the president ever actually apologizes). "Some people can't take it. As much as they want to, they can't take it." Conversely, some thought that Trump's people have done rather too much taking it, not nearly enough giving of the kind public service usually demands.

For the most part, Trump stayed in salesman's mode during our conversation. He is always selling, even if we have already bought—however reluctantly and regretfully—the thing he has been hawking, even if it is obviously improbable that he believes a pompous grifter like Ben Carson will help return the nation to greatness.

"There are those that say we have one of the finest cabinets," Trump claimed. That is not a commonly held view. In fact, I can't think of anyone even halfway credible who has said anything approaching that. Even some of Trump's most ardent supporters have expressed dismay at the people he has hired, which is why it fell to Fox News prime time anchor Laura Ingraham to push Trump to fire Pruitt. And as much as his detractors despise Trump, they despise the people he has brought into his administration even more.

"They're really talented people," Trump said, but he did not seem to believe it. He later did acknowledge that "some of them got burned out." That seemed closer to the truth, if not quite all the way there.

It wasn't supposed to be this way. During the presidential campaign, Trump had promised to hire people utterly free of self-interest, people fully committed to his populist agenda. People for whom self-dealing and personal enrichment would be utterly anathema because they were so utterly committed to carrying out the populist vision of Trump and his campaign manager Steve Bannon.

Trump admitted that, during the presidential transition, he allowed himself to be influenced by outside groups, whether the Heritage Foundation or energy magnate Robert E. Murray. "I wouldn't say that I agreed with all of the people," he told me, "but I let them make their decision. In some cases, I was right." As for the other cases? Well, he left that unsaid.

Once he got into office, Trump quickly signed a stern ethics order that seemed to close the notorious revolving door that allowed people to move freely between working for the federal government and lobbying the federal government on behalf of private interests. But he just as quickly granted waivers that allowed political appointees to violate the rules that Trump had just put in place. Promising to drain the swamp, he merely stirred its murky surface.

When I confronted him with this fact, Trump bristled. "We need certain people to run the country well, at the top level," he argued. We have granted waivers. How often do we grant waivers? Have you seen? Not too much, right?" At the same time, he seemed clearly discomfited by the fact that where Trump saw a political movement, others saw nothing but a means for profit. He did not know, for example, that Ryan Zinke, the Interior secretary he had fired the previous December, had joined Turnberry Solutions, a Capitol Hill lobbying firm started by Corey Lewandowski, Trump's first campaign manager.

"I didn't know that Zinke…" Trump began.

In fact, Trump didn't know at all about the existence of Turnberry Solutions. "That's an interesting name," he said sharply. The name was interesting because Turnberry was also the name of a Trump-owned golf course in Scotland. Nobody who wanted to exert influence in Washington would have missed the association. "That's amazing," the president said, though his amazement was plainly not of the happy variety.

Trump tried to rationalize how Zinke becoming a lobbyist did not fly in the face of the promises he had made as a candidate. "I guess you can't stop people from going out and doing what they do," the president said. "In some cases, they've been here from day one, when people said I didn't have much of a chance. Then they work for years. Then all of a sudden they're in a position where people are calling them because they think they're geniuses and they want them to work for them. That's been going on from George Washington until the present, let's face it. That's what happens."

Zinke wasn't the only one. Five days before we spoke, ProPublica had found that there were 33 former Trump administration officials who were either lobbying the federal government or were more or less doing the work of a lobbyist without actually registering as such. And it was true that lobbying was as old as the republic itself, but had not Trump's promise been that his administration would be unlikely any other? He wanted to claim that he was exceptional, except for those instances when it suited him to claim that he was just like his predecessors.

There was also the matter of more than one hundred key administration positions that remained unfilled. These needed Senate confirmation, and though some nominees have withdrawn, many of those positions never had a nominee in the first place, allowing some agencies and departmental offices to languish like unwatered plants.

Trump contradicted this, unsurprisingly. "I have 10 people for every job," he added. "The hard part is choosing, because I have great people."

Everything was great in Trumpland, especially Trump himself. America was great again, as were its constituent parts: "the hottest economy ever," "a lot of great trade," a "great relationship" with Kim of North Korea, "great success" in fighting the Islamic State stemming from Trump's visit to Iraq. "I think I'm doing great service for the country," Trump said. There was the matter of "the Russian bullshit witch hunt," but as Trump said, "I think we're doing nicely on that one, too." He did not explain what was nice about the way he had handled the investigation by special counsel Robert S. Mueller III, who some thought was going to bring down the Trump administration.

Then it was time to go. Trump complained about the books that had been written about him, which he said were uniformly unfair, though he also did not appear to have read any of them. He called Michael Wolff "a dopey guy," referring to the journalist's book as "*Sound and Fury*," apparently conflating Wolff's book, *Fire and Fury*, with a William Faulkner novel.

Trump also became upset at senior adviser Kellyanne Conway, who was sitting in on the meeting, for apparently keeping *Washington Post* associate editor Bob Woodward from interviewing the president for his own book, *Fear,* which was also critical of Trump. "Kellyanne didn't tell me he asked ten times for a meeting. I wish she did," he said bitterly of Conway. "I'm sure it would have been a little bit of a different book." This obviously bothered him. "You should have told me," he went on. "Honestly, you should have told me."

Conway just sat there, taking it as she has doubtlessly taken it from the boss many times before. You couldn't last in this administration unless you were willing to take it daily, take it with a smile and a "yessir," take it even while knowing that much of the country loathed you, considered you complicit in one of the great political crimes in American history. And you would take it in this way that Conway was taking it now only if you truly believed in the man who was giving it, in his vision for the country. Unless, of course, there was something in it for you. There was that, too, sometimes.

It was now late afternoon, a winter dusk descending on Washington. On Capitol Hill, members of Congress were debating Trump's declaration of an emergency at the border with Mexico, and outside the gates of the White House, protesters were denouncing the same, mingling with religious pamphleteers and tourists in Make America Great Again hats. On any given day, you could stand out on Pennsylvania Avenue and watch the gorgeous squalor that was American democracy at work. If you stood there long enough, you might be converted into a Jehovah's Witness, or a member of the anti-Trump resistance, but would you be any closer to understanding what all of it meant, what *any of it* meant?

These were questions for another time. I rose to go.

"Get the hell out of here, now," the president told me. "All right. Good. Have a good time."

PREFACE: THE END
OF SOMETHING

What a happy night it was supposed to be for the people who gathered at the mansion in Massachusetts Avenue Heights on November 8, 2016. They were immensely accomplished, and they had gathered to celebrate the handing-over of the federal government to people just as accomplished as they, people who harbored the same convictions, people who were colleagues and friends, people who were going to serve President Clinton as ably as the men and women now congregating at the elegant Georgian manor in Northwest Washington had served President Obama.

Few suspected they were about to witness the end of something, and the beginning of something else, something they could have scarcely imagined only hours before. That the night would attain a mythic quality, that people would talk about where they were the way an earlier generation remembered the precise details of learning that Kennedy had been shot.

That day in November had transformed the nation. And so would this one.

The Trump people knew, or so they would later claim. Speaking almost exactly two years after the election, someone who had been with Trump from the very start said he awoke that Tuesday without any doubt about who the victor would be. He said he'd known as far back as August 2015, when Trump held a rally in Mobile, Alabama. The campaign initially estimated that a couple thousand might show. Instead, they got thirty thousand.

As for the polls? The Trump veteran took the suggestion with something like disgust. Fuck the polls. That was precisely what the establishment had never understood, what the prattling pundits on cable news failed to grasp. This was never about the polls.

Relatively early in the evening, a few White House staffers decided to leave 1600 Pennsylvania Avenue and troop up to the party in Massachusetts Avenue Heights, a small neighborhood of large homes sitting beneath the three soaring towers of the National Cathedral.

The host of this affair was Penny S. Pritzker, the commerce secretary. Pritzker was not an ordinary government official: Ordinary government officials, even high-ranking ones, did not buy 1929 mansions for $7.95 million. A member of the Chicago family that founded the hotel company Hyatt, she had gone to Stanford and Harvard, becoming an accomplished entrepreneur in her own right. In 2008, she served as Obama's campaign finance chair. By the time he selected her as his commerce secretary in the summer of 2013, she was worth close to $2 billion.

Obama staffers—young, well educated, diverse—were known to like a party, and they had enlivened a city that had grown dull during the eight years of the George W. Bush presidency. The party at Penny Pritzker's house was not, however, a beer-fueled affair of the kind one might have found that evening in an Adams Morgan row house. This was instead a sumptuous, catered evening, with a buffet dinner and large-screen televisions set up in every room to show the results of the presidential election.

Several top Obama administration officials were present: Susan E. Rice, the national security advisor who had struggled to formulate the administration's response to the killing of four Americans at the consulate in Benghazi, Libya; Treasury Secretary Jacob J. Lew, who had continued the work of his predecessor Timothy F. Geithner in keeping the nation from backsliding into financial calamity; Sally Jewell, the secretary of the interior, one of several cabinet members to advance the administration's focus on global warming; W. Neil Eggleston, a veteran of Democratic politics who was finishing a term as White House counsel; Michael Froman, the U.S. trade representative, who'd recently helped negotiate the Trans-Pacific Partnership.

The men and women who had come to mark the night with Pritzker, in other words, were custodians of the order Obama had ushered in. That order was not always popular, even among some liberal Democrats, but it was based on empirical observations conducted by people who were certain that reason and data would triumph over feeling and fear. Among these officials, there was little argument: The future was going to be neoliberal, technocratic, inclusive, and diverse. The GOP was dying, the conservative movement stuck in a rut roughly corresponding to the length of the George W. Bush administration. All this was obvious, at least to the columnists and commentators who repeated it incessantly in late October and early November, in the days leading up to the presidential election.

The several people who came from the White House reported that Obama was upbeat about the prospects for Clinton, whom he defeated in 2008 and endorsed in 2016. Later, he would voice public complaint about how Clinton ran her campaign, which employed data scientists who could tailor an appeal precisely to one Cleveland suburb or another, a campaign that could summon Jay-Z or Bruce Springsteen to headline rallies. But the Clinton campaign's impressive mechanics disguised the fact that this was a machine. It lacked heart. It knew everything about the voters in suburban Cleveland, but it could not tell those voters a story they wanted or needed to hear.

None of this was apparent yet, in the early evening of November 8, or at least not as apparent as it would become in the days and months to come.

The first signs of trouble came around 10:39 p.m., when Ohio was called for Trump. It wasn't close, either, with Trump up by nearly nine percentage points. "It is remarkable, what we're seeing here," Jake Tapper said on CNN. Tapper observed that in the reliably Democratic suburbs of Philadelphia where he had been raised, the margins for Clinton were also not as high as they should have been. Something was amiss.

And there it was, the thing they feared, now upon them. Florida went to Trump, as did North Carolina. Michigan should not have gone, but there it went, right along with Pennsylvania. At 2:30 a.m., Trump won Wisconsin. It was all over but the shouting. And there would be plenty of shouting to come.

At Penny Pritzker's house in Washington, a few senior commerce officials gathered in a room once it was clear that Trump was going to win. These officials routinely made decisions of consequence, and there would be time later to wonder if some of those decisions had led to the night's result. For now, one question haunted them, demanding an immediate answer: "What do we say to our career professionals the next day?"

Only the upper ranks of the federal government were filled by political appointees. Of approximately two million jobs in the federal government, only four thousand were appointed positions. Most "politicals," as they were known in Washington, expected to be out of a job when a new president came into office, even if that president was of the same party as her predecessor. Experts in their fields who had enjoyed at least some proximity to state power, they were likely to find easy work on Wall Street or K Street. Some got teaching jobs. A few got book deals. Most would be fine.

For career employees of the federal government, Trump's victory was ominous not just politically but professionally. Often depicted as gray pixels in a featureless bureaucracy, these employees included paleontologists working for the Department of the Interior, civil rights lawyers at the Department of Education, financial investigators at the Department of the Treasury unraveling transnational money-laundering schemes. Throughout the 2016 campaign, Trump had explicitly and implicitly threatened their jobs, suggesting that he might get rid of certain agencies altogether. He had showed open contempt for government work, for government workers, and for the notion of government itself. He was coming not to save Washington, but to destroy it.

INTRODUCTION: THE BEST PEOPLE

They were the best people, the finest in the land, tasked with returning the nation to greatness. It was June 2017, and for the first time, they sat in a room together, the principals around a table, some others in chairs along the walls. And at center table sat the man who brought them together, the general who had recruited this elite unit, the man who had introduced the very idea that the nation had fallen from greatness and needed him to return it to glory, the forty-fifth president of the United States, Donald J. Trump.

By and large, these best people were also new people as far as the public sector was concerned. In this, they were just like the man who selected them and who himself had performed no public service until taking the oath of the presidency five months before. There was the producer of films that included *Batman v Superman: Dawn of Justice*. There was a former Navy SEAL who tried to take credit for the raid that killed Osama bin Laden. There was also, in that crowded room, a former second baseman for the University of Kentucky baseball team. Soon, he would be the target of a dozen investigations into his penchant for first-class flights, top-notch restaurants, and other benefits not generally available to government bureaucrats, or to middling second basemen.

But these were not regular government bureaucrats, as the confirmation hearings of the previous winter had made so vividly clear. There was a fundamentalist from Michigan who, during her Senate hearing, warned about "potential grizzlies" when asked about arming school staff. There was a former U.S. senator from Alabama who had been deemed too extreme for the federal bench during the Reagan administration. Now, he was the top law enforcement officer in the land, even as he struggled to say just how many times he had met with the Russian ambassador when he was Trump's campaign surrogate, or why he needed to meet with the Russian ambassador at all.

In the chairs along the wall sat other members of the retinue Trump had assembled to serve as his White House advisers. There was the potentially sociopathic former contestant from *The Apprentice*, and there was the right-wing media impresario who owned enough of the *Seinfeld* back catalog to have become very rich, who had a thing for obscure philosophers, and who did not like to wear ties, which men in the White House were expected to do. Then again, this was going to be a White House outside the bounds of the expected and not just when it came to neckwear.

There was a thirty-six-year-old of vague accomplishment and faltering voice whose father had paid $2.5 million to help get him into Harvard, despite an academic record any admissions counselor would have regarded as significantly beneath the Ivy League. That father went to prison on a variety of tax-related charges, one of which involved him covertly taping his brother-in-law's encounter with a prostitute.

It was June 12, 2017, and President Trump was holding his first full cabinet meeting, in the same Cabinet Room of the White House where Franklin D. Roosevelt convened his "war cabinet" in the 1940s. Here, John F. Kennedy and his advisers searched with increasing desperation for ways to defuse a nuclear standoff with the Soviet Union during the Cuban Missile Crisis and, half a decade later, Lyndon B. Johnson tried and failed to contain the escalating war in Vietnam.

And now it was Trump's turn to wage his own battles, whether against Mexican gangs, Middle Eastern terrorists, or liberals from San Francisco.

No concrete code dictated who belonged in that room. "The cabinet itself is not defined in statute," explained Andrew Rudalevige, a presidential historian at Bowdoin College in Maine. "It's really at the discretion of the president." At its most basic, it was the fifteen heads of the executive departments. Then there were cabinet-level positions like director of national intelligence and ambassador to the United Nations, as well as high-ranking assistants to the president, the top layer of advisers within the White House itself who formed a crucial membrane between the chief executive and the rest of the executive branch.

Unlike other aspects of the American system of government—the Congress, for example, to which sixty-five chapters were devoted in the U.S. Code of Laws—the cabinet was not narrowly circumscribed by settled law, tending to evolve (or devolve) with each new administration. The vagaries of who belonged in a presidential cabinet, and what the responsibilities of cabinet members were, could sometimes play to presidents' strengths. Just as often, the uncertainty played to their weaknesses.

The first cabinet meeting was convened on February 25, 1793, by the first president, George Washington, who desired input on "interesting questions of national importance." Those questions were put to only four cabinet members, two of whom were Thomas Jefferson and Alexander Hamilton. Departments were added as the federal government's role in everyday life grew. The most recent addition came in 2002, with the advent of the Department of Homeland Security. There were subtractions, too, like that of the postmaster general, who left the cabinet after Richard M. Nixon reorganized the nation's postal operations in 1970.

Sitting in the Cabinet Room of the White House on that June

afternoon in 2017, at a table that had been a gift from Nixon to the U.S. government in 1970, Trump looked pleased, even as his approval rating earlier that month had slipped to a precarious 34 percent. Those dismal polling numbers made him the least popular president in modern American history at this point in his term, confirmation to his critics that he was simply incapable of holding the most challenging elective office in the world. To supporters, however, he was still learning, and this first cabinet meeting was a sign of progress, a much-needed team huddle.

"This is our first cabinet meeting with the entire cabinet present," Trump said in the flat monotone he tended to reserve for prepared remarks, which he clearly disliked delivering. "The confirmation process has been record-setting long—and I mean record-setting long—with some of the finest people in our country being delayed and delayed and delayed." He blamed those delays on Senate Democrats, whom he called "the obstructionists."

Trump also complained that "the ethics committee" had become "very difficult to deal with," by which he meant the Office of Government Ethics, a federal agency that reviewed financial disclosures for potential conflicts of interest. Conflicts of interest were practically a job requirement in this administration. Jared Kushner, the senior White House adviser, presidential son-in-law, and Harvard alumnus, would eventually update his financial disclosures more than forty times, so knotted were his family's real estate dealings with entanglements in Qatar and Israel, not to mention in Russia and China.

Wilbur L. Ross Jr., the crusty corporate raider who had been named commerce secretary, neglected to mention that he had investments in a Russian shipping company with ties to Russian neo-czar Vladimir V. Putin. Treasury Secretary Steven T. Mnuchin, he of *Batman v Superman* fame, somehow left off $95 million worth of real estate. Tom Price had traded medical stock even when, as a member of Congress, he'd pushed for legislation that would benefit the companies in question. Now he was the secretary of the Department of Health and Human Services. That controversy, like most others involving Trump's cabinet, had proved inconsequential during Price's confirmation process. Not only had the Republicans won the White House the previous November, but they'd maintained their majority in the Senate. That ensured safe passage for Trump's nominees, relegating the Democrats to a bound-and-gagged minority that watched helplessly as the man responsible for *Get Hard* assumed the office once occupied by Hamilton.

But on that humid day in Washington, D.C., all the struggles of the previous months could be set aside, however fleetingly. Here was reason to rejoice, at least as far as the man responsible for that odd and improbable conclave was concerned. "There's an incredible, talented group of people in this room: generals, governors, congressmen, entrepreneurs, business leaders, and many, many others," Trump said in the crowded Cabinet Room, as cameras clicked away like crickets on a summer night. He had personally chosen all of them, he said, to achieve a "very simple, but very beautiful, goal: serving and defending our beloved nation."

Eight years before, President Barack Obama had opened his first cabinet meeting by soberly discussing the ramifications of the financial crisis, which he had inherited from President George W. Bush. As was custom, the secretary of state was seated to his right (each cabinet member had an assigned seat at the table). In that case, it was Hillary Clinton. For the portion of the meeting that was open to the press, Obama spoke in the clipped, confident tone that would be a hallmark of his public persona. He asked his cabinet chiefs to find $100 million in savings. He knew it would not be much, given the hundreds of billions of dollars involved in the response to the Great Recession. Still, it would show that the federal government was a responsible steward of taxpayer money, not the profligate spender some conservatives claimed it was. Obama's remarks lasted about six minutes. Then the cameras went away.

Trump's first cabinet meeting had a distinctly different feel, something closer to nervous children gathering together on their first night at sleepaway camp, aware that they are under enormous scrutiny, desperate to make themselves liked.

Vice President Mike Pence went first. "It is just the greatest privilege of my life" to serve in the Trump administration, said the former governor of Indiana. Pence added that the women and men seated around the table were "bringing real change, real prosperity, real strength back to our nation," echoing the central (and errant) Trump conviction that Obama had left him with an ailing economy, a country in the grips of malaise.

So they went around the table, saying little about what they planned to do, revealing much about the devotion with which they would treat Trump, who had improbably won the presidency and, in doing so, had suddenly elevated these backbenchers of public and private life to powerful posts they could have scarcely imagined back when it seemed that a Clinton rout was imminent.

"There was no prep for this or advanced warning," later confided one of the department chiefs seated at that table. "So I was just watching with amazement as people answered like they did, trying to figure out if this was [as] unusual as I thought it was."

After Pence, Attorney General Jeff Sessions spoke about the rising crime rate, even though violent crime was actually on a decades-long downward trajectory, with very minor upticks in the recent past. Sessions had been the first senator to endorse Trump, back when that chamber was uniformly skeptical of the Manhattan billionaire. Now he had the job he long coveted, only it would later come with unimaginable humiliation, most of it orchestrated by the man who hired him, a needy man who demanded loyalty but gave no loyalty in return.

The cabinet members who followed strove to outdo each other in their groveling. R. Alexander Acosta, the labor secretary, said he was "deeply honored" to serve Trump. It was a "great honor" for Ben Carson, who headed Housing and Urban Development, and who had only recently said that he did not think he had the capacity to lead a federal department. Earlier, during the Republican presidential primary, when Carson was an unlikely front-runner, Trump had impugned the former neurosurgeon's honesty and even compared him to a child molester. That slight was forgotten, at least for now.

Rick Perry, the energy secretary, was merely "honored" to be part of Trump's team, but he made sure to laud Trump because he was "not going to be held hostage to some executive order that was ill thought out," a reference to the Paris accords on climate change, which Trump had recently announced the United States would be leaving.

"I can't thank you enough for the privileges you've given me and the leadership that you've shown," said Price, the new Health and Human Services secretary, who as a Georgia congressman had been an avid assailant of the Affordable Care Act, President Obama's signature achievement. Now, five months into full Republican control of Washington, efforts to repeal the health law were as inauspicious as they had ever been, because neither Trump nor Price had shown the ability to persuade recalcitrant legislators or to convince a skeptical public.

Ryan Zinke, the interior secretary, immediately referenced his service in the Navy SEALs—"Mr. President, as your SEAL on your staff..."—just as he had done during his political rise in Montana some years before. He was chastised back then by members of the military for unseemly self-promotion. Luckily, he found a presidential administration where self-promotion was a virtue.

"I want to congratulate you on the men and women you've placed around this table," said Sonny Perdue, the new head of the

Department of Agriculture. "This is the team you've assembled that's working hand in glove with—for—the men and women of America, and I want to, I want to thank you for that. These are great team members and we're on your team," continued Perdue, who as governor of Georgia had signed a tax bill that seemed to benefit him personally and once supported a proposal to return Confederate iconography to the state flag. Now he was in the White House.

The cabinet itself was very much unusual, though not quite for its record of altruism or public service. It was the whitest in generations, with one African American and one Hispanic. It was overwhelming male, and overwhelmingly old, with an average age exceeding sixty. Trump had never shown much curiosity about the world outside Trump Tower, and the people he surrounded himself with in Washington were a reflection of his self-centered outlook: white men grown thick around the waist with the comforts of middle age, rich but not especially cultured, married but trailed by divorce. The sport of the Obama administration had been basketball. Trump guys played golf.

Many of them were not just rich, but quite a bit richer than Trump. Shoddy financial reporting by Trump's cabinet made its collective wealth difficult to estimate, but some credible news outlets said the aggregate number was as high as $4.5 billion. Some of these riches were inherited, as in the case of Betsy DeVos, the education secretary, whose father had built an auto-parts fortune in Michigan. But some were also ill-gotten gains. During the financial crisis of 2008, Mnuchin's bank, OneWest, relentlessly pursued homeowners delinquent on their mortgage payments. This earned him the nickname "Foreclosure King."

Among the richest of Trump's cabinet members was Wilbur Ross, who like Trump was given to inflating his wealth. "Mr. President, thank you for the opportunity to help fix the trade deficit and other things," said the new chief of the Commerce Department. He added that "other countries are gradually getting used" to the fact that "the free rides are somewhat over with." *Somewhat?* The month before, he had managed a deal with China involving chicken and beef. It would remain his greatest accomplishment.

So it went for eleven minutes, a gathering that was the equivalent of cotton candy: high in sugar, light on substance. The high (or low) point was Chief of Staff Reince Priebus telling Trump, "On behalf of the entire senior staff around you, Mr. President, we thank you for the opportunity and the blessing that you've given us to serve your agenda and the American people."

Priebus was the former Republican National Committee chairman who had been installed in the West Wing to pacify mainstream Republicans and ensure that Trump didn't stray too far from party dogma. He was an emissary from the very establishment Trump had come to slay. And even as he sat there in the Cabinet Room, as he praised the president, everyone in Washington knew what a miserable time he was having in the White House, what a nightmare the babysitting gig at 1600 Pennsylvania Avenue was turning out to be.

By the time Trump held another cabinet meeting on December 20, several of the best people who had gathered in that room six months earlier were already gone. Bannon would be forced to leave by Priebus's replacement, General John F. Kelly, who was himself constantly fighting for influence in a West Wing that both badly needed a military discipline like his and desperately resisted it. Shortly after that, Tom Price became the first departmental chief to resign, after his penchant for travel on private and government jets came under unrelenting scrutiny.

More than a half dozen other of the best people were under investigation for ethical lapses. Scott Pruitt alone would face some sixteen different inquiries, from a variety of different agencies, including his own. Ryan Zinke, by one count, was the subject of eighteen. The previously anonymous figure of the agency inspector general suddenly became a Washington heroic archetype to some, a defender of American democracy whose secret weapon was the annotated and appendicised report.

Trump's supporters tried to dismiss these controversies, sometimes suggesting they were part of a "Deep State" plan to undermine the president. But this was becoming increasingly hard to do, especially since many of Trump's best people were just as eager for publicity as he was. Pruitt provided his most disastrous interview, in which he lied about giving raises to political appointees, with the most friendly outlet imaginable: Fox News. His minders in the White House had advised him against it, but Pruitt refused to listen. Watching him, they knew he was done.

This was all a remarkable turn for a president who pitched himself to the American people as a singularly skilled chief executive, one with an uncanny ability to spot and cultivate talent. He promised to untether the federal government from the bureaucrats and their crusted-over bureaucracy, to run it as profitably and efficiently as he did his family business, the Trump Organization. Trump was precisely as competent and successful as he said he was, at least according to many of his supporters.

Reality told a different story. As shocked by his election night win as many of his most strident foes, Trump had done little to prepare for becoming the leader of an enterprise that employed two million people, owned or leased 361,000 buildings and operated on a $4 trillion budget. At times, he did not seem especially interested in learning.

Was the president erratic? A person who spent time with him daily had to think about that for a while. No, that was too strong, he finally concluded. But Trump was undisciplined, he said, and he was unpredictable, and he would take the federal government where he wanted it to go. He would visit the Bastille Day procession in Paris and decide that Washington, too, must have a military parade, that it was outrageous that France showed off its military might but the

United States did not. The issue of whether to hold a military parade, which no one had been seriously considering, became a matter of national debate. Eventually, the Pentagon concluded that a military parade would incur the obscene expense of $92 million. Trump raged, blamed Washington's mayor for her supposed lack of enthusiasm. Then he, too, dropped the issue, and just like that the matter of a military parade, which had occupied the nation for months, was entirely forgotten.

Trump allowed various factions—wealthy donors, establishment Republicans, his friends at Fox News, the conservative Heritage Foundation—to dictate who was going to carry out the various imperatives he so expertly packaged into slogans during the presidential contest. Foremost among these was his promise to "drain the swamp" that was Washington, D.C., a cesspool of former politicians and congressional aides who'd turned to the far more lucrative business of lobbying, the lawyers who enabled it, and the members of the media who eagerly accepted free drinks from them. Republicans desperate to intellectualize Trump's appeal arrived at the image of an enthralling iconoclast who would do to Washington's permanent class what Jesus Christ had done to the money changers in the temple.

Now, more than halfway through Trump's term, it is clear that this promise has remained unrealized. He said he would usher in a political revolution; what we have instead is a national twilight in which lurid things thrive. The swamp runneth over, and the federal government is more dysfunctional than it has ever been. Where the government does still work, it works principally because it has been left alone.

What follows is a story of how a presidential campaign that promised nothing short of radical transformation of the American political system succumbed so frequently to its own worst impulses. The administration's staunchest critics will allege that Trump did so intentionally. And in some cases, perhaps that is true. But more often than not, inattention was at work, a collective carelessness that allowed the likes of Pruitt and Zinke to turn the Trump administration into a low-class orgy of first-class kleptocrats.

Some in the White House began to understand, by mid-2017, that they had not paid enough attention to the executive branch outside the campus of the White House and the Eisenhower Executive Office Building, where the president's top advisers worked behind a black iron fence (West Wingers referred to "the building," as opposed to "the campus," a pointed reminder that they worked in the White House itself). There were earnest efforts to curb the abuses, and though these were made in earnest, they were also delinquent.

This administration has included some thoroughly decent, highly capable people, including Secretary of Defense General James N. Mattis, who resigned in December 2018, and U.S. Ambassador to the United Nations Nikki R. Haley, who announced two months before Mattis that she was leaving. Mike Pompeo has been a steady, relatively reassuring presence as the secretary of state. Ask administration officials about cabinet members who haven't caused them grief, and they will cite Linda McMahon of the Small Business Administration and Elaine L. Chao, the transportation secretary.

But they are the exception. Too many of Trump's cabinet members took to behaving like middle managers let loose in the supply closet for the first time, stuffing their pockets with notepads and pens, hoping the stern secretary doesn't notice. A few learned their lessons. The highest praise that could be lavished on Steve Mnuchin was that, after a colorful dalliance with scandal, he went to ground and disappeared from the news. History will have to judge if that qualifies him as truly one of the best people.

Before history has her say, the electorate will. Come the 2020 presidential election, Americans will want to know how and why their government was turned over to men and women with a profound antipathy to government, not to mention a disconcerting ignorance about how government works. They will marvel at scandals like Carson ordering a $31,000 dining room set or Mnuchin arranging government travel in order to witness a solar eclipse at taxpayers' expense. They will surely wonder how these people did it and, even worse, why they thought they could.

The many scandals of the Trump administration have been a boon to late-night comedians and writers of newspaper headlines. At the same time, those scandals obscure some disconcerting truths. Bumbling and inept as it may be, the Trump administration has undertaken a project that would shrink the federal government and its role in American citizens' lives. For the most part, that project has been clumsy and poorly articulated, if articulated at all, so that its contours can get lost in the daily haze of outrage. And yet the project continues, even if its executors do not always understand quite what they are doing.

Joel Clement, a Department of Interior whistleblower, figured a grand design informed all this. He had been driven out of government, as had hundreds of federal employees at agencies like the EPA and the Department of Education, where once meaningful work had become meaningless. And that was the intent, as Clement saw it. "They're put in there to screw up," he said of his former boss Zinke and other department heads. "You don't want people respecting or trusting government," he continued. So you install people who will break government, thus confirming the conservative view that government is broken.

"That'll take decades to repair," Clement offered. Some believe that it will take longer. Some believe that no repair will be possible, so thorough is the damage Trump is doing to the federal government. His strongest critics believe the only America that will ever be possible again is the America remade by Trump.

Things could have gone differently. Trump could have declared war on Washington's entrenched interests—the lobbyists, the lawyers, the think-tankers, the numberless other peddlers of influence and opinion—while undertaking a whittling-down of the federal government that even some liberals know is necessary. But this would have required enormous courage and discipline, an ability to stick to conviction even when every pundit and poll screamed for that conviction to be cast aside. Few presidents have had such conviction, and most of them hailed from a time before focus groups directed every policy decision.

Long after he'd left the White House, Bannon remembered how and why the promise to "drain the swamp" went awry. It was a winter morning in New York City in late 2018, and he was lounging in his top-floor suite at the Loews Regency Hotel. This was the city he loved. Washington, he hated. Washington, he could not fix. Now, he was fomenting populist revolution in Europe while continuing to push for a confrontation with China over trade. The war over Washington itself he knew was lost.

"The swamp draining...we had all these potential things," Bannon reminisced. "They just got ground up and it just turned out not to be a priority." And so Trump's promise to remake government went unfulfilled. He would have successes, just as he would have failures. But this was less a failure than a promise broken, both by Trump himself and the people he charged with running the federal government. They did not share his populist convictions, or his iconoclastic impulses. Some seemed to have no conviction of any kind, aside from personal glorification and enrichment.

Trump understood as much, even if he would never say it. Speaking at a Rose Garden event in the spring of 2018, he said that he had "been fighting to drain the swamp," adding that "sometimes it may not look like it, but believe me, we are draining the swamp." As a matter of fact, evidence strongly contradicted Trump's assertion.

Even as the swamp-drainers turned out to be swamp creatures, they managed to inflict harm on the people they were charged with protecting.

Under the leadership of Betsy DeVos, the Department of Education drastically reduced its oversight of for-profit colleges, allowing them to prey on unsuspecting Americans once again. Scott Pruitt directed the Environmental Protection Agency to roll back dozens of Obama-era rules, including those involving the regulation of toxic pesticides and the health of the nation's waterways. Carson has scaled back enforcement of the Fair Housing Act, allowing housing discrimination to flourish once again. Ross, at the Commerce Department, has perverted the census into a weapon of political warfare.

As 2018 came to an end, Trump signed an executive order freezing the pay of federal workers. They were responsible for none of the scandals and abuses of his administration, yet they were taking all of the blame. How galling it was for them to languish amid a government shutdown as men like Mnuchin and Ross, men with no business in Washington, continued to ape the role of the public servant, and to convince the president of their act.

Few others were convinced. These were the best people, Trump said, but by the summer of 2018, only 30 percent of Americans agreed with him. The best people failed on Trump's own terms, not to mention the terms on which public servants were judged before Trump. They failed, yet they kept smiling. They failed, but they called it victory. They failed and, finally, Americans saw them for who they were.

PART ONE: THE SIEGE

Chapter 1

······

THE ACCIDENTAL VICTOR

National Harbor, Maryland, was an unlikely cradle for revolution. Ten miles south of Washington, on the eastern bank of the Potomac River, it was essentially an open-air mall built on the site of a former plantation. A Ferris wheel rose from a river dock, while outlet stores clustered on the land below. Ersatz statues of historical figures like Frederick Douglass lined the insipidly named American Way, the figures looking like they'd been petrified while hawking trinkets and sweets.

For several days each winter, National Harbor became the most compelling place in American politics, a mecca for the adherents of Ronald Reagan, for the believers in limited government and personal liberty. For several years, the Gaylord National Resort & Convention Center, a boxy behemoth on the edge of what passed for National Harbor's downtown, had been home to the Conservative Political Action Conference. Hosted by the American Conservative Union, CPAC had come to be regarded as an audition for Republican presidential candidates looking to make overtures to movement conservatives. The centerpiece of the conference was a straw poll that crowned the right's favored rising star. In the eyes of many attendees, the more at odds that star was with establishment Republicans, the better. These were the faithful, only it was a faith that called for Washington's demise.

3

Donald Trump first spoke at CPAC in 2011, when it seemed like he might challenge Barack Obama in his attempt to win a second term (Trump had mused about a presidential run since the late 1980s, but had never taken the requisite steps). He came into the event knowing that many there favored libertarian representative Ron Paul, the aging but energetic Republican from Texas who was staunchly against the kinds of bloody, expensive military interventions George W. Bush had initiated in Afghanistan and Iraq. Though he had no record as a party activist, Trump lectured the base during his speech on the folly of aligning with Paul, who "just has zero chance of getting elected." While he didn't announce a run, Trump made a pitch remarkably similar to the one he would issue from the lobby of Trump Tower four and a half years later. "If I run and if I win, this country will be respected again," he said, adding later, "Our country will be great again."

Paul easily won the 2011 CPAC straw poll, with Mitt Romney, the former Republican governor of Massachusetts and the eventual 2012 GOP nominee for president, earning second place. Trump—who'd been invited to CPAC by GOProud, a conservative gay group—failed to register as anything more than a sideshow.

Trump kept returning to CPAC, like a persistent suitor determined to make his case. He came back in 2013 ("We have to take back our jobs from China"), 2014 ("With immigration, you better be smart, and you better be tough"), and 2015 ("Our roads are crumbling; everything's crumbling"). He had become one of CPAC's intermittently charming oddballs, punctuating a four-day precession of paeans to more guns and lower taxes with his freewheeling New York shtick, delighting the anti-abortion activists from Duluth or Dallas who knew not to take the reality television star seriously.

After he announced his run for the presidency, some of the GOP grass roots remained suspicious, even as he seemed to be eliminating

Republicans one by one on his way to the presidential nomination. Some attendees at CPAC 2016 decided they would stage a walkout of Trump's speech; having learned of the plan, and apparently fearing embarrassment, he decided to campaign in Kansas and Florida instead.

"He's not a true conservative," one attendee explained. Many in the GOP waited for the principled right to provide a final bulwark against Trump, to embrace a more moderate candidate like the junior senator from Texas, Ted Cruz. They kept waiting and waiting, but the moment never came.

In 2017, CPAC took place just a month after Trump's inauguration and was a purely celebratory affair. Trump remembered his first speech at the convention in 2011, "I love this place," he said, even though "this place" had not always loved him.

The centerpiece of the conference was an appearance by Steve Bannon, the chief executive of Trump's campaign in its closing months and subsequently the president's chief political strategist. With him on stage was Reince Priebus, the new chief of staff. The Bannon-Priebus CPAC duet was meant to tamp down rumors of West Wing squabbling and dysfunction, but also to show that an alliance had formed, finally, between Bannon's nationalist forces and Priebus's mainstream Republicans. It was all "phony," one person formerly close to Bannon would later say dismissively, but it looked halfway believable at the time. Everyone was getting along in the White House, and the White House was getting along with Capitol Hill. The right was united, while the left remained in wounded disarray.

Bannon and Priebus walked onto the stage to a standing ovation. "President Trump brought together the party and the conservative movement," Priebus told the crowd. Bannon seemed to agree, but it wasn't long before he resorted to his familiar pose of the pugnacious sage. "There's a new political order that's being formed out of this," he said, contradicting the earlier suggestion of cohesion. Bannon was a warrior. True to form, he promised war.

Among the new president's main goals, Bannon said, would be "the deconstruction of the administrative state." Some clapping followed, some whooping. Bannon smiled, continuing in that dark, insistent way of his. "If you look at these cabinet appointees," he added a little bit later, "they were selected for a reason, and that is the deconstruction. The way the progressive left runs is if they can't get it passed, they're just going to put in some sort of regulation in an agency. That's all going to be deconstructed and I think that that's why this regulatory thing is so important."

Deconstructing the administrative state was not quite the same thing as draining the swamp, but if they were not identical twins, they were at least siblings. The swamp, which Trump invoked without ever defining, was the ill-defined membrane that had grown between the public sector and the industries that haunted its borders: the lobbyists, the contractors, the consultants, the media, the law, the defense-industrial complex, the nonprofits, the think tanks. And all these industries thrived because as the administrative state—that is, the federal government, in all its regulatory might—grew, it became ever more inefficient and unwieldy, the lithe prince grown into a fat king propped up by his servile court. Bannon wanted to banish the court, force the king onto a diet, make him lean again.

Bannon was not wrong in his belief that government had grown into a beastly organism far beyond what the Founding Fathers envisioned. Some of that growth reflected westward expansion, as well as a population boom caused in part by immigration. But government also grew because it was deliberately grown by those in power.

An adherent to the progressive movement of the early twentieth century, Woodrow Wilson pushed for an expansion of federal powers that accorded with modern views of what the fortunate owed their supposed inferiors.

Government was not only to protect property rights, but to protect those being trampled on by factory bosses, slumlords, and bankers. Wilson oversaw the creation of the Federal Reserve System, the Federal Trade Commission, and the National Park Service, which quickly became hallmarks of the federal behemoth that, a century later, Bannon would yearn to dismantle.

Franklin D. Roosevelt's New Deal dramatically expanded Washington's role in domestic affairs with creations like Social Security, the Securities and Exchange Commission, and the Tennessee Valley Authority. World War II and the Cold War led to the rise of what Dwight D. Eisenhower would come to call "the military-industrial complex," with contractors like Northrop Grumman and Boeing coming to dominate the defense industry, acting like a shadow Pentagon. Lyndon B. Johnson's domestic program, the Great Society, was a broadening of the social welfare programs Roosevelt had started, this time with a particular sensitivity to racial inequality.

Even as the government grew, the number of federal employees remained flat, having reached two million in the 1950s and staying there ever since. Some saw that stasis as little more than an illusion. In 2017, conservative commentator George F. Will argued that government has "dispersed to disguise its size." Citing the research of Brookings Institution scholar John J. DiIulio Jr., Will estimated that if one were to add to the federal workforce state and municipal workers dependent on Washington for their employment, and also include contractors, the true number of government employees was actually fourteen million. This was the administrative state, splashing happily in the swamp.

Just weeks after Trump announced his run for the presidency in June 2015, the musical *Hamilton* moved from the Public Theater to Broadway. As Trump obliterated his competitors in the Republican primary, *Hamilton* became a musical and cultural sensation. Lin-Manuel Miranda's creation was celebrated as a paean to immigrants, multiculturalism, and the ascendancy of hip-hop as an art form. It was also a celebration of big government, albeit indirectly. Hamilton was a proponent of a centralized, powerful federal government. In the first of his *The Federalist Papers* essays, Hamilton praised an "enlightened zeal for the energy and efficiency of government" while warning against demagogues who would let loose a "torrent of angry and malignant passions."

Conservatives preferred another Founding Father, one whose views on federal power directly opposed Hamilton's. They eagerly cited the limited-government philosophy of Thomas Jefferson, whose ideal American was the gentleman farmer. In his 1801 inaugural address, Jefferson called for "a wise and frugal Government which shall restrain men from injuring one another, which shall leave them otherwise free to regulate their own pursuits of industry and improvement, and shall not take from the mouth of labor the bread it has earned."

More than two centuries later, conservatives were still promising the same thing, convinced that if government receded, liberty would flourish. Liberty, in their conception, could endow people with a dignity that the regulatory state never could. Reagan's experiment with trickle-down economics and George W. Bush's pro-business agenda had not borne these ideas out, suggesting that people often craved more government, not less, even as they demanded that government act efficiently and responsibly. And yet the right clung to its sacred nostrum.

Trump was not a scholar of Jefferson, nor a disciple of Reagan. As an enthusiastic but undisciplined builder of real estate, he frequently relied on the government, whether to seize properties by eminent domain, reap tax incentives in exchange for development, or to embrace the protections afforded by declaring bankruptcy. But political opportunity tended to make for quick converts, and by the presidential campaign of 2016, Trump was a zealous believer in the limited government cause.

As presidential expert Elaine Kamarck saw it, Trump and Bannon had a "fundamentally monarchical" understanding of the presidency. "We fought an entire fucking revolution to get away from kings and queens and get to the rule of law," she said derisively, still in disbelief two years after the presidential election where so many Americans had fallen for a vision contrary to the very notion of America. For all its unwieldiness, the administrative state enshrined and protected freedoms. As for the swamp, it was often just Americans exercising—however profitably or unwholesomely—their First Amendment right to petition the government.

Kamarck had worked for the Clinton administration, and her office at the Brookings Institution was decorated with Democratic memorabilia: her in the West Wing, jumping for joy after the passage of a bill that would, as a matter of fact, help reduce the size of government; a poster for the 1988 Democratic National Convention in Atlanta, another showing 1984 vice presidential candidate Geraldine Ferraro as Lady Liberty from Eugène Delacroix's famous depiction of the French Revolution.

Having worked on Clinton's downsizing effort, Kamarck freely acknowledged that the federal bureaucracy had become a wild, unweeded garden. Yet she had nothing but contempt for those who wanted to swing the scythe without understanding what they were doing, what it was that they were aiming to slash. "The federal government is the most highly educated workforce in the world," she said. "It's no longer a government of clerks, filing away your social security records."

For conservatives, the unelected bureaucrat was a vastly more convenient symbol than the specialist—whether in tax law or nuclear waste—who could triple her earnings in the private sector but decided to stay in public service out of conviction and dedication, maybe even old-fashioned patriotism. The unelected bureaucrat was a creature of infinite entitlement and could thus be easily dispensed with for the sake of the republic.

"It's been forty years since these conservatives have been talking about shrinking government," Kamarck said, growing animated and annoyed. "They don't ever manage to do it." Not managing to do it was, paradoxically, what allowed them to promise that they would. All they ever needed was four more years.

Trump first made his most consequential campaign promise during a rally in Green Bay, Wisconsin, on October 18, at a time when Clinton was leading by six points and seemed destined for surefire victory. He used it again the next day in Colorado Springs, Colorado. "We're going to end the government corruption," Trump said after his opening remarks about local military bases, "and we're going to drain the swamp in Washington, D.C." He then recited a litany of accusations regarding Clinton and her use of a private email server. "This truly is many worse than Watergate," he said. "And we are going to put an end to it November eighth."

"Drain the swamp" became a popular refrain in the final weeks of the presidential race, shaping the campaign's conclusion just as "Build the wall" had shaped its opening. But while talk of a border wall thrilled Trump, he was not animated by the swamp stuff. He said as much in an October 26 rally in Charlotte, North Carolina, in one of his unsettling bouts of honesty: "I said that about a week ago, and I didn't like it that much, didn't sound that great. And the whole world picked it up. Funny how things like that happen…So drain the swamp, I didn't like it, now I love it, right?"

In his final campaign stop in Grand Rapids, Michigan, just as polls were set to open nationwide on November 8, supporters chanted "Drain the swamp" along with that other, more sinister rallying cry of Trump rallies: "Lock her up." "Drain the swamp" dovetailed perfectly with Trump's complaints about a "rigged system" that was going to hand Clinton the election, thereby excusing what some said was going to be his historic, McGovern-sized defeat. He was going to lose precisely because he knew how much of a "disaster" Washington had become, because he knew who was responsible for it, because he was not afraid to call the malefactors out by name.

At a rally earlier that October, he had warned that the United States was "controlled by a small handful of global special interests" that had fostered an "illusion of democracy." It was dark stuff, the justification for a loss he must have felt coming as keenly as did the Clinton camp.

In truth everyone felt it, even if some claimed they had known all along that Trump was going to win. The evening would be confirmation of what everyone had known all along. Across the country, journalists were ready to file their "Clinton Wins in Historic Romp" articles, in hopes of getting to bed at a decent hour. (I know, because I wrote two such articles myself, and have them somewhere on my laptop still.)

Trump and his closest aides were at Trump Tower, watching the returns. The Trumps lived in a fifty-eighth-floor triplex (he claimed the tower had sixty-eight floors, but this was a bit of creative marketing), while the campaign headquarters were below: Bannon's "crack den" on the fifth floor, in the same space where *The Apprentice* was once filmed, and the "war room" on the sixth floor (or, in Trump's alternate universe, the fourteenth) where communication aides Andrew Surabian and Steven N. Cheung put out what media wildfires they could.

Trump came down to watch as Bannon and another staffer analyzed the returns from Florida, which Bannon had predicted Trump was going to win. Then he went back up to the residence. Some of his top aides followed, and soon they were in the unusually cramped kitchen of the otherwise opulent penthouse, crowded around a small television set. At 9:18 p.m., the *Detroit Free Press* called Michigan for Clinton. This was a sign that her midwestern "firewall" was holding, however tenuously. It had been a tense night for the Democrats, more tense than it needed to be, but the whole affair had finally come to its predicted, predictable end.

It took about an hour for the Michigan prediction to be discounted and reversed. People around Trump exploded in cheering. Some cried. But the more serious of Trump's advisers were probably closer in feeling to their Democratic adversaries. "We were not jubilant," Bannon would remember much later. He was talking about himself but also about the man who, in a matter of hours, would be the president-elect of the United States. Trump permitted a smile but otherwise refused to partake in the increasingly celebratory mood around him.

"You could tell the wheels were spinning," Bannon said. "It was reality."

Chapter 2

......

"I WIPE MY ASS WITH THEIR THING"

As the presidential election of 2016 neared, Jared Kushner, the husband of Ivanka Trump and one of Donald Trump's most influential advisers, reached out to Aryeh B. Bourkoff, founder of LionTree, a Manhattan investment bank with interests in media and telecommunications. Kushner was not looking for funds to allow the Trump campaign to buy more television ads, hire more staff, or perhaps start to close the seemingly intractable gap between Trump and Clinton in the polls.

Kushner wanted Bourkoff's help in "setting up a Trump television network after the presidential election in November," reported the *Financial Times*, which broke news of the Kushner-Bourkoff talks. In the gentle, understated way of the British newspaper, the report allowed that "the approach suggests Mr. Kushner and the Republican candidate himself are thinking about how to capitalise on the populist movement that has sprung up around their campaign in the event of an election defeat."

Others were not nearly so circumspect. In the *Atlantic* magazine, Derek Thompson wrote an article headlined "Trump Is Finished. Trump TV Is Next." To be fair, this made perfect sense. During the campaign, Trump hadn't needed CNN or the *Washington Post* to talk to his loyal supporters. He did need Fox News, but the network needed him more. After the election, his base would crave the feeling of a Trump rally, only twenty-four hours a day, delivered to their phones and televisions, an outlet to relentlessly prosecute President Clinton on the very issues Trump had raised during the campaign: the off-site State Department email server, the handling of the Benghazi consulate attack in Libya, the inveterate greed of the Clinton Foundation, Bill Clinton's treatment of women. He had promised to be their voice at the Republican National Convention. Their voice he would remain, for a modest subscription fee.

In those final days of the election, there was much talk of whether Trump would accede to the peaceful transfer of power after his inevitably disastrous defeat to Clinton, who was projected by some to win Republican redoubts in the Sun Belt and maybe even in the South.

Trump, who was famously incapable of handling public embarrassment, was about to be embarrassed worse than any major-party presidential nominee since 1984, when Democratic candidate Walter F. Mondale managed to defeat Ronald Reagan only in his home state of Minnesota. "Donald Trump is going to get his ass kicked," predicted a writer for the news site Deadspin. He added that "this isn't close, and never was."

Some people on Trump's own team plainly saw it that way too, especially after the revelation of Trump's boorish remarks on the *Access Hollywood* tape. Hillary was going to campaign in Arizona. Donald was going home. Bannon later said he remained certain that Trump would win even after *Access Hollywood*, but many others thought the renegade campaign was being finally handed the comeuppance it had long deserved.

Among those who apparently figured doom was approaching in those final weeks of the campaign was Chris Christie. The portly, bombastic Republican governor of New Jersey had spent the years before the 2016 presidential election as head of the Republican Governors Association, boosting the prospects of GOP candidates while raising his profile in midwestern and southern states. He planned to run for president as a sensible, solution-seeking Republican, one who would take on public-sector employees and Islamic terrorists, and still have time to watch a ball game, hotdog in hand.

That image of the capable chief executive suffered greatly from the Bridgegate scandal, the 2013 politically motivated lane closures on the George Washington Bridge between Fort Lee, New Jersey, and Manhattan, ordered by Christie's top aides. Though Christie's popularity plummeted at home, his campaign advisers believed he had a chance to prevail in a crowded primary field by being louder, and punching harder, than Republican counterparts unsuited to the style of combat that was Christie's expertise. If anyone dared to bring up Bridgegate, he would simply shout them down.

There was one unexpected problem with this approach: Trump. There was room on the right for many varieties of conservatism, but there was not room for two bombastic bridge-and-tunnel strivers. Christie understood this, jabbing at Trump as the primary season commenced. Trump answered with shattering uppercuts. Ahead of the critical New Hampshire primary, Trump gave it to Christie on the nose: "Chris can't win because of his past. I don't believe you've heard the last of the George Washington Bridge, because there's no way he didn't know about the closure of the George Washington Bridge. And all of his people are now going on trial in the very near future. And they're going on criminal trial. There's no way he didn't know about it."

Trump won New Hampshire, while Christie, who had been campaigning there relentlessly since as early as 2014, finished an inconsequential sixth. The following day, February 10, 2016, Christie suspended his presidential campaign. "I have both won elections that I was supposed to lose and I've lost elections I was supposed to win and what that means is you never know what will happen. That is both the magic and the mystery of politics—you never quite know when which is going to happen, even when you think you do," Christie wrote on Facebook.

Two weeks later, Christie surprised just about everyone by endorsing Trump, becoming the first national Republican figure to do so. "I will lend my support between now and November in any way for Donald," Christie said at an event in Fort Worth, Texas. He looked pained as he spoke, as if praising Trump's character and political acumen caused him deep physical discomfort. Here was a man humiliated, for all to see and many to mock.

The mockery was relentless, but Christie's calculation looked increasingly clever as Trump muscled Republican competitors out of the way. Remaining a loyal surrogate for Trump, Christie hoped for a position in an eventual Trump administration, should that unlikely reality ever come to pass. But his ambitions were always going to have a check in Jared Kushner. In 2004, when Christie was a U.S. attorney in New Jersey, he prosecuted Jared's father, the developer Charles Kushner, on charges of tax evasion, improper campaign contributions, and witness tampering. The last of these referred to a scheme in which Charles Kushner had a prostitute seduce his brother-in-law, who had become a government witness. The covertly recorded encounter was sent to his wife, Charles Kushner's sister Esther. This was preposterously illegal. Charles Kushner went to prison for fourteen months. Jared Kushner never forgot the insult. When it came time for Trump to select a vice presidential nominee in the summer of 2016, Christie yearned for the job, only to have Kushner frustrate his desires. The vice presidential nomination went instead to Mike Pence, the conservative governor of Indiana who had as much in common with Trump as he did with the emir of Qatar.

Still, Christie had endorsed Trump when few others would, and now he wanted something, anything, in return. Christie remained by Trump's side despite his wife Mary Pat's loathing for the candidate.

The loyalty paid off, if perhaps not nearly to the extent Christie had hoped. On May 9, Trump named Christie to lead his presidential transition team. The Republican National Convention was still months away, but Trump had just won the Indiana primary and, in doing so, vanquished his last two Republican rivals for the nomination: Senator Cruz of Texas and Governor John R. Kasich of Ohio. Though some wanted them to keep fighting, no remotely realistic configuration of delegates gave either one a shot at victory. Trump was their man, whether Republicans liked it or not.

Presidential campaigns customarily began planning for the transition long before any votes were counted on Election Day. The precedent was set by Jimmy Carter, who during the 1976 presidential election started his transition planning after winning the Pennsylvania primary that spring. Early transition planning came to be seen as a public good, something to be encouraged. In 2010, Congress passed the Pre-Election Presidential Transition Act, which deemed "that certain transition services shall be available to eligible candidates before the general election." The goal was to stimulate transition planning by partly subsidizing it.

Even so, few campaigns devoted sufficient time to the presidential transition, which Max Stier, founder and head of the Partnership for Public Service, deemed "the moment before the Big Bang," when all the ingredients for the presidency itself had to be meticulously assembled. "You're talking about the takeover of the most complicated, largest, consequential organization not just on the planet, but in history," explained Stier, the nation's foremost expert on the presidential transition, both as it had been and as it should be. "Transition planning has to begin a year out."

Yet transition planning would be worthless unless and until preceded by a November triumph. Accordingly, most campaigns put off the former while focusing on the latter. Hillary Clinton did not start planning her own transition until mid-August, though the pace of transition planning accelerated in October, when her victory seemed certain.

In a statement announcing the formation of his transition team, Trump called Christie "an extremely knowledgeable and loyal person," while Christie vowed that he'd be "putting together a first rate team." There were ominous signs, however: Kushner would also be involved in the transition, making it unlikely that Christie would have as much freedom as he wanted. There was also the inevitability of Clinton's win, which loomed like a thunderhead over the Trump campaign. Any moment now, she was going to finally dispatch her pesky primary challenger, Vermont senator Bernie Sanders, and make a tight, fast turn toward the general election. It took her a little longer than many thought it should, but by late August, she had finally shaken off Sanders and was leading Trump by twelve points.

Though signs of defeat were legion, Christie set about doing his work with the help of trusted New Jersey aides like Richard H. Bagger and William J. Palatucci, the governor's closest adviser. Both had been through many a Trenton brawl, but this was the presidency, not New Jersey. Some saw them as unsuited to the task of building out an administration. Bannon, never one to police and moderate his own views, came to regard them as "total fucking New Jersey scam artists."

Stylistic differences aside, they committed what Bannon saw as an unpardonable sin: "They never had any faith in Trump." It was a charge that Bannon and other loyalists would later level—sometimes fairly and sometimes not—when things would go awry in the White House. As they saw it, at least Democrats were open in their loathing of Trump. More insidious, in their eyes, were Republicans who quietly subverted Trump's will even as they made public shows of loyalty.

Just hours after Bannon was appointed to lead the Trump campaign in August, he watched as the candidate ripped into Christie.

The reason was a news report about Christie's fund-raising on behalf of the transition effort.

"What the fuck are you doing?" Trump bellowed at Christie, who sat across from the candidate on a sofa, trying desperately to defend himself. "I want to shut the whole thing down."

Bannon stood to the side, watching. He had never met Christie before, but he knew that the New Jersey governor was right. He tried to pacify Trump by explaining that they had to run a transition, and that to run a transition, they needed money. Trump wouldn't have it. "You're jinxing me," he complained, pointing to the wasted transition effort of Mitt Romney's failed 2012 presidential campaign. It also felt like Christie was raising money that should have been directed to the Trump campaign itself. Finally, though, Bannon won out.

"Fine," Trump conceded. "But no more fucking raising money."

The campaign continued, with Clinton remaining ahead but never quite pulling away. Then came October 7, a Friday. A hurricane threatened Florida. In Wisconsin, House Speaker Paul D. Ryan prepared to campaign with Trump the following day. Trump and his advisers were at Trump Tower in Manhattan, getting ready for a presidential debate. That afternoon, the *Washington Post* published its account of the *Access Hollywood* tape. The denunciations of Democrats were expected; it was the denunciations of Republicans that were astonishing. Condoleezza Rice, who had served as secretary of state under George W. Bush, voiced the conclusion many of her mainstream conservative colleagues had reached, some of them long before the infamous recording emerged: "He should withdraw." Speaker Ryan told congressional Republicans on a call to "do what's best for you and your district," a signal that he was leaving the Trump campaign to its own devices. The joint rally in Wisconsin never took place.

Bannon later said that *Access Hollywood* was when he knew that Trump was going to win. Whether this was retroactive mythology or an understanding of what motivated Trump's base would be impossible to say. The way he would tell it, he wanted the campaign purged of anyone of wavering conviction. In this group was Christie. Bannon focused his ire on the bombastic but insecure governor. "The plane leaves at eleven o'clock in the morning," Bannon said of what he would come to call Billy Bush Saturday, and of Christie's fall from grace that day. "If you're on the plane, you're on the team. Didn't make the plane."

Christie stayed off the plane in the days to come. The second of three presidential debates was that Sunday evening in St. Louis. Despite supposedly being one of Trump's closest advisers, Christie was not there. Nor had he appeared on the Sunday talk shows that morning, though he had been slated to do so. The following Tuesday, Christie, a sports radio enthusiast, did speak to WFAN Sports Radio, a New York–area station, where he denounced Trump's comments on the *Access Hollywood* tape. "It is completely indefensible, and I won't defend it and haven't defended it," Christie said. "That kind of talk and conversation, even in private, is just unacceptable."

That may have been the moment when Christie doomed his chances of a job within the Trump administration. It would be impossible to overstate just how much those around Trump came to dislike the New Jersey governor. Even though the lines of enmity and suspicion in the eventual Trump administration were complex, they also coalesced around a couple of well-known nodes. One was Reince Priebus, routinely dismissed by colleagues as a "nice enough guy," in the words of someone who saw plenty of Priebus in the West Wing. The other was Christie. There were words for him, but they were not nice words. They were words like "pussy" and "coward," which those around Trump spat out with magnificent loathing.

Even as Christie seemed to go missing, the transition continued, however pointless the task may have seemed. Scott H. Amey, a lawyer for the Project on Government Oversight, remembered meeting in late October with Palatucci inside Trump's transition offices in

Washington. Amey came with Norman L. Eisen, who had served as the chief ethics lawyer for President Obama, and Thomas M. Susman, a veteran Washington lawyer with an expertise in government affairs. The trio wanted the presidential campaigns to sign on to a "new and improved ethics pledge," as Amey described it, that would curb the influence of lobbyists and access-peddlers on the federal government. At least the Trump campaign had agreed to meet; the Clinton campaign ignored the request.

The three lawyers sat with Palatucci for about an hour, presenting him with their pledge. "He leafed through it and asked a few specific questions about the contents and definitions," Amey recalled. But what really stood out to him was the apparent state of the transition, just three weeks from the presidential election. "It was very dead." There were "empty cubicles and empty desks." The lights were off.

"Not a good sign," Amey thought as he left the desolate offices.

A staffer told Bannon the same thing, that the Trump transition headquarters in Washington was "crickets."

Bannon asked why.

"Palatucci and those guys," the staffer answered.

Bannon wasn't surprised. He thought "the New Jersey mafia" had only gone to work for Trump because, if he managed to win, "they were going to be the lobbyists and beat the inside fixers and make a shit ton of money." Yet he was too concerned with the campaign's endgame to care much about the New Jersey guys in their empty Washington offices.

(This author attempted to engage Palatucci in conversation about the transition on a number of occasions. Eventually, Palatucci agreed to answer some questions by email, then decided against it. He sent a statement that said the Christie transition had been "professional, comprehensive, and ready on election day to advise the president-elect on all matters." Suffice it to say that of the many high-ranking transition staffers I spoke to for this book, not a single one shared anything even remotely approaching this sunny view.)

Christie showed up at Trump Tower on election night, and attempted to ingratiate himself with the man about to be elected president. Trump was "cold as ice," remembered Bannon, who also didn't take well to Christie's transparent last-minute attempts to sidle back into the fold. At one point, Christie told Trump that Obama had called him. Christie said that Obama would call back on the governor's phone, at which point he would pass that phone to Trump. A notorious germaphobe, Trump grew enraged. "Hey Chris," he said, "you know my fucking phone number. Just give it to the president. I don't want your fucking phone." Christie tried to write some of Trump's victory speech, delivered early that Wednesday morning, and tried to sidle into photographs of the Trump team as the president-elect addressed a gobsmacked nation. This too went over poorly.

The transition was to hold its first meeting on Thursday, two days after the victory, with a presentation to Trump on Friday. That Wednesday, Trump was preparing to head to Washington to meet with Obama when Kushner called Bannon. "Trump wants to get rid of Christie tonight," said Kushner, who despised Christie for having sent his father to prison. "Immediately."

Vicious as Bannon could be to underlings and opponents, he had no interest in dealing with Christie when so many more important matters were at hand. "I don't know Christie," he pleaded. "You're the guy." Kushner said he was not going to be the guy. Bannon would have to be the executioner.

It happened as the full transition team met on the twenty-fifth floor of Trump Tower. Bannon's assistant summoned Christie, sending him down to the crack den, where Bannon had a glass-walled office near the elevator banks.

Anyone who walked by that afternoon would have seen a spectacle. For four hours, Bannon remembers, Christie pleaded with Bannon to keep his job. People put their faces up to the glass, wondering what was taking so long. Bannon wondered too. Long after, he remained incredulous about the episode. "I mean, I'm the head of this, and I'm taking four hours with this guy." If other enmities had cooled by late 2018, this one still had not. Bannon could only remember Christie with oceanic revulsion, wondering if the New Jersey governor was "psychologically fucked up." Bannon had no reason to believe this, but he believed it all the same. "He's not an adult in the way he thinks about things," he said. "I don't know if it's because he's so grossly overweight or if it's something else. There's something that is psychologically not right with this guy." Two years of many other battles waged had done nothing to soften this view.

Christie only deepened his own humiliation, making ineffectual appeals he had to have known were not going to sway Bannon. "She's going to be all over my ass," he said of his wife, Mary Pat, who had been telling him for months to "cut bait on Trump." He had stayed, waiting for the reward he knew he deserved. He was supposed to have been the vice president. And now what was he? "The only reason I took the transition is I'm supposed to be chief of staff," he said. Now he had nothing to show for staying with Trump, not to himself nor to Mary Pat nor to what few political supporters he still had. Christie sunk into self-pity. "I'm so fucked," he said.

Bannon was annoyed at having to play "father confessor" to a man he did not know well or hold in especially high regard. "You're not getting fired for the work," Bannon told Christie, desperate to have this uncomfortable episode over with. "Trump doesn't want you around, and Kushner can't stand the sight of you. You're gone."

That Friday, vice president–elect Pence was named to head the transition. This was only a nominal designation. In truth, a triumvirate would oversee the process: Bannon on the cabinet, Priebus on the White House, Kushner on foreign policy.

They had to start somewhere. That starting point would be the binders Christie compiled in the months before the election. It may not have been the soundest of foundations, but they figured there would be something there to work with.

The Christie binders would take on a mythic quality, like a lost ancient scroll. To some, they were symbols of work needlessly squandered. "Leave aside their decision to fire Christie, but their decision essentially to ignore all the work was a big mistake," said Stier of the Partnership for Public Service, who called what Christie compiled "a very credible set of preparations." By ignoring these, Stier was convinced, Trump "fell behind from the very beginning."

Others bristled at the notion that Christie was a savior banished by jealous rivals from the king's court. One staffer involved with the transition said that Christie's effort amounted to a "shallow hole." He said that when he and others looked at the documents Christie had put together they were left with a single question: "What the fuck is this shit?"

Bannon may not have known Christie personally, but he knew the man's work, and that was all he needed to know. To him, the transition plan reflected not only a lack of effort but a lack of expertise, a crippling unfamiliarity with national Republican politics. "Christie doesn't know anything about the federal government," Bannon complained later. "He just doesn't. He's not a Washington guy."

Christie's not being a Washington guy was apparent in the appointments he recommended. In top national security positions, he had General Stanley A. McChrystal, who had already said he wanted nothing to do with Trump, and Admiral William H. McRaven, who, although he did not endorse anyone in the 2016 election, was considered a potential vice president for Clinton and later came out as a Trump critic. Another spot in the national security pantheon would have gone to a relatively minor defense manufacturer in New Hampshire who happened to have been a major Christie campaign donor.

"He's a joke and his fucking transition was a joke," Bannon said. "I wipe my ass with their thing." (He asked this author to convey the message to Palatucci, precisely in those terms.)

Bannon liked to tell a story that in his view perfectly captured the imperatives of Christie's transition team. The day after the election, he said he called one of Christie's top men and told him he was needed at Trump Tower in Manhattan.

That was going to be impossible. Why? Bannon delivered the punch line. "He's in the Bahamas. What the fuck? Been there for five days, been there for the weekend before, because they didn't think we were going to win. Now the thing is a joke." Others said that Bannon got this wrong, that if there was a vacation on the part of the transition figure—who later became a U.S. ambassador to an Asian nation—it had been long planned and not intended as a slight to Trump. But as a slight is precisely how Bannon saw it.

There was another problem. "Drain the swamp" had been the popular closing refrain of the Trump campaign, only Christie had stocked the transition team with lobbyists. Rich Bagger, the governor's New Jersey confidant, was a pharmaceutical lobbyist. Just days before the election, he had convened a meeting for the transition team with some of Washington's top lobbyists. The meeting took place at the offices of BakerHostetler, the immensely influential law firm whose Washington offices were steps from K Street, a thoroughfare synonymous with the influence trade. (Among those present was J. Steven Hart, who would figure in the undoing of Scott Pruitt.) This was the swamp in all its fetid glory. It would not do.

Bannon's complaints aside, others within the transition found plenty to dislike about the work Christie and his associates did. Another top transition staffer, who was by no means a Bannon ally, took issue with the legal documents Palatucci drafted, which he described as bordering on the imbecilic. So poor was the work, incoming White House counsel Donald F. McGahn II had to spend considerable time doing it all over again.

A person who worked on the transition from Washington was stunned by how little work Christie had done beyond compiling lists of names. He was young, this person, and he was new to Trump's staff, but he was also a Republican who wanted the president to succeed. How could you succeed under conditions like these? Christie's vision of a Trump administration consisted mostly of scraps from the outdated Romney transition plan.

That was only a small part of the problem. As this newcomer saw it, the transition was "absolute chaos," with no clear lines of authority.

The Washington transition was led by Rick A. Dearborn, who had been chief of staff to Senator Jeff Sessions, the Republican from Alabama. Sessions was small and talked slow. Dearborn had presence and intensity. He was known to show little patience for fools. He ran the show as best as he could, but with limited powers and with little sense that the work in Washington was being taken seriously by the people in New York.

Another powerful figure in the transition was Stephen Miller, also a former Sessions aide, though one who was much closer than Dearborn to Trump. Jewish though he was, hailing from Santa Monica and educated at Duke, Miller could channel Trump's lunch pail nativism better than anyone. "A weird little guy," one campaign veteran called him, reflecting a popular view. Slight in stature, perhaps, but not in influence. During the transition, Miller gave off the impression of wielding power without having to fight for it. "Everything will flow through me," he declared.

As the transition careened toward January, pundits and columnists grasped desperately for every sign of normalcy, trying to convince themselves that a "presidential pivot" was imminent—even as others noted, correctly, that a polar bear was more likely to pivot toward the tropics. Sure enough, as November turned into December, it was clear that the Trump transition would have no stability, and no peace.

As agencies in Washington awaited the arrival of Trump "beachhead teams" to begin the changeover, Trump remained sequestered in Trump Tower, high above Manhattan. Protesters gathered below, as did tourists, who suddenly had an entirely new attraction during their visits to New York. Meanwhile, a variety of factions jostled for the attentions of the supremely impressionable neophyte, who—and all his courtiers understood this—could be prevailed upon quite easily, as long as his own vanities were nurtured. Christie, for all his faults, had at least erected the scaffolding of an administration around Trump. That was torn down, and what now went up was a teetering edifice held together by duct tape.

In those weeks between the election and the inauguration, Trump received Peter Thiel, the libertarian cofounder of PayPal, and Tulsi Gabbard, the far-left U.S. representative from Hawaii. To Trump Tower came Maurice "Hank" Greenberg, the former chief of the American International Group, and Larry King, the CNN host who had been married five more times than thrice-wedded Trump. Kanye West came, Bill Gates came, Elon Musk came, and Tommy Hilfiger came. Why they came nobody knew, though they seemed happy enough to do so. Al Gore came, and suddenly environmentalists were cheered. A few days later Scott Pruitt came, and was announced as the new head of the EPA, and environmentalists knew they were in for a long, cold winter.

Eventually, Bannon prevailed on Trump to conduct his transition meetings from the president-elect's golf club in Bedminster, New Jersey. If a photograph was framed just so, the colonnaded entrance resembled that of 10 Downing Street, the London address that was the residence of the United Kingdom's prime minister. The resemblance wasn't much, but Bannon would take it over the hordes foisting anti-Trump signs on Fifth Avenue, providing television audiences with endless evidence of a furious anti-Trump resistance.

To Trump, whose starring turn in *The Apprentice* thirteen years before had revived his flagging business fortunes, theatrics were an imperative, though he also knew the show would get bad ratings if it tipped too quickly into the absurd. As television crews camped out in Bedminster and midtown Manhattan, the president-elect used his Twitter feed to push back against a precession of reports about the transition team's dysfunction and inaction, while promoting the selection of cabinet members as if they were reality television contestants:

- November 15: "Very organized process taking place as I decide on Cabinet and many other positions. I am the only one who knows who the finalists are!"
- November 17 (at 4:45 a.m.): "My transition team, which is working long hours and doing a fantastic job, will be seeing many great candidates today."
- November 22: "Great meetings will take place today at Trump Tower concerning the formation of the people who will run our government for the next 8 years."
- December 11: "Whether I choose him or not for 'State'—Rex Tillerson, the Chairman & CEO of ExxonMobil, is a world class player and dealmaker. Stay tuned!"
- January 13: "All of my Cabinet nominees are looking good and doing a great job. I want them to be themselves and express their own thoughts, not mine."

These exhortations could only have reassured his true believers, the ones who had already been sold on the myth of the ruthlessly capable chief executive. To the liberal opposition, the situation was closer to that of a jester thrust into the royal chamber. The president-elect seemed especially fixated on candidates for office who were, in his words, "out of central casting," a phrase at once hopelessly outdated and fully tethered to the superficial. Mitt Romney called Trump a "fraud" in an eviscerating speech delivered during the Republican presidential primary. Because he had the look of an elder states-man, Trump considered him for secretary of state. The two had an immensely awkward dinner at Jean-Georges, an upscale restaurant located in the Trump International Hotel and Tower that featured a $138-per-person tasting menu. The job would eventually go to Rex W. Tillerson, the chief executive of ExxonMobil.

Ben Carson, the pediatric neurosurgeon turned conservative com-mentator, had no experience administering public housing programs; he even admitted that he was not prepared to take on a cabinet post, a disquieting truth coming from someone who had just run for pres-ident. Bannon loved Carson and wanted him for Health and Human Services, but congressional Republicans had other ideas, so Housing and Urban Development was "the thing he got," as Bannon put it. "He was going to be in the cabinet from the beginning. It was just finding a slot for him."

Nikki Haley was an unexpected choice to join Trump's cabinet. The South Carolina governor had earned plaudits for calling to have the Confederate flag removed from the statehouse grounds in Columbia after a white supremacist slaughtered nine people in an African-American church in Charleston. Haley's principled stance earned favorable national attention. So did her criticism of Trump during the Republican national primary race (which some wanted her to join). She once said that Trump was "everything a governor doesn't want in a president," an opinion many Republicans shared but few uttered. Never one to hold back a counterpunch, Trump claimed that South Carolina was "embarrassed" by her, which was untrue: Haley's near 60 percent approval rating from South Carolinians ahead of the presidential election made her significantly more popular than Trump would ever be in his first two years as president.

When it came to nominate an ambassador to the United Nations, Trump picked Haley. She had no diplomatic experience, having spent her entire career in South Carolina. Then again, Nimrata

Randhawa was the daughter of Indian Sikhs who had moved to the United States in 1969. That was enough. Central casting had done its work.

John R. Bolton was not a central casting standout, looking rather like an aging adjunct professor annoyed at having to still teach undergraduates. Bolton was a frequent presence on Fox News, where he attacked Obama, Clinton, and the Democrats with such zeal, you might have thought they had conspired to kill his hamster. Because of his prolific punditry, Trump considered Bolton for secretary of state. When the job went to Tillerson, it was not because Trump was a protectionist and Bolton was an interventionist. It was because Bolton had a mustache. Mustaches looked sloppy. Trump had to find someone else.

While Trump was holding auditions at Trump Tower and Bedminster, Washington waited for the transition to begin. One member of President Obama's 2008 transition team issued a warning: "It is hard to get the government to do things. It's not like you flip a switch. Even reversing regulations, as Trump has said he wants to do, is a long process." Deconstructing the administrative state was not quite the same thing as letting the administrative state languish under a cloud of ineptitude. The warning was a sound one. Only nobody heard it. Or, if they heard it, if they knew that the transition was faltering badly, they also knew they couldn't tell Trump.

Trump's management style in private business was autocratic. But this imperious manner masked what many who had worked with him believed to be an insecure and anxious personality. Barbara A. Res saw Trump's character at a proximity few outside his family were afforded. In 1980, he hired her as the head of construction for Trump Tower, making her the most influential woman in the building trade in New York. The Trump she knew was the same man who now sat in the Oval Office. "He would pit people against one another," she said, playing divide and conquer with his own staff. One usually divided and conquered enemies, not allies, but Trump had no allies other than himself. If his subordinates were fighting, it meant they were not conspiring against him.

Much as he loved to insult people, he did everything he could to avoid direct confrontation.

One episode in particular stayed with Res. Trump Tower needed a residential manager, and she found a German who seemed up to the task. He was not, it quickly turned out. The German proved inexperienced and unpleasant, so as a senior executive, Res did the natural thing: she fired him.

Upon learning of his dismissal, the German promptly went to Trump himself, who offered him another chance. The German returned to work at Trump Tower, where he showed himself to be no more capable than he had been before. Again, Res fired him. Again, the German went back to Trump, who again gave him his job back.

"Took us three times to get rid of the guy," Res said with disbelief. The act of recollecting all this pointless back-and-forth exasperated her, even many years after the fact. Exasperating others was always part of Trump's style. He ran people ragged. He used them, and after they were all used up, he sent them away.

One day, someone called in a bomb threat to Trump Tower. Res went to Trump, asking if they should evacuate the building. Trump Tower had just opened; evacuating a skyscraper because of a potential terrorism threat was not the kind of publicity one wanted. Except thousands of lives could be in danger if the threat were genuine.

Trump did not know what to do. He was the chief executive, only he wanted the chief's trappings without the chief's responsibilities. The responsibilities, someone else could have. He told Res that she would be the one to decide whether an evacuation was necessary. Res thought it "crazy" that he would leave her with a decision that significant. Decades later, she thought that still.

Trump retained many of the character traits Res saw in the eighteen years she worked for him. But like instruments in an orchestra, some of those traits would grow quieter, while others would grow louder. Res remembered that when she knew him, he was a "borderline human being," which were about the kindest words she could summon for her former boss. The figure arriving in the White House was someone else entirely: as careless a manager as the budding real estate tycoon of 1986, but much more deluded about his own powers, much less able to summon equanimity when the alarm went off.

As would be the case so often during the Trump administration, the transition proceeded along two tracks, the real and the illusory. In the illusory transition, Trump was stocking his administration with the most able men and women the Republican ranks had to offer. In reality, he and his top advisers were completely overwhelmed, happy to take recommendations from anyone. Those who grasped this, like the Heritage Foundation, were eager to supply him with names. He would get to tout the selection, while their influence in the new administration would increase.

"I wouldn't say that I agreed with all of the people," Trump told me, "but I let them make their decision. In some cases, I was right."

In the early months of his presidency, Trump would routinely blame Democrats for delay in staffing his government, though his own party, the Republicans, controlled both chambers of Congress until the 2018 midterm election. But he also did not think he needed to staff up, because all policy emanated from his own person, as if he were not president but king. In late 2017, the president was asked by Laura Ingraham of Fox News about understaffing at the State Department. He responded with a cross between confidence and contempt. "Let me tell you, the one that matters is me. I'm the only one that matters, because when it comes to it, that's what the policy is going to be," the president said. This outlook governed the Trump administration from the start.

When I spoke to him in 2019, Trump put it differently. "Everybody wants to work here," he said, though only months before he had struggled to find a chief of staff before finally prevailing on Mick Mulvaney to take the job. "I have so many people that want jobs here." Those people had a funny way of showing their desire for an executive branch job. This was as true in 2019 as it had been in 2017.

Trump's hubris doomed his own transition more than any Democrat ever could. "The process he ran can pick your twenty," said Stier of the Partnership for Public Service, "but can't pick your four thousand." Four thousand was the total number of political appointments a president had to make. Of those, the Partnership for Public Service deemed 706 to be "key positions." As of January 2019, only 433 of those positions had been confirmed by the Senate, while another 264 positions had no nominee at all. At the departments of Interior and Justice, only 41 percent of key positions had a Senate-confirmed official.

Christie relished this disorder. "I think what folks who were involved in that transition have now painfully learned at the expense of the country is that experience matters," he said in early December 2017, as the president-elect's harrowing reality show lurched in any number of directions but forward. The following spring, Christie leveled an even more damaging accusation at the transition: "brutally unprofessional."

Even as he gloated, Christie continued to yearn for a role in the Trump administration. The perfect opportunity finally came in December 2018, after Trump announced that John Kelly would be leaving his position as White House chief of staff. The president's top choice to replace Kelly was Nick Ayers, the thirty-six-year-old chief of staff to Vice President Pence. Notoriously ambitious, Ayers surprised Washington by turning down the job. Maybe he really did want to spend more time with his family, though he may have also wanted to avoid potential scrutiny of his fortune—somewhere between $12 and $55 million—as well as questions about his ties to Missouri governor Eric Greitens, who resigned in 2018 amid allegations of sexual misconduct and campaign finance violations.

Others also indicated they had no interest in the position, which is how Trump alighted on Christie. Some reports had him as the top candidate, but then the former New Jersey governor, who wanted power so badly, who sought it out so shamelessly, declared that he did not want the job after all.

Some thought they knew what had actually transpired. Still stewing about his ouster from the transition, Christie had spent some of 2018 writing a book, *Let Me Finish: Trump, the Kushners, Bannon, New Jersey, and the Power of In-Your-Face Politics*. Tightly held by the publisher until its January 2019 release date, the book charged that Trump was surrounded by "amateurs, grifters, weaklings, convicted and unconvicted felons." The obvious implication was that Christie, and Christie alone, could have stopped this calamity. And so the governor publicly exacted revenge on the men he believed to have ousted him from the transition, Bannon and Kushner in particular. But in doing so, Chris Christie ensured that he would never work in the Trump administration, that he would be relegated to cable news, where the grim-faced governor would shake his head at what was while hinting at what could have been.

Things seemed to be headed in the other direction for Bannon. He and Trump had had a falling out in early 2018, over some rather too frank comments Bannon had made to *Fire and Fury* author Michael Wolff. But if Trump was quick to anger, he was also quick to forget. When I asked Trump, about a year after their spat, whether he would hire Bannon for his 2020 presidential campaign, Trump did not reject the idea. In fact, he almost welcomed it.

"I watched Bannon a few times, four or five times over the last six months," Trump said. "Nobody says anything better about me right now than Bannon." This was a certain sign that Bannon was back in the president's good graces, though of course it also did not mean that he would be running the president's re-election campaign.

Trump was certainly open to it. "I will say this," he said, returning to a subject to which he had clearly given some thought. "Bannon, there is nobody that has been more respectful of the job I'm doing than Steve Bannon."

And maybe Christie could have come back into the fold, too. Only he had books to sell and cable news appearances to make.

Chapter 3

······

THE STRONGEST MEN OF THE PARTY

Every new presidential administration had to pay debts: to the donors who contributed millions of dollars to the campaign, to elected officials who made endorsements and accompanied the candidate to fish fries and town halls; finally, to the voters who voted for him or her because they had seen something good, heard something true, found something to believe.

One promise Trump had made during the campaign was unusual and dangerously superlative, to a degree he did not grasp at the time. It didn't just tether him to a specific policy promise, or to an influential think tank that provided critical support, but, rather, to the explicit vow that his government would be unlike any other, in the grandest way possible.

Relatively early in the Republican primary, Trump fired his longtime adviser Roger J. Stone Jr., the former Nixon operative who had been urging Trump to run for the presidency since the late 1980s. Trump explained to the *Washington Post* why Stone had to go: "I'm going to surround myself only with the best and most serious people. We want top of the line professionals."

"The best people" became shorthand for the unconventional administration over which Trump would preside: skilled corporate swashbucklers, not process-obsessed bureaucrats writing reports that nobody read. "I would use the greatest minds," he told Sean Hannity of Fox News right around the time of the Stone firing. "I know the best negotiators. I know the ones that are no good that people think are good. I know people that you've never heard of that are better than all of them."

This continued into 2016. "I am self-funding and will hire the best people, not the biggest donors!" he wrote on Facebook in April, as primary challengers fell away and the battle against Hillary Clinton neared. It was unusual for a president to brand his own cabinet, especially before that cabinet had been chosen. History usually did that work, though most cabinets were too lackluster and transitory to collectively demand much more than a passing note in the historical record.

Once in a while, the members of a cabinet did rise collectively out of obscurity and take a place in the national imagination, alongside the president himself. Historian Doris Kearns Goodwin famously branded Abraham Lincoln's cabinet a "team of rivals" because he selected three formidable political adversaries—William H. Seward, Salmon P. Chase, and Edward Bates—to important posts in his administration. Asked about the wisdom of this choice, Lincoln answered, "We need the strongest men of the party in the Cabinet. We needed to hold our own people together."

The politics of a presidential cabinet could be as complex as a French ballet (and to a certain breed of person, a lot more riveting). Few understood the intricacies of the dance as well as James P. Pfiffner, a scholar of the presidency at George Mason University. In 1986, Pfiffner published a paper, "White House Staff Versus the Cabinet: Centripetal and Centrifugal Forces," that meticulously combed through the historical record to discover the forces that could either elevate or ruin a presidency.

Pfiffner, who served in Vietnam before becoming an expert on government, argued that there were "strong centrifugal forces at work pulling the cabinet secretary away from the president." Pfiffner wrote that those forces included "the cabinet secretary's duties to the law and to Congress and their dependency on their career bureaucracies and the constituencies their departments represent."

The lack of a formal organization for the cabinet meant that every president got to have his own way, which he assured himself and those around him would harness the power of government as no previous administration had. Every president was intent on making his own mistakes, in learning the lessons of history anew.

Franklin D. Roosevelt assembled a "brain trust" during his first presidential campaign. (It was initially "the brains trust," an offhand reference to FDR's advisers made by *New York Times* reporter James Kieran in 1932.) Headed by Columbia University economist Raymond C. Moley, the brain trust would guide FDR's response to the Great Depression, helping to implement new regulations aimed at banks, market stimulations to promote economic growth and jobs programs that returned millions of Americans to employment. They were a shadow cabinet, leading one journalist to observe that on "a routine administrative matter you go to a Cabinet member, but on matters of policy and the higher statesmanship you consult the professoriat."

Even though the New Deal policies implemented by the brain trust rescued the nation from its greatest economic calamity, there was also a populist backlash to this injection of professorial expertise into a government that had previously been—in image, if not always reality—the domain of rough-hewn men who fought in wars and tilled the land. As the political historian Richard Hofstadter wrote in his 1963 classic *Anti-intellectualism in American Life*, "the notion became widely current that the professors were running things, and a veritable brain-trust war began which reawakened and quickened the old traditions of anti-intellectualism," a suspicion of learning and expertise that, Hofstadter argued with cutting eloquence, had informed the American experiment from its inception.

It was not lost on FDR's opponents that many of his advisers were Jewish, leading some to dub his programs "the Jew Deal." A writer in the *Saturday Evening Post* posited that no "thoughtful man can escape the conclusion that many of the brain trust ideas and plans are based on Russian ideology."

Dwight D. Eisenhower, president from 1953 until 1961, probably ran the most disciplined cabinet in modern White House history. Eisenhower earned fame as a military commander, but his cabinet was stocked with business executives, leading Richard Strout of the *New Republic* to call it "eight millionaires and a plumber," the latter being Martin P. Durkin of the Journeymen Plumbers and Steamfitters Union, who was to head Eisenhower's Department of Labor.

Under Eisenhower, cabinet "meetings were relatively formal, with fixed agendas and focused discussions and follow through," Pfiffner wrote. "Eisenhower used his cabinet by delegating as much as possible to his cabinet secretaries and by using the collective cabinet as a deliberative, though not a decision making, body."

John F. Kennedy's cabinet was less military band and more free-wheeling jazz quartet. He presided over a "loosely structured White House," as Pfiffner described it, one in which intelligence, grace, wit, and breeding were more important than anything to be found on an organizational chart. It was an administration in love with intelligence, principally its own. Like Kennedy himself, many of the best and brightest—as that cabinet would come to be known, in a sobriquet loaded with tragic irony—were bred in the boarding schools of the East Coast and, after that, the Ivy League. If they were not born into the highest reaches of society, like Secretary of State Dean Rusk, they had long ago assimilated into the ruling class and adapted its affects, from the Brooks Brothers suits to a paternalism about the affairs of government.

The best and the brightest would be principally remembered as the flawed heroes of David Halberstam's 1972 book, where that phrase originated (there was also an 1811 Christian hymn, "Brightest and Best," but Halberstam claimed he was not trying to play on its title). Convinced that the world was precisely as they believed it to be, even as the world offered increasing evidence to the contrary, they walked into a Southeast Asian trap just as the French—humiliated at Dien Bien Phu—were slinking out of it. By the time we walked out, 58,000 Americans, and perhaps as many as two million Vietnamese civilians, would be dead.

None of that was apparent on January 20, 1961, as John F. Kennedy stood on the East Portico of the U.S. Capitol and, taking the oath of office, vowed an end to "tyranny, poverty, disease, and war itself." Coming from the handsome and articulate young president, this seemed a credible promise. Halberstam told the story of how impressed Vice President Lyndon B. Johnson, who had emerged untutored from the Texas scrublands, was by the men whom Kennedy had hired to bring the nation across the New Frontier. "After attending his first Cabinet meeting," Halberstam wrote, Johnson "went back to his mentor [fellow Texan and Speaker of the House] Sam Rayburn and told him with great enthusiasm how extraordinary they were, each brighter than the next."

Rayburn was less impressed. "You may be right and they may be every bit as intelligent as you say," he told Johnson, "but I'd feel a whole lot better about them if just one of them had run for sheriff once."

Tellingly, Steve Bannon was spotted reading *The Best and the Brightest* by an observant *New York Times* college sports reporter while waiting to board a flight at Hartsfield-Jackson International Airport in Atlanta. This was in late December 2016, about a month before Trump's inauguration. "I'm having everyone in the transition read it," Bannon said to the reporter about Halberstam's book. "It's great for seeing how little mistakes early on can lead to big ones later." (He subsequently explained that, actually, only some people on the transition were made to read *The Best and the Brightest.* Maybe more should have.)

Nixon, like Trump, governed without seeking advice from his cabinet members, especially since much of the cabinet was focused on domestic policy, and Nixon found domestic policy beneath him. Accordingly, the cabinet was beneath him, too. "I am only interested when we make a major breakthrough or have a major failure," Nixon decreed. "Otherwise don't bother me." To make sure he wasn't bothered, he had chief of staff H. R. "Bob" Haldeman, who said of his job, "Every President needs a son of a bitch, and I'm Nixon's. I'm his buffer and I'm his bastard. I get done what he wants done and I take the heat instead of him."

Shielding a president from lower-level administrative disagreements was a crucial task, as some in the Trump administration would discover. Haldeman may have done it too well. He and another top Nixon aide, John D. Ehrlichman, were accused of forming a "Berlin Wall" around the Oval Office, isolating Nixon by severely restricting the flow of information to him. Both men went to prison for their involvement in Watergate. Their boss did not.

Gerald R. Ford, who became president after Nixon resigned, kept most of his predecessor's cabinet, in what proved an unwelcome continuity. In 1975, he fired several members of that cabinet, which had succumbed to vicious rivalries. The most notable victim of what came to be known as the Halloween Massacre was Henry A. Kissinger, who was deposed from his position as national security advisor (though he stayed secretary of state). Ford also named Dick Cheney his chief of staff. Cheney worked quietly but efficiently to consolidate power. "Somebody has to be in charge," he explained. Cheney was happy to be that somebody.

Jimmy Carter's management of the executive branch was much like the rest of his administration: high-toned, idealistic, and hopelessly ineffective. Coming into office, the former Georgia governor vowed a definitive break with the administrations of Nixon and Ford. "I believe in Cabinet administration of our government," Carter said. "There will never be an instance while I am President when the members of the White House staff dominate or act in a superior position to the members of our cabinet." This did not work out as planned. In July 1979, Jimmy Carter accepted the resignations of six cabinet members during a national crisis of confidence that many charged the White House had done too little to quell. The dismissals did nothing to rescue Carter's prospects for a second term.

Ronald Reagan won the presidency at least in part on the promise of a conservative revolution, but his cabinet lacked the ideological warriors some yearned for and others feared. That infuriated evangelicals, who had been disappointed with the liberalism of Carter, a practicing Baptist, and had gone with Reagan less out of conviction than convenience. His cabinet choices felt like a betrayal. Complained Patrick J. Buchanan, "Where is the dash, color, and controversy—the customary concomitants of a Reagan campaign?"

Reagan was a famous delegator of responsibility; his White House was largely run by the "troika" of Edwin Meese III, James A. Baker III, and Michael K. Deaver. This arrangement seemed to function for much of the first term, though signs of breakdown became increasingly evident by 1983. "I've never worked in an organization like this," one White House staffer complained. "There is no one person to give orders, except the President. This lends itself to jockeying for position and not letting anyone else get too far ahead."

Bill Clinton's cabinet was centrist and cerebral, but the *West Wing* mythology obscured the chaos of the early years of his presidency. There were remarkable similarities to the Trump administration. For one, Clinton had invested too little in the transition, which "led to a White House staff that was constructed late, on the fly and almost by remainder," as adviser William A. Galston would remember in 2004. In the summer of 1994, Clinton replaced chief of staff Thomas

F. "Mack" McLarty III with Leon E. Panetta, which he hoped would, as the *New York Times* put it, "dispel the notion around the country that the White House is a chaotic operation in which decisions are made largely on impulse." Things did get better after that, though then Monica Lewinsky came along, and Clinton succumbed to something worse than impulse, causing something worse than chaos.

The cabinet of George W. Bush seemed to largely reflect the desires of Dick Cheney, probably the most powerful vice president in the history of the United States. Naming him as a running mate was Bush's "most remarkable organizational achievement" in the words of Fred I. Greenstein, one of the great scholars of presidential power. Bush was the first president to hold a graduate business degree, which led him to govern by what Greenstein generously called "a corporate model" of promiscuous delegation. Others were less generous. After he left the administration, Treasury Secretary Paul H. O'Neill would describe Bush at cabinet meetings as "a blind man in a room full of deaf people." O'Neill complained that cabinet members had "little more than hunches about what the president might think."

Trump desperately needed a Cheney of his own, who would guide his thinking on unfamiliar topics, translate inchoate wishes into policy goals and make sure that even in the far-flung reaches of the administrative empire, presidential directives were being followed.

Trump proved his own best saboteur. On November 13, he announced that Reince Priebus would serve as his chief of staff, making the Republican National Committee chairman from Wisconsin the air traffic controller of the incoming administration. The same announcement declared that Bannon would serve as the White House "chief political strategist." Was this a power-sharing agreement? Nobody knew, including, it would quickly become clear, Trump himself.

It was clear that Bannon was not going to play the Cheney role in the Trump administration, since he was a rogue operator at heart, one who hated organizational charts as much as he hated wearing ties. Close as they were to Trump, Jared and Ivanka lacked the experience. That left Priebus.

Even people who liked him would quickly come to see him as an unsound guardian of the Oval Office. The importance of the position could not be overstated, especially for a president with no experience in politics. "Without a great chief of staff, a president frankly doesn't know what he is doing," Bill Clinton's labor secretary Robert B. Reich told the historian Chris Whipple.

One veteran of both the Trump campaign and the Trump administration tried to explain just how preposterous the Priebus pick was. Priebus should have had the wisdom to turn the job down, said the Trump veteran, who had worked for other Republican presidents and knew how things were supposed to run. It was winter, and it was dusk, and we were sitting in a bar in Northern Virginia. The gruff GOP hand pointed out the window, where commuters were on their way home. Imagine, he said, if a nurse came through that door and demanded we go with her to a hospital to perform heart surgery. We would have to beg off, the reason being that we knew nothing of cardiology. Only she would insist: We had to be the ones. She would drag us to the hospital, into the operating room. She would hand us scalpels, instruct us to get on with the quadruple bypass. And we would cut into the flesh, because either too much vanity or too little courage kept us from stepping away. That, he said, was what it was like to have Reince Priebus as the White House chief of staff.

The best chiefs of staff understood the mechanics of governing, which gears depended on each other, as well as where the machinery of policy overlapped with the machinery of politics. This was not Priebus's expertise. "The guy couldn't tell you how a bill becomes a law," scoffed another Republican operative, a top Trump campaign and transition official.

It would not be fair to blame Priebus entirely for the chaos of Trump's first year. Some of that chaos was natural to a new administration. But some of it—particularly on the cabinet level—resulted from inattention, an inability to tame eruptions of self-importance, carelessness, and greed. This would have been Priebus's job, as it had been the job of previous chiefs of staff. Eisenhower's cabinet was counterbalanced by a powerful chief of staff in Sherman Adams, the first man to officially hold that position. Adams wielded so much power in the West Wing that he became the subject of a joke: What if Adams should die and Eisenhower becomes president of the United States?

Nobody was going to mistake Reince Priebus for Sherman Adams. He was a fund-raiser, and fund-raising was courtship, not management. He quickly set about transfusing as much of the RNC as he could into the West Wing. He hired Katie Walsh, a high-ranking RNC deputy, and Sean Spicer, an RNC spokesman. The communications shop quickly became a refuge for young RNC alumni. A joke about Priebus went around the building, much as there had once been a joke about Adams: If a journalist wanted a reaction from one of the White House press staffers, she needed to write a hit piece not on Trump, but on Priebus. If the Adams joke was about power, the Priebus joke was about petulance.

As for that cabinet itself, it came into focus in the weeks following the election. And as it did, it also came to look suspiciously like Trump himself. His cabinet was 85 percent white and 75 percent male, with an average age of sixty-two, according to Politico's calculations. It appeared to have been constructed in intentional opposition to the cabinet of Barack Obama, who had tried to inject a measure of multiculturalism into the upper ranks of the executive branch. Trump got rid of all that, dispensing with even the most remote pretense of gender or ethnic parity.

The cabinet was stocked with men and women of terrific wealth—DeVos, Mnuchin, Ross, McMahon—but they were not captains of industry or brilliant innovators, men and women whose wealth was a mark of singular achievement. DeVos had inherited her wealth, while McMahon and her husband Vince presided over WWE, the gaudy professional wrestling concern that was little more than a pageant of steroidal muscles and unhinged theatrics (Trump would sometimes appear at their matches, honing his dramaturgic skills). Mnuchin and Ross were both finance bottom-feeders, neither particularly respected in Wall Street's highest echelons. They would not command much respect in the Trump administration, either. It was a cabinet of wealth that was tacky and vulgar, wealth desperate for recognition, wealth that could only have been an insult to the average citizens whose tribune Trump vowed to be in Washington.

Senate hearings for cabinet nominees had not made for compelling television in the past. In the Trump administration, they were riveting, constituting the first real battle between Trump and Senate Democrats. They were a minority party without the power to block a nominee on their own. Their only hope was to seriously damage a nominee, causing him or her to withdraw, or to raise so many doubts that moderate Republicans may decide to cast a "nay" vote.

They succeeded most clearly in the case of Andrew F. Puzder, who withdrew his nomination to head the Department of Labor in mid-February. Puzder was the chief executive of Carl's Jr., the fast-food chain best known for advertisements featuring voluptuous women performing fellatio on hamburgers. "I like beautiful women eating burgers in bikinis. I think it's very American," Puzder once explained.

Puzder never even got to a Senate hearing. Unflattering reports hounded his nomination from the start, and the salacious ads that once seemed genius were now marshaled as evidence that Trump was hiring men just as blasé about sexual harassment as he was.

The "slutburger" ads, as they came to be known, portended greater troubles for Puzder. In a divorce filing from 1988, Puzder's then-wife testified that he had assaulted her. Just a few days before his nomination hearing, Politico unearthed an interview that ex-wife, Lisa Fierstein, had given to Oprah Winfrey in 1990. It was a sickening conversation. "The damage that I sustained you can't see. It's permanent," Fierstein said. "They don't hit you in the face. They're too smart. They don't hit you in front of everyone."

There were other embarrassments, too, of the sort that would plague many other Trump nominees in the weeks to come. During the presidential campaign, Trump had boasted of an unrivaled toughness on undocumented immigration, whereas Puzder once employed an undocumented woman at his Southern California mansion. And he was against increasing the minimum wage, even as Trump promised economic salvation to low-income Americans.

In a book he published in 2018, Puzder blamed his downfall on a popular Trump-era enemy: the media. He dismissed the allegations of spousal assault, writing that his ex-wife "acknowledged that the charges she had made were wholly untrue." Those charges, Puzder argued, should never have become a story. But they did, because of "the Left's attack campaign," which was "designed to defame and disparage."

Puzder withdrew his nomination two days after Lieutenant General Michael T. Flynn resigned as the national security advisor. Flynn had been a close Trump adviser during the campaign. Before that, he had been head of the Defense Intelligence Agency in the Obama administration, only to be fired from that position. Obama warned Trump against hiring Flynn, but as with so much else, the cocksure new president ignored his predecessor's advice. It took only twenty-four days for Flynn's return to public service to unravel, with reports of mystifyingly improper calls to the Russian ambassador outside the usual diplomatic channels, as well as lobbying work on behalf of foreign governments, work that Flynn did not see fit to report.

Puzder's withdrawal and Flynn's resignation refuted Trump's claims that his administration was coming together smoothly. If anything, the exact opposite was true.

Puzder aside, the Democrats at least partly succeeded in arguing to the American public that Trump was making poor choices. They did so by subjecting nominees to intense scrutiny before Senate committees, even if they knew that Republicans would ultimately move the nomination forward, and that the entire chamber, narrowly controlled by Republicans, would confirm that nominee. The question was how much the nominee could be wounded before he or she became a cabinet member, how much the nominee could be shamed, interrogated, and browbeaten, so that he or she never afterward had the feeling of job security.

Trump's people knew this, of course. The transition headquarters on F Street, moribund in the weeks and days before the presidential election, came to life as winter settled over Washington. In a wood-paneled room that resembled a Senate hearing chamber, transition officials conducted intense preparation sessions—known as murder boards—for the nominees. They had Republicans familiar with the confirmation process ask the nominees the kinds of difficult, uncomfortable questions they could expect from Democrats; one person who was there even remembers a few former U.S. senators taking part.

Not everyone took the murder boards seriously. Jeff Sessions, who was nominated to be the U.S. attorney general, spurned invitations to come to F Street, instead conducting his own preparations, with his own staff. Much later, it became clear that Sessions lied to the Senate about the extent of his contact with the Russians. Would having gone to the murder boards have changed that? Maybe not. But people did not forget that he had failed to show.

Nominees were encouraged to bring family members to the murder boards, in order to simulate the sensation of having your spouse and children sit behind you as political adversaries delved into your history, holding every potential embarrassment, no matter how small, up to the light. Wilbur Ross brought his wife to the murder boards, but also a younger man. Someone asked who this younger man was.

As one person who was there remembers, Ross answered that it was his tennis trainer. They were scheduled to play later, so it only made sense to bring his tennis pro to the murder boards. It was a hint that Ross would do things his own way, as he had always done them. He was too old, and too rich, to do them any other way.

Nominees were also dispatched to Capitol Hill to meet with senators to build support and quell incipient anxieties. The importance of these meetings was directly related to the level of unease transition officials expected from Democrats. Among those who worried the transition most was Scott Pruitt, a favorite of energy executives and climate-change deniers. Concerned that his extreme anti-environmentalism might lead some Republicans to drop support, the transition sent him to meet with forty-two senators.

The nominee was usually ferried to Capitol Hill by a "sherpa," a liaison who had the requisite congressional experience, from a knowledge of what legislators wanted, or feared, to a mastery of the labyrinthine underground passageways beneath the U.S. Capitol. For some reason, Pruitt did not like his original sherpa, so he went to the transition offices and picked another. This new sherpa, who would accompany Pruitt to his meetings with senators, was Rob Porter, who at the time was chief of staff to Orrin G. Hatch, the senior Republican senator from Utah.

Working on Pruitt's confirmation was the first step in Porter's elevation within the still largely unformed Trump administration. Porter would be a key White House figure in the second half of 2017, as the White House struggled to curb the disorder of the administration's first months. But then he would be undone by a scandal that prompted him to leave the White House, and some of that disorder would return.

The confirmation hearings began on January 10, with Sessions facing the Senate Judiciary Committee. It was a tough hearing; Sessions was asked about his views on race, his contacts with Russia, and his independence (or lack thereof) from Trump. Most of the hearings that followed did not get much easier, with Democrats doing their best to override the triumphalist narrative of Fox News and Breitbart, to portray the incoming department chiefs as incompetent and unprepared.

Education secretary Betsy DeVos proved the most confounding of Trump's nominees. Some of the intense dislike she engendered was probably the result of sexism, as well as some bias against her conservative brand of Christianity. It did not help that her brother Erik Prince was the founder of Blackwater, the infamous military contractor responsible for several bloody excesses during the war in Iraq.

But most of all, it was DeVos who hurt herself. Asked by Senator Christopher S. Murphy, a Democrat from Connecticut, about guns in schools (he had become a ferocious gun control advocate after the 2012 shooting at the Sandy Hook Elementary School, which left twenty children dead), she said that was "best left to locales and states to decide," like a woman ordered not to stray from Republican dogma on the Second Amendment. Pressed to explain, she referenced rural schools in Wyoming and the need "to protect from potential grizzlies," thus inadvertently giving birth to one of the first great memes of the Trump presidency (there would be many more in the months to come).

Questions from Senator Al Franken, a Democrat from Minnesota, revealed that DeVos was totally unfamiliar with the difference between measuring student growth and student proficiency, a crucial distinction in the debates over standardized testing and teacher effectiveness. "It surprises me that you don't know this issue," Franken said sourly. DeVos kept on smiling.

There were many things DeVos did not know. In an exchange with Senator Maggie Hassan, she failed to grasp that the Individuals with Disabilities Education Act was a federal law, meaning it could not be selectively applied. DeVos pledged her "sensitivity," but that hardly allayed Hassan. "With all due respect, it's not about sensitivity," the Democrat from New Hampshire retorted. "Although that helps." (The sensitivity would turn out to be a ruse; the following fall, her Department of Education canceled seventy-two guidances for special education and disabled students because they were supposedly "outdated, unnecessary, or ineffective.")

Not every nomination hearing went quite so badly, but enough did to make one wonder if they were being staged by the comedic minds of *Saturday Night Live*, especially since Senator Franken of Minnesota was an alumnus of the program.

"Did you enjoy meeting me?" Franken drily asked Rick Perry, the former governor of Texas nominated to head the Department of Energy.

"I hope you are as much fun on that dais," a beaming Perry answered, "as you were on your couch." The salacious implications being rather blatant, Perry pleaded to "rephrase that." He was easily confirmed, the Senate untroubled by recent reports that Perry had no clue that the Department of Energy oversaw all of the nation's nuclear facilities and was responsible for the management of some ninety thousand metric tons of nuclear waste, which could leak into the groundwater or fall into the hands of terrorists. That he would have to learn on the job, along with much else.

By and large, the Senate was powerless to properly take stock of Trump's cabinet choices, with all their conflicts of interest and ethical lapses. Republicans didn't have the courage to oppose Trump, and Democrats didn't have the numbers. And no one with access to the Oval Office pointed out to the president that bad advice, or an errantly wired decision-making process, was leading him to select people who were far more likely to subvert his agenda than to execute it. He was draining the swamp by filling it with sewage, but there would be no reward in blaming him for the stench.

Wilbur Ross was the perfect embodiment of the power elite

Trump had run against. His key trait was loyalty to Trump, or at least loyalty perceived. "Wilbur maxed out," Bannon said of his contributions to the Trump campaign. That earned him the distinction of being nominated for the Department of Commerce, which would in effect make him the nation's chief negotiator on a potential trade war with China, which Trump promised was coming, or a reworking of the North American Free Trade Agreement, which Trump had labeled a "disaster" during the campaign.

In 2009, Ross had invested $100 million in Longyuan Power, a Chinese wind power producer. He was also an investor in Diamond S Shipping Group, Inc., a Chinese concern that would benefit from continued open trade with the United States. And a ProPublica investigation published that December found he had invested in and sat on the board of ArcelorMittal, the world's largest steel producer. He would therefore have a personal stake in any tariffs the Trump administration decided to levy.

"It's never happened that a Commerce secretary has been so directly involved in the fallout, and rewards, from previous trade deals," one former treasury official told ProPublica.

This did not subject Ross to the scrutiny he deserved. Sitting in front of the Commerce Committee, he mumbled his way through his testimony in the manner of a municipal accountant reading from his ledger before a deserted city council hearing. No one who hoped that Trump would rebalance the American economy through better trade deals could have been heartened by the droning performance.

Maria E. Cantwell, the junior Democratic senator from Washington State, and one of the youngest members in the chamber, teased out the problem with magically converting billionaires like Ross into public servants. "The President-elect's administration is trying to bring in a lot of private sector experience," Cantwell said as Ross sat before her. "I appreciate private sector experience, but oftentimes that experience is about answering to shareholders and other special interests.

This is about answering to the public interest." Her analysis of the tension between private wants and public needs would haunt Trump's administration in the months to come. Ross promised to be "quite scrupulous about recusal and any topic where there is the slightest scintilla of doubt." Soon enough, this assurance would prove to be disingenuous.

Ross and other nominees benefited from the crosswinds buffeting Capitol Hill that winter of 2017. Republicans were eager to confirm Trump's cabinet and begin the business of government. They weren't thrilled by some of Trump's choices, and they were confused by others, but if they wanted to repeal the Affordable Care Act and install conservative justices on the U.S. Supreme Court, they needed to get through this awkward first round of dating.

Steve Mnuchin, the oleaginous Santa Monica banker who clung to Trump's side throughout the campaign, was a cluster bomb of ethical shortcomings, if not of glaring illegalities. His riches were about as ill gained as riches could get, predicated on his 2009 purchase of IndyMac, the California bank in part responsible for driving the foreclosure crisis. Mnuchin and his partners drove it harder, and further, at one point foreclosing on a ninety-year-old woman who'd mistakenly sent Mnuchin's bank three cents, when she in fact owed thirty.

As Mnuchin went to Capitol Hill to testify before the Senate Finance Committee, it was revealed that he had failed to disclose about $100 million in assets on the financial disclosures he had filed. He claimed this was mere oversight. The mistake was worthy of leniency, unlike the mistakes of IndyMac mortgage-holders he had foreclosed on.

Democrats wanted badly to sink Mnuchin's nomination, but got no help from their GOP counterparts, who praised Mnuchin for a nonexistent commitment to ordinary Americans. Republicans could have easily argued that Mnuchin was spectacularly unsuited to the task of carrying out Trump's message of economic populism. But they had all seen what Trump's tweets could do to a political rival. And now, those tweets would be coming from the Oval Office. So they stayed silent.

Sometimes, Democrats simply gave up, recognizing the odds they faced and the ammunition (in particular, outrage and indignation) they needed to conserve for the coming years. This was true even with nominees like Ben Carson, who was as qualified to lead the Department of Housing and Urban Development as he was to coach the Washington Capitals. Carson said so himself. When it was first rumored that Trump was considering his former campaign adversary for a cabinet position, an adviser shot down the notion: "Dr. Carson feels he has no government experience, he's never run a federal agency. The last thing he would want to do was take a position that could cripple the presidency." Now the man who once mused about whether the Holocaust could have been avoided if Europe's Jews were better armed would oversee the nation's public housing.

Troubling as this was, Democrats let Carson pass. His cluelessness was treated as amusing, perhaps even a sign of genius. He compared Senator Sherrod Brown, the customarily shrewd and brittle Democrat from Ohio, to the television detective Columbo. That was hilarious. He misspoke (one assumed) and said he would do nothing "to benefit any American." That was pretty funny, too. "I know that Trump is probably gonna destroy the world," joked *Daily Show* host Trevor Noah, "but at least Carson is gonna make it fun on the way out."

By April 27, with the successful confirmation of Alex Acosta to head the Department of Labor, Trump's cabinet was finally confirmed. They had surrounded Washington. The city was theirs for the taking.

Chapter 4

·······

FREE COMMERCIALS

The White House was his, and it was empty. It was January 20, 2017, and Donald Trump had taken the oath of office some two hours before. After traveling down Pennsylvania Avenue in the inaugural parade, the presidential limousine pulled through the northwest gate and toward the North Portico of the White House. For the next four years, this was going to be home. Hell, maybe for the next eight.

It did not feel like that right away, would not for months to come. There were ushers waiting on the upper floors, there was staff moving through the basement, but in the gray light of that January day, the White House seemed a deserted mansion. There was no instruction manual, no one waiting to give them a leisurely tour. But there were millions waiting for the president and first lady to emerge, as well as an evening ahead of them studded with celebratory galas.

An advance man helped the Trumps find a bathroom where they could fix their hair. Then it was back into the world, where a wintry mix of jubilation and anger awaited.

Steve Bannon couldn't care less if the Trumps felt cozy at 1600 Pennsylvania Avenue. That was not why he'd fought through the darkest days of the campaign, when the smirking visage of Billy Bush ("How about a little hug for the Donald? He just got off the bus.") seemed to fill every television and smartphone screen in the land, when pundits debated just how badly Trump would be embarrassed.

The first two weeks of the Trump administration would be the closest that his presidency would ever come to the assault Bannon had envisioned. He wanted to "flood the zone," as he put it, to utterly overwhelm Trump's critics and opponents before they could throw up any legal or legislative barricades in their way.

Trump was happy to sign executive orders, which gave the appearance of work diligently accomplished. But he also remained furious about debates over the size of his inaugural crowd, which were compared unfavorably to President Obama's.

Even as he pushed ahead on Bannon's agenda of restricted immigration and decreased regulation, Trump sent ominous signs about what he expected from the people who were coming to work for him, about what excellence in service of the public was going to look like under President Trump.

After the release of the *Access Hollywood* tape, a San Francisco woman named Shannon Coulter started a boycott campaign called Grab Your Wallet, a name that referenced the crudest of Trump's remarks on that recording. The goal wasn't just to boycott Trump's own products—the wine, the throw blankets, the ties—which would have been distasteful in the first place to urbane liberals like Coulter. Rather, the boycott was aimed at retailers that enabled the Trumps by carrying their products.

After his victory, Grab Your Wallet became the best, if still very much inadequate, means of making Trump feel some of the pain of the anti-Trump resistance. Among the largest retailers to respond to the pressure was Nordstrom, which operated close to four hundred department stores across North America. On February 2, Nordstrom announced that it would no longer carry the clothing line of Ivanka Trump. Nordstrom did not say that the boycott movement had anything to do with that decision, issuing a statement about the need to "refresh our assortment."

If the point was to enrage Trump, the objective was achieved, and in very public fashion. The president tweeted about the Nordstrom affair on Wednesday, February 8, around the time he would have been reviewing his presidential daily briefing a summary of the most significant threats to the nation's security. "My daughter Ivanka has been treated so unfairly by @Nordstrom," the president complained. "She is a great person—always pushing me to do the right thing! Terrible!"

This came from Trump's own Twitter account, but since he was intent on using that handle instead of the one specifically allotted to the president, the message had the force of a presidential announcement. The use of public office for private gain was strictly illegal, but the president was not a midlevel bureaucrat at the Department of Labor. He held the most scrutinized office on earth, but that office also put him on complex legal terrain, if not exactly outside the law, then somewhere on its fraying boundary. Much of a president's behavior depended on decorum, his understanding of what it meant to sit where Lincoln and Kennedy once sat. When a president defiled that office (and Trump certainly wasn't the first), it was unclear what price he had to pay.

Even some in the pro-Trump brigade were discomfited by the tweet—and they had been discomfited by so little else during his journey to Pennsylvania Avenue. On Fox News, one young conservative offered that the "White House is not QVC." For this to come from the president's favored source of insight and information was nothing short of cruel.

A remedy was at hand. The morning after Trump's tweet criticizing Nordstrom, one of Trump's top advisers, Kellyanne Conway, appeared on his most beloved Fox News program, *Fox & Friends*, the network's flagship morning show. It was 7:48 a.m. in Washington, and

Conway was standing in the James S. Brady Press Briefing Room, which was usually empty at that hour. Speaking about Ivanka, Conway sounded like a cross between an aggrieved-yet-proud aunt and a junior publicist who had been handed talking points by her client only moments before.

"You can certainly buy her goods online," Conway informed viewers. She mused that Trump's adversaries were "using her, who's been a champion for women empowerment, women in the workplace, to get to him." She then offered, with a carefree wave of the hand, a way to counter Nordstrom, Grab Your Wallet, and all the other forces aligned against the Trump family: "Go buy Ivanka's stuff is what I would tell you. I hate shopping, but I'm gonna go get some myself today."

In the Manhattan studio of *Fox & Friends*, host Steve Doocy smiled at the suggestion, noting that a campaign in favor of Ivanka Trump's merchandise had been launched on Twitter. But next to the perennially upbeat Doocy, cohosts Brian Kilmeade and Ainsley Earhardt looked like they were witnessing an execution. They must have been aware that Conway's endorsement had crossed a line that no presidential administration had crossed before (though the Clintons' treatment of the Lincoln Bedroom as an Airbnb for political donors came close). Kilmeade fiddled with a pen, glancing uneasily off-camera for help that was not coming.

Conway evidently saw no problem with the endorsement, because she repeated it a few moments later, after a gratuitous but unsurprising barb at Hillary Clinton's "failed" appeal to the American voter. "It's a wonderful line; I own some of it," Conway said. "I'm just gonna give a free commercial here, go buy it today, you can buy it online."

The commercial would not be free. Trump was now the president, and Conway was a top White House staffer whose $179,700 salary was paid by the American taxpayer. And while Trump had promised in his dark inaugural address that "buy American" would be one of his governing principles, nobody expected that principle to be so quickly reduced to "buy Trump."

Maybe they should have expected just that. On January 11, nine days before the presidential inauguration, Trump held a press conference at Trump Tower in Manhattan to address ethics issues surrounding his administration. "I could actually run my business and run the government at the same time," he boasted. His tax lawyer, Sheri A. Dillon, described a vague arrangement in which Trump would not manage his businesses, but also not fully disassociate from them. On a table next to Trump were stacks of papers, presumably relating to his finances. A reporter's photograph showed that the papers were blank.

The press conference sent two signals. The first was that Trump did not think public service was worth sacrificing whatever gain he stood to make in private enterprise. The second was to the men and women he was then in the midst of recruiting for this administration. They could do the same, without fear of consequences, without worrying about how glaringly their desires to hold on to stock options or offshore accounts clashed with Trump's promises. Trump was telling them it was okay.

Remarkably, Trump held to this when he spoke in early 2019. "It sometimes makes it very difficult," he said, "because people can't go to work here because the rules and regulations are very strict, afterwards." This raised an obvious question: Why would he want to employ people whose main concern would be their post-White House source of income?

"The tone was set by the president when he decided not to divest," said Walter M. Shaub Jr., who'd been appointed by Obama as the head of the Office of Government Ethics, which served as the referee of the executive branch. Shaub would remain in that post during the transition and for the first five and a half months of Trump's tenure, growing increasingly dismayed by what he saw, finding few reasons for optimism. After leaving the White House, he described how the administration "came in unprepared for the rigors" of working within the federal government, "unaware of the fact that there are many requirements and a culture of accountability to the public."

Shaub blamed a lot of the ethical lapses on White House Counsel Don McGahn, whom he charged with fostering an anything-goes atmosphere by interpreting rules and laws in ways that allowed Trump to skirt them. That may have been an overestimation of the power McGahn wielded in the West Wing, of the energy with which he approached his responsibilities. Quickly falling out of favor with Trump, he sequestered himself in his office, almost never coming into the Oval Office to offer Trump the counsel he so desperately needed.

If Washington was a swamp, McGahn was a creature from its deepest depths. He was a close ally of Mitch McConnell, while his wife Shannon was a Republican operative on Capitol Hill. An expert in the financing of political campaigns, he was appointed to the Federal Election Commission by George W. Bush near the end of his second term in the White House. He served on the FEC for the next five years, doing what he could to make it easier for wealthy donors and corporations to contribute to political campaigns. This would be the very culture Trump would run against, promising a campaign where dark money and corporate cash would have no say. But not especially concerned with incongruences, even flagrant ones, he hired McGahn—who by 2015 had moved to Jones Day—to be his chief campaign lawyer. Two years later, he followed Trump to the White House.

McGahn "had no business being a White House counsel," said a lawyer who worked with McGahn in the West Wing. He was a "judge guy," happy to push through judicial nominees preselected by the Federalist Society or McConnell. But he utterly abdicated the role of offering sound legal advice to the president and his staff.

Trump grew to despise McGahn, who had a law degree from

fourth-tier Widener University, in marked contrast to peers who had been trained at Harvard or Yale Law. Trump blamed McGahn for the immensely sloppy executive order restricting travel from Muslim-majority countries, which the president thought should have received better legal vetting. He also blamed McGahn for Jeff Sessions recusing himself from the Russia investigation. In response, McGahn grew ever more distant.

Reince Priebus was another enabler. A week before the inauguration, he warned on national television that Shaub "ought to be careful" about criticizing Trump's conflicts of interests. Priebus complained to ABC's George Stephanopoulos that Shaub was "becoming extremely political" and thus squandering his credibility.

"I'm not sure what this person at government ethics, what sort of standing he has anymore in giving these opinions," Priebus said.

Trump liked having his way, but he also respected people like Bannon who would stand up to him, tell him to his face that he was full of shit. The diminutive Priebus lacked charisma or a blazing wit, not to mention courage. He was "the little guy from Kenosha," as Bannon put it. Priebus's attack on Shaub was revealing of a desperation to be liked by the chief executive, even at the expense of the presidential credibility he was charged with protecting. Lacking conviction, searching for approval, Priebus hastened his own irrelevance.

Kellyanne Conway's "free commercial" from the Brady Briefing Room became an early test of how seriously the administration took the promises Trump made to the American people. It was also an opportunity to see if the immune cells of the body politic worked as they were supposed to, whether they recognized that something was amiss and reacted as they were supposed to.

Four days after Conway's appearance on *Fox & Friends*, Shaub sent a letter to Deputy White House Counsel Stefan C. Passantino, in hopes that the capable young ethics lawyer would see things his way. Passantino was decent and bright, eager about toiling in the federal

government's employ. Upon his appointment to the Trump administration, he had earned unlikely praise from Howard Dean, the former
head of the Democratic National Committee.

In his letter to Passantino, Shaub wrote that "there is strong
reason to believe that Ms. Conway has violated the Standards of
Conduct and that disciplinary action is warranted." Shaub noted
that the regulations, which were put in place by George W. Bush,
contained a hypothetical example of such a violation: a White
House official "appearing in a television commercial to promote a
product." The letter drily observed that "Ms. Conway's actions track
that example almost exactly."

Passantino bristled at being lectured by Shaub. He wrote back that
Conway "made the statement in question in a light, off-hand manner while attempting to stand up for a person she believed had been
unfairly treated and did so without nefarious motive or intent to benefit personally." In a footnote, Passantino interpreted federal rules to
conclude that Shaub lacked oversight power over the executive office
of the president, meaning that he could not sanction Conway over
the endorsement even if a sanction were warranted.

Shaub was stunned. "The assertion is incorrect, and the letter cites
no legal basis for it," he wrote back to Passantino. To him, Passantino's
pushback was evidence that the Trump administration sought not
only to disregard ethics rules, but to actively dismantle them. "They
just wanted maximum latitude to do anything they wanted," Shaub
complained.

Shaub announced that he was leaving OGE on July 6, 2017 (the
following summer, Passantino would follow him out the gates). Upon
his departure, he deemed the administration he was leaving behind
"pretty close to a laughingstock." He watched in dismay as, two
months later, Trump used his response to Hurricane Harvey's devastation of Texas to promote a line of campaign hats.

Although he would hesitate to admit it, Trump modeled his

political approach after that of Michael R. Bloomberg, the financial services entrepreneur who became mayor of New York in 2002, despite having never held elected office before. Bloomberg was one of the wealthiest people in the United States, which made him impervious to the sleazy machine politics that had governed the city since the days of Tammany Hall. Trump promised to do for the White House what Bloomberg had done for City Hall: stock it with serious, incorruptible people whom only he could attract to the public sector.

Trump did make one crucial move in the direction of good government. That was the signing of Executive Order 13770 on Saturday, January 28.

EO 13770 was titled "Ethics Commitments by Executive Branch Appointees." Political appointees to executive branch positions came from outside the civil service and were nominated to their posts by the president. Under the new order, all such appointees had to pledge that they would not lobby the agency to which they were appointed for five years after leaving it; they would abide by restrictions regarding contact with agency officials; would not lobby foreign governments after working for the administration; would not accept gifts from lobbyists; and would follow other regulations.

Raj S. Shah, the deputy White House press secretary, grandiosely called it "the most sweeping Executive Order in U.S. history to end the revolving door" between 1600 Pennsylvania Avenue and the lobbying firms of K Street, singling out the injunction against foreign lobbying in particular. In some ways, the order was not dissimilar from what the Obama administration had in place: in fact, some parts of the executive order appeared to have been taken wholesale from the Obama version, thus making for an ironic and telling ethical transgression of its own.

The news of EO 13770, and any debate over its relative merits, was utterly lost in the furor over Executive Order 13769, which had been signed that Friday night, banning travelers originating in seven majority-Muslim countries from entering the United States. Hastily written and announced to the public like a minor-league pitching change, EO 13769 sent protesters to airports and into the streets. That made EO 13770 something between an afterthought and a joke.

The difference between making a rule and enforcing it was the difference between consulting a map and actually traveling the route. With his farcical transition press conference on January 11, Trump had indicated that Bannon's populist revolution was not on his agenda. That project, however dubious, would have required selfless men, not men like Steve Mnuchin and Wilbur Ross.

According to Norman L. Eisen, who served as President Obama's chief ethics lawyer, the executive order on ethics was sabotaged by the very people in the executive branch charged with implementing it. Eisen claimed that the widespread granting of ethics waivers by the administration—in effect, permits to violate the new rules—completely undermined the executive order. "They've made a mockery of the executive order and of ethics in general," he said, claiming that the Trump administration had "virtually no standard" on how such waivers are granted.

Eisen found Trump officials' contention that their executive order was virtually equivalent to the one that guided the Obama administration preposterous: "It's an ethics calamity of a kind we have never seen in modern presidential history." Only six months into the presidency, there were seventy-four lobbyists already working in the administration, forty-nine of them in agencies they once lobbied on behalf of clients.

There were plenty of men and women in the Trump administration who had no interest in doing free commercials for Ivanka Trump. Many of them had served under George W. Bush, and they understood the contours of federal employment: what they could do, what they could never get away with, what bad optics would do to their careers, which could involve working in Washington, *with*

Washington, long after their terms in the Trump administration were through.

Trump's cabinet members, for the most part, lacked this same awareness. Some were new to government. Some were new to Washington. Conway's free commercial, Priebus telling Shaub to not meddle in presidential affairs, were signs that they could do as they pleased. The boss would not mind, and the public would never know.

Chapter 5

......

ALLIGATORS AND LILY PADS

For such a pedestrian word, "lobbyist" summoned up a glorious carnival of sleaze. If scandal was upon Washington once more, a lobbyist was most definitely to blame. Not that any such blame would ever be credibly pinned in time for the public accounting the lobbyist had long deserved. Others would be dragged before congressional committees, forced into shows of contrition. The lobbyist was too quick, too smooth, the firm he worked for too powerful. Washington would never expel him because Washington needed him too much.

That was how lobbying had come to be seen by the early twenty-first century, and if that depiction was not entirely fair, it was also not entirely undeserved. It would be impossible to understand how Washington worked—and thus the reality of what truly powered the legislative and executive branches of government, cabinet departments included—without understanding lobbying, for no other reason than that lobbyists were the bees that pollinated the flowers.

What replenished K Street was the steady flow of talent from Capitol Hill. There were 425 former members of Congress as of 2018 who worked as registered lobbyists. The number of former congressional staffers plying the same trade was in the thousands: 69 alumni of Hillary Clinton's time as the junior U.S. senator from New York are or were registered lobbyists, giving her first place in this category.

There was nothing surprising about this migration. A junior legislative aide in Congress could expect to make about $40,000 per year. As a lobbyist, she could easily triple or quadruple her salary.

Lobbying the federal government was by 2018 a $3.3 billion annual enterprise, one that until 2016 had a lobbying group of its own, the Association of Government Relations Professionals. In 2018, the Center for Responsive Politics concluded that there were 11,444 registered lobbyists in Washington, as well as thousands more working as "shadow lobbyists," doing the work of lobbying without adhering to the rules. There was the National Association of Ordnance and Explosive Waste Contractors, as well as the U.S. Association of Reptile Keepers, not to mention the Beer Institute. If there was a cause, there was a lobbyist.

America's first lobbyist was William Hull, hired in 1792 to advocate for Virginians who had fought in the American Revolution. Some decades after that, gun-maker Samuel Colt found himself in need of a patent extension. To this end, he hired Washington lobbyists who "have at different times presented pistols to certain members," as a later investigation found.

As for the dreaded term itself, a popular—though, unfortunately, probably apocryphal—story dates it to the administration of Ulysses S. Grant, the decorated Civil War general who would come to preside over one of the most corrupt presidential administrations in American history. Grant took an evening drink and cigar at the Willard Hotel, a couple of blocks from the White House. Those looking to win an audience with the president convened in the lobby of the Willard, a work of baroque splendor. (Historians have disputed that Grant's postprandial habits had anything to do with the advent of "lobbying" as a term of art, as it appears to have shown up in the English language as early as 1777.)

In 1875, Congress began an investigation into the granting of an improper subsidy to the Pacific Mail Steamship Company. Among the culprits was Samuel Cutler Ward, known as "the King of the Lobby." Ward defended his honor before the House Ways and Means Committee: "I do not say I am proud—but I am not ashamed—of the occupation." Ward knew that lavishing lawmakers with food and drink was often all it took and "proceeded upon the comfortable axiom," as a biographer would write, "that the shortest distance between a pending bill and a Congressman's 'aye' lies through his stomach."

No one lived this lesson as thoroughly as Jack A. Abramoff. By the time his career in Washington was over in 2005, and prison loomed, Abramoff had become the symbol of the Washington that Trump would run against. He was the swamp creature nonpareil, dragged from its lightless deep so that the whole nation could see what had become of American politics.

"I hope he goes to jail and we never see him again," said a Republican U.S. senator from Montana who eventually returned campaign contributions from the man who had come to be known as Casino Jack. "I wish he'd never been born, to be right honest with you."

By 2018, the façade of 801 Pennsylvania Avenue was shared by outlets of Wells Fargo, the coffee chain Paul, the salad chain Chopt, and several other unremarkable shops. Across the street was the concrete brutalist headquarters of the FBI, while on the next block, set back from the street, was the Trump International Hotel.

There was a time, nearly twenty years ago, when 801 Pennsylvania Avenue—located almost exactly between the White House and the U.S. Capitol—was the place to be. Between 2002 and 2005, this was the home of Signatures, one of the restaurants Abramoff owned in Washington, during a brief period when he owned all of Washington, or at least acted like he did.

There were places around Washington, like the charmingly fusty Tune Inn of Capitol Hill or the warm and rambling Old Ebbitt Grill across the street from the White House, that did not care to announce themselves as refuges for the powerful, which is probably why the powerful sought them out, savoring the chance to have a beer and burger without being bothered.

Signatures was for people who hungered to announce their arrival on the scene. A May 2002 review in *The Hill*, a paper for the city's political class, gushed that "Signatures has the feel of a successful venture, including some silent investors with deep pockets, a prime location...a skilled chef and imaginative menu," which included the then rare delicacy of Kobe beef from Japan. The review noted that the restaurant was owned by a group called Livsar Enterprises, among whose silent partners was "a prominent lobbyist" recently profiled by the *New York Times*. That lobbyist was Abramoff.

A product of Beverly Hills, Abramoff had gone to college at Brandeis University in Boston, where he headed the College Republicans chapter. He graduated in 1981 and went to Washington. He became the national chairman of the College Republicans upon his arrival in the district, then went to law school at Georgetown, graduating in 1986. He made a couple of movies, did some work for the apartheid South African government. In 1994, Jack Abramoff joined his first lobbying firm.

Abramoff's genius was in his understanding Washington exactly as it was, not as it should be or had once been. He saw Washington without her makeup and loved her anyway. Judging by the politicians who sold their votes to him, Washington loved him right back. He worked by seducing staffers on the Hill and, eventually, their bosses, the members of Congress themselves, while convincing interests foreign and domestic that he was a figure of Rasputin-like influence within the Republican Party. His method was simple, but effective. Horace M. Cooper, who had been an aide to Representative Dick Armey, the influential Republican from Texas, was feted with tickets to see all the major Washington sports teams in action, as well as with seats to performances by Bruce

Springsteen, the Dixie Chicks, and other acts. Who could say no to such largesse?

Plenty said yes. Republicans who turned out to have had dealings with Casino Jack, whether directly or not, included President George W. Bush, Texas attorney general John Cornyn (later the senior U.S. senator from that state), and Iowa senator Charles E. Grassley. There were Democrats, too, including U.S. Senate Minority Leader Harry Reid of Nevada and Tom Harkin of Iowa.

Abramoff's clients were stunningly diverse. They most famously included six Native American tribes from which he reaped $66 million, even as he derided their members as "plain stupid" and "monkeys." Other clients included the governments of Malaysia and the Northern Mariana Islands.

Downfall awaited Abramoff in 2005, after a whistleblower—another lobbyist—brought his trade secrets to light. The following year, a pained-looking Abramoff appeared on the cover of *Time* magazine as "the man who bought Washington." He was supposed to be a symbol of the city at its most venal, but the truly frightening thing was not what Abramoff got wrong but, rather, what he got right.

Abramoff left prison in 2010. He wrote a book about corruption and became a spokesman against lobbying. This did not last. By 2016, he was back at it, trying without success to broker a meeting between Trump and the Congolese president, Denis Sassou-Nguesso. The effort failed. As the Trump administration approached the end of its first year, Abramoff appeared on Fox News, where Tucker Carlson asked him if Washington had changed since the halcyon days when Signatures was a hot table.

In response, Abramoff laughed. "Washington, basically, is the same swamp it used to be," he said, "but they rearranged the alligators and the lily pads." From anyone else, this would have come across as calculated cynicism. Coming from Abramoff, it had the harsh texture of truth.

Every president had done such rearranging. In 1992, about a month and a half before the presidential election, the *Washington Post* reported, "High-profile staff members from various Washington lobbying firms are actively campaigning for Democratic nominee Bill Clinton," further noting that "Democratic lobbyists see the chance of expanding their influence and gaining new business if Bush is ousted."

The *Post* spoke to one lobbyist who predicted a Clinton victory, and the windfall that would bring to firms like his, Hill and Knowlton. "I think Clinton is going to win," that lobbyist said. "And we may well be the place to go if you want advice and counsel about how the new administration will affect your business, your cause or your country." The lobbyist's name was Frank Mankiewicz. He was once a top aide to Robert F. Kennedy. When Kennedy was assassinated in Los Angeles in 1968, it was Mankiewicz who announced the killing on television. There was nothing uniquely ignoble about his turning to lobbying, but it was a sign of where true power had come to reside in Washington.

Barack Obama's eight years in office were marked by a remarkable lack of major corruption-related scandal, but that was not because his administration shunned lobbyists. To the contrary, it welcomed them like every other administration. There were lobbyists on his transition team, despite promises they would be kept out. Democratic power lawyer Lanny Davis, a top Clinton aide, dismissed this incongruity. "From George Washington to George W. Bush, there has been a role for the lobbyist that is perfectly appropriate and good for democracy," he told the *Washington Post*. "The notion that there is something wrong per se with lobbying is ridiculous."

Lobbyists had access to the Obama administration, if not always to the White House itself in the most literal terms. Diagonally across the street from the White House, on Pennsylvania Avenue and Seventeenth Street, there was an always crowded outlet of Peet's

Coffee, the Berkeley-based chain, by the time that Trump took office. During the Obama presidency, this was Caribou Coffee, and it played more or less the same function as the Willard's lobby may have in Grant's time.

Inviting lobbyists on campus would have required them to be recorded in Secret Service visitor logs, which could be subject to Freedom of Information Act public disclosure. But there were no disclosure laws pertaining to a coffee shop, even if privacy would be in short supply. Some other meetings with lobbyists were held at the White House Conference Center and at the Council on Environmental Quality, both located in the genteel row houses of Jackson Place, in sight of the White House. These could also be kept secret.

"We don't believe there's anything untoward about these meetings, and we don't think that represents any special access for lobbyists," one White House official told the *New York Times* in 2010 about the Caribou Coffee klatches. This was untrue. The Obama staffers were trying to keep their lobbyist meetings secret by, paradoxically, holding them in public. The Obama administration did release its visitors' logs, though only after a lawsuit. Even then, the logs were incomplete.

Lobbyists were never more empowered than with the election of Donald Trump. He ran as their scourge; he would govern as their benefactor.

Trump may have banished Chris Christie from his transition, but when it came to actually making the four thousand political appointments for the executive branch that were the responsibility of the president, Trump inevitably turned to K Street, whose lobbying firms were clustered just north of the White House. That gave lobbyists enormous power in molding the Trump cabinet. Once the right people were in place, they could steer the federal government where they pleased.

What happened to draining the swamp and deconstructing the administrative state? There was no time, no will, at least not for the project as Bannon had envisioned it. He understood this as well as anyone. Washington was, as he put it, a "company town," and Trump was now its mayor. Trying to tear everything down was not going to be a very smart program, even if that had been the program he promised. But there were other promises, other imperatives, namely on trade, healthcare, and national security. "Draining the swamp is very important, don't get me wrong," Bannon said. "But you need to get the economy going again."

Opportunists rushed in. Savviest in gaining access to the new administration was the Heritage Foundation, the conservative think tank that opposed virtually every idea Bannon championed. The man who ran Heritage until the spring of 2017, Jim DeMint, made no pretenses about being an intellectual. A former U.S. senator from South Carolina, he was associated with the Tea Party and spent the first term of the Obama presidency in a state of perpetual resistance. When he took over Heritage in 2013, the think tank forswore its philosophic roots, taking on the reactionary dogmatism of its new leader.

Trump's lack of commitment to conservatism, his disregard for that movement as anything other than a means of winning the presidency, was not a problem for DeMint, who moved toward Trump as others backed away. The gamble proved auspicious, and Heritage was rewarded with dozens of appointments within the Trump administration, even as other conservative groups struggled to gain a foothold in the West Wing. The foundation was also instrumental, along with the Federalist Society, in selecting Trump's two successful Supreme Court nominees, Neil M. Gorsuch and Brett M. Kavanaugh.

"Here's the brutal reality," Bannon explained. "There was not a deep bench of talent that could step in to the government and run things. Now, we should have done a much better job of getting Trump people into the administration," the former chief strategist added, showing a reflectiveness that did not come across in his spirited public appearances. "Absolutely, much better job. It's one of the things that Trump didn't fight."

The presence of Heritage in the executive branch made the mainstream conservative movement—whose articles of faith Trump so floridly flaunted in his candidacy—the primary lobbying group within his administration. As of early 2019, Heritage had a remarkable 114 former employees or interns who were either serving or had served in the Trump administration. Heritage was not alone in influencing policy by influencing staffing. There were also, ProPublica discovered, 35 disciples of the free-market libertarians Charles G. and David H. Koch, not to mention 187 registered federal lobbyists.

What made the Trump administration unique was that its mundane reality contrasted so sharply with the grandiose vision of the presidential campaign. At the crux of that campaign was the idea that Trump himself was so rich that he would be above influence. "While I'm beating my opponents in the polls," he'd tweeted in late July 2015, a month into his campaign, "I'm also beating lobbyists, special interests & donors that are supporting them with billions."

Later, tweeting from the White House during the hours of "executive time" devoted to Fox News marathons, Trump frequently invoked the Deep State, an invention of that network and its Internet subalterns. He applied the term to a ruling elite made up of career federal lawyers and bureaucrats, rank-and-file Pentagon staffers, what little remained of the public intelligentsia, and the failing, fawning media that clung to this group like a barnacle. The Deep State was the stuff of second-rate spy fiction, only it was coming from inside the Oval Office.

In a sense, Trump was right. There was a shadowy cabal of expert operators manipulating the American government. Only he was wrong about who they were. It was the lobbyists he appointed, not the bureaucrats he inherited, who came closest to forming a Deep

State. Its agents were like cancer cells, activated by the Heritage Foundation and the Koch network to eat away at the federal apparatus from the inside.

These cells had names.

Nominated as a top lawyer at the EPA, Erik Baptist had worked for the American Petroleum Institute, fighting the good fight for the oil and gas industry. Because the API was a lobbying group, Baptist's appointment would seem to be in direct contravention of Executive Order 13770, the one White House officials touted as the toughest edict on ethics to ever emerge from 1600 Pennsylvania Avenue. That executive order would mean nothing if new hires were granted waivers, as Baptist was. His (partial) waiver was signed by EPA acting general counsel Kevin S. Minoli, who said it was "in the public interest" to have Baptist join the agency because of his "expertise," neglecting to mention that his expertise was in dismantling environmental protections. Baptist eventually became a high-ranking administrator in the EPA's Office of Chemical Safety and Pollution Prevention.

Trump used such waivers—sixteen granted by the spring of 2017—as a loophole through which he could evade his own decree. That explained how David L. Bernhardt became a federal employee. Bernhardt lobbied and worked for at least a dozen corporate concerns: the Rosemont Copper Company, Cobalt International Energy, Alcatel-Lucent Submarine Networks, Garrison Diversion Conservancy District. What did one make of a man like that? Naturally, one made him a top deputy in the Department of the Interior.

Kelly Marie Cleary went from a lucrative position at the white-shoe firm of Akin Gump, where she spent ten years working on behalf of clients in the medical industry, including insurance companies, to serving as the chief legal officer for the Centers for Medicare and Medicaid Services at the Department of Health and Human Services. Maya Michelle Noronha had been a Republican operative who worked on voter suppression efforts for the Republican National

Lawyers Association, which inexplicably qualified her to serve as a special adviser on civil rights at HHS.

Kevin O'Scannlain, an associate counsel to the president, had an astonishingly prolific lobbying profile: Discover, the credit card company; Cathay Pacific, the Asian airline; Rite Aid, the pharmacy chain; First Kuwaiti General Trading & Contracting; Emirates Investment and Development. One might have thought that a former lobbyist for Lehman Brothers, the failed investment bank identified with the worst excesses of the housing and financial crisis of 2008, would not be the person to help enact Trump's populist agenda. And yet there O'Scannlain was, a White House special assistant.

In one of the Trump administration's most brazen nominations, Andrew R. Wheeler was picked to be the deputy administrator of the Environmental Protection Agency. Wheeler was a former coal lobbyist who did not appear to believe in climate change. It mattered little. With Democrats defeated and Republicans cowed, Wheeler was confirmed in the spring of 2018.

Did all these people succumb to their own worst impulses once installed in the federal government? Of course not. They simply did not belong there, in a White House that was to be above influence, above cronyism, above the buying-and-selling that had marked earlier administrations.

Only the task was too great. No one was up for it at the start. Later, no one bothered to revive it. "Draining the swamp is very difficult," Bannon would come to concede. "People have to go in with a maniacal focus if they're going to do it, and in this administration, there just has been no center of gravity to do that."

Chapter 6

······

"KIND OF A ROUGH START"

B y the early twenty-first century, limited government had become a religion for the right, one whose central conviction of "less is best" was mouthed by virtually every candidate seeking office on the Republican line. Through the dint of repetition, the phrase lost all meaning, other than to serve as a show of faith to the legacy of Ronald Reagan, who did so much to demonize the federal government but so little to actually contract it.

Reagan famously charged that government was the problem, not the solution, but during his time in the White House, he tempered this animosity, adding some 95,000 civilian (i.e., nonmilitary) employees to the federal rolls. He also raised taxes on eleven separate occasions. Reagan did so little on the regulatory front that a 1988 report by the libertarian Mises Institute compared Reagan unfavorably to his predecessor Jimmy Carter, the Georgia liberal.

Bill Clinton reduced the federal workforce by 351,000, in good part because of reorganization efforts like the one undertaken by Elaine Kamarck. After he left the Oval Office, the federal workforce increased again, with the Foundation for Economic Education, a think tank promoting free-market principles, estimating that George W. Bush and Obama together added 399,000 government employees. Curiously, the rate of growth was greater under Bush (17.2 percent for nonmilitary jobs) than it was for Obama (10.1 percent).

John DiIulio Jr. was that rare political scientist who argued in favor of an expanding bureaucracy, but only as a means of limiting the reach of the federal government. Author of the 2014 book *Bring Back the Bureaucrats*, DiIulio called the federal government "a grotesque Leviathan by proxy, in which an expanding mass of state and local government workers, for-profit contractors, and nonprofit grant recipients administers a vast portion of federal money and responsibilities."

DiIulio believed that any limited government conservative should want the return of these outsourced functions to the government, away from the secondary state on which the government had come to rely. "Paradoxical though it may sound," he wrote in a 2014 *Washington Post* op-ed, "more federal bureaucrats means less big government, and more direct public administration means better government."

DiIulio's counterintuitive ideas could have actually helped Trump form a leaner, more efficient government less reliant on outside interests. This would have taken surgical precision: knowing where to cut, where to graft, where to leave things as they were.

There was no time for this, nor much interest. Trump did not so much hack away at the limbs of the federal government as inflict a couple of cuts that were left to fester, until the surrounding tissue died.

The disastrous results of this approach became apparent in the spring of 2017, after the cabinet confirmation battles that took up the first two months of the Trump administration. Hints, however, had come during the transition, when the future administration's DNA was being cobbled together in Trump Tower and the F Street headquarters in Washington.

Every administration sent landing teams into federal agencies.

These were meant to prepare incoming political appointees for the job of managing thousands of people in what were, in essence, public corporations. Awaiting these landing teams at each agency were career staffers and political appointees from the outgoing administration who were to show the newcomers how to keep the place running.

A department head at Housing and Urban Development thought that calling the administration arrivals "beachhead teams"—an advent of the Trump transition—was, in itself, a "combative" move, one with hints of a military invasion. "Doesn't set a great tone," she would recall thinking.

Only the invasion was not especially fearsome. "It wasn't clear what they were seeking to do," remembered the HUD official, who has since left the federal government. Many had only an "elementary understanding" of federal housing policy and asked career staffers "very basic questions." Another, less senior housing staffer said he had "zero" interaction with members of the Trump beachhead team.

The HUD transition was led by Shawn Krause, who had no experience working for the government. For more than two decades, she had made an impressive climb to the top of Quicken Loans, the nation's largest issuer of loans backed by the Federal Housing Administration. By 2016, Krause was the top Quicken lobbyist in Washington, where the company was facing a Department of Justice lawsuit into deceptive underwriting practices. Quicken's chief executive defended her appointment to the housing beachhead team. "When you think about draining the swamp, this goes right in line with that," he said to the *Wall Street Journal*, without explaining what he meant.

"We started planning for the transition before the election," said one high-ranking treasury deputy who left the department in July 2017. She had been there for thirty-five years, had seen three previous transitions, those of Clinton, Bush, and Obama. But she had never seen anything like this. There was, she remembers, "a whole week before we saw anyone," after which people "sort of trickled in." Those people appeared to lack treasury experience. Some, she remembers, were unfocused and lost.

What little trust existed between the Trump transition teams and career staffers in the federal agencies eroded altogether in early December 2016, about a month into the transition, when someone at the Department of Energy leaked a memorandum in which transition officials sought the names of programs focused on climate change, and the names of the people who worked on those programs. To critics of Trump, this confirmed that his administration would be both anti-government and antiscience; Trump loyalists saw an effort to undermine his presidency before it even began, evidence of what would come to be known as the Deep State at work.

About two weeks later, there was another leak, this time of a transition team memorandum to the State Department, asking about "existing programs and activities to promote gender equality," leading the denunciations and counter-denunciations that would become standard political discourse in the Trump era. The more substantive outcome was that the business of staffing the government, while never exactly dispassionate, now fully succumbed to politics.

Still, a transition needed to happen; that a Trump presidency awaited on the far shore made that no less imperative. Gina McCarthy, the outgoing EPA administrator, practically pleaded for the transition team to arrive, even if she knew perfectly well that her successor, Scott Pruitt, was going to undo much of her work. In early December, she admitted to being "most anxious to have the transition team around. We have had one individual who came the day before Thanksgiving, and we have not heard from anybody since."

Some agencies, like Commerce, saw their transitions go relatively well. Penny Pritzker, the outgoing secretary, was a marathoner who told her deputies that they were going to "run through the tape," finishing out their term at Commerce forcefully and with grace. She wrote her then unknown successor—this would turn out to be Wilbur Ross—a twenty-page, single-spaced letter, a playbook of the kind nobody had provided her with when she stepped into the federal bureaucracy for the first time.

"The Department that you will be leading," the letter began, "is a special place that has high-impact missions carried out by dedicated public servants, but it is a place that is often underestimated from the outside." She proceeded to outline what the department did, and what it could do better.

Commerce, which employed 46,000 people, had an impossibly broad mandate. Among its twelve bureaus were the National Oceanic and Atmospheric Administration, or NOAA, the U.S. Census Bureau, the U.S. Patent and Trademark Office, and the International Trade Administration. Pritzker explained how these and other parts of the department worked, showing an appreciation for the sophistication and importance of the job. There was something humble, almost inspiring, in the Harvard-educated billionaire delving into the minutiae of the federal bureaucracy. It was clear from the letter that Pritzker had come to appreciate that bureaucracy, though knotted and unwieldy it could be.

The incoming Trump administration sent in a beachhead team led by William "Willie" C. T. Gaynor II, a Washington lobbyist, who oversaw a competent turning-over of the department. On the last day of the administration, Pritzker literally ran through racing tape that had been placed across the hallway of her fifth-floor office, thus signifying the end of the Obama administration.

"That was so cool," one person present remembered Gaynor saying.

Things were not cool at the EPA. Christopher S. Zarba started working at the EPA in the early 1980s when it was led by Anne Gorsuch Burford, the conservative politician from Colorado (her son

Neil was Trump's first pick for the Supreme Court). That had been a divisive time, but he outlasted it, and twelve years under two Bushes, neither exactly a conservationist. During the Obama administration, he was made the staff director for the agency's science advisory board.

Then came Trump. Instead of the "seasoned professionals" Zarba expected, the beachhead team that arrived at EPA headquarters on Pennsylvania Avenue was full of "junior" people, including many from the office of Senator James M. Inhofe, the Republican from Oklahoma who was the most notorious climate-change denier in Congress.

"The people that came were just so unqualified," Zarba said. They were led by Myron Ebell, a director at the Competitive Enterprise Institute, a conservative think tank, who had devoted his life to combating the growing certitude of climate science. Once a fringe figure, he was now presiding over the EPA transition.

Sometimes, the transition played out like a tragicomedy. At the Department of Agriculture, which employed 100,000 people and had a budget of about $140 billion, the Trump beachhead team was for a time comprised of a single person, Brian A. "Klip" Klippenstein. Klippenstein's sole qualification appeared to be his leadership of Protect the Harvest, a clever name for a group that advocated for the factory farming of animals. Klippenstein's advocacy extended to the defense of "puppy mills," grindingly inhumane operations where dogs were bred purely for profit.

Klippenstein was supposed to have help from Joel Leftwich, a former Pepsi lobbyist who was the Republican staff director of the Senate Committee on Agriculture, Nutrition, and Forestry. Leftwich joined the transition in November, only to be pushed out a month later. That left Klippenstein as the sole delegate of the incoming Trump administration at Agriculture. This was less a beachhead than a toehold.

"Kind of a rough start." That was the frank verdict delivered in

January 2017 on the transition by Senate Majority Leader McConnell. He offered that Democrats were gumming up the transition because they were "in a bad mood."

He was right about the bad mood, wrong about its power to sway a process that had withstood many previous waves of post-election ill will. Former administration officials would say frankly that they hadn't planned for a transition because they hadn't planned to win. Once they won, they had more important things to do than concern themselves with the particulars of management, especially of agencies like the EPA that they were suspicious of to begin with. So they outsourced the job, did it on the quick.

Or they simply left the job undone. According to the Partnership for Public Service, Trump should have had about a hundred officials nominated by the time he took office. He had all of twenty-eight. "The Empty Trump Administration," read a Bloomberg headline.

Back in the spring of 2016, Trump had envisioned "a government based on relationships. I want people in those jobs who care about winning," he said in a *New York Times* interview. A year later, this team of winners was proving remarkably difficult to assemble. Aware that he was being criticized for turning the federal bureaucracy into a ghost town, Trump took to his favorite outlet, Fox News, to argue that the understaffing was strategic, even philosophic. "I look at some of the jobs and it's people over people over people," he told the network in February. "I say, 'What do all these people do?' You don't need all those jobs."

Trump's premium on "relationships" turned into an obsession when it came to the histories of potential hires, in particular of whether they'd been critical of him or supportive of Hillary Clinton's candidacy. Secretary of State Rex Tillerson, for example, wanted Elliott Abrams, a respected statesman, as his top deputy. Trump met Abrams and liked him, but in 2016, Abrams had written a column critical of Trump in the *Weekly Standard*. The criticism in "When You

Can't Stand Your Candidate" wasn't even all that strong, but it did predict a Trump defeat. Trump wasn't known to be a reader of the *Weekly Standard*, but someone showed him the column, almost certainly someone from the West Wing's nationalist faction. The Abrams nomination was scotched.

Throughout the winter and spring, First Lady Melania Trump remained in New York. There was much gossip about the Trumps' marriage, about her perceived coldness toward the president. But more important was the fact that she was simply not there. Elaine Kamarck, the Clinton veteran and Brookings scholar, thought the lack of a "functioning political wife" was even more detrimental to the Trump administration than Reince Priebus's ineffectual turn as chief of staff.

A first lady was the only adviser who could not be fired, Kamarck reasoned, the only one who could see the president in the residence as she wished. Ivanka Trump had her father's ear, but also an official position, from which she could be dismissed. She also had an inheritance to think about. She was his favorite child, but breaking with the president too strongly could ultimately cost her hundreds of millions of dollars.

Even if Melania did come to Washington earlier (she finally moved there in June 2017), she was not likely to have filled the role of trusted adviser the way Eleanor Roosevelt or Hillary Clinton had. "This first lady, whose clothes I admire terrifically, she doesn't know anything," Kamarck said. She did not say this cuttingly. She said it with compassion. "She has no instinct for this business. She is not a help," nor ever would be.

Priebus and his RNC allies made things worse. People who worked with him liked him, but that work was in the service of the presidency, which demanded qualities other than likability. "The guy you want to be your neighbor, but not your chief of staff." That was the verdict delivered by one senior administration official. Another person, who was in the Oval Office daily, saw Priebus as perpetually skittish, his time occupied by "daily survival stuff." That often involved leaking to the press, not to bolster the president, but to weaken his own enemies in the West Wing.

It didn't help. He was caught between Steve Bannon and Jared Kushner, unable to ever gain sufficient trust from the president. With his flappy suits and wan smile, Priebus was a man desperately out of his element. People noticed. During staff meetings held in his office, others would openly make jokes at his expense. They would mock the president's chief of staff, and he would do nothing to rebuke them. It was stunning stuff, remembered one person who witnessed this brutally impudent behavior.

Priebus's deputies leaked incessantly to the press to protect his reputations and their own. Katie Walsh was a source for Michael Wolff's *Fire and Fury*, a bracingly unflattering portrayal of the first months of the Trump administration. Yet some colleagues in the West Wing saw her own reputation for competence as entirely undeserved.

Sean Spicer had no such reputation. His own leaking was well known and perplexing to those who knew how a White House was supposed to work. A press secretary was indeed supposed to have off-the-record and background conversations with journalists, but only on behalf of the president, either to boost a favorable story or knock down a malicious rumor. That was how it had been done for generations. Spicer leaked for an entirely different reason: to protect himself and Priebus, most often by casting aspersions on their West Wing rivals.

It was all so knotted and confusing, bewildering even to Americans who wanted to support Trump, *had* supported Trump, but could not make sense of what this administration was turning out to be. While Spicer barked at reporters in the Brady Briefing Room, on Fox News, emissaries like Kellyanne Conway and Sebastian Gorka portrayed themselves as close confidants of the president. Often, they gave their interviews from Pebble Beach, a space near the northwest gate where administration members conducted interviews with the press. That gave the impression that they had just stepped out of the Oval Office, even though that was almost certainly not the case.

"I'm not entirely sure what Kellyanne did," one person said contemptuously of Conway, who graced the English language with "alternative facts" but did little else of note. Charged with solving the opioid crisis, she dispensed nutritional advice: "Eat the ice cream, have the French fry, don't buy the street drug." (I asked Conway for interviews several times, but all she would say is that she was "not a leaker." I suppose that settles it, then.)

As for Gorka, the notion that he was a bearded Kissinger was "bullshit." He was rarely in the Oval, and he had no evident duties, no portfolio to work on, other than meddling in the National Security Council at Bannon's behest. His greatest contribution to the Trump administration was finally leaving it, in typically graceless fashion, during the summer of 2017.

Groveling courtiers at a madcap court, Gorka and Conway generated pointless controversy, then retreated into the shadows, only to return for another round a few days later, like addicts looking for a fresh fix. Much as with the RNC whisper campaign, this self-promotion infuriated the serious men and women in the White House who wanted to get things done, who understood that publicity was the enemy of productivity. And there were such people, only one never heard their names, for they had not come to the White House to make their names known.

Whether they were products of the RNC or Fox News, it was the insecure and the incompetent who frustrated the president's own agenda—however scattershot that agenda was—often because it suited their own ends to do so. If they formed an "internal resistance" to Trump, they did so inadvertently and vaingloriously.

As they frequently would do in the months to come, Trump's allies tried to cover up disorder in the White House with groundless accusations of conspiracy. Speaking at a Republican Party event in early March, Representative Mike Kelly, a Republican from Pennsylvania, alleged that President Obama was maintaining his family's residence in Washington—the first president to do so since Woodrow Wilson—"for one purpose and one purpose only, and that is to run a shadow government that is going to totally upset the new agenda." His staff retracted the impolitic remark, but only after it had been made public. Kelly's silly insinuation offered a revealing look at the contradictory Republican mind-set: broadly suspicious of all government, but wanting the Trump government to succeed, so that Trump could dismantle government once and for all. It was, understandably enough, much easier to engage in conspiracy theories than try to honestly resolve these contradictions.

The utter unpredictability of the new administration meant that little could be taken for granted in Washington. On any given day, the city might wake to a sense of stability, however modest and hard-won, only to plunge into disorder by afternoon. In early April, the Trump administration dismissed many of the onetime campaign workers who had come to Washington and been placed in various federal agency beachhead teams. The White House said that it was merely reorganizing staffers, but this was not an especially convincing explanation, including to those who were being pushed out of jobs they thought were permanent. As one of the dismissed complained to CBS News, "The perception is, we were Mr. Trump's goons who were good at knocking on doors, but can't do much else."

That was the perception. Career staffers at Treasury were not thrilled to be working for Steve Mnuchin. But they were glad that he got rid of the beachhead team, which signaled some measure of independence from the White House. "They weren't his people," one top treasury staffer explained, and Mnuchin "didn't have much patience" with them. He may not have had much patience with career staffers, either—many found him arrogant and aloof— but at least the new secretary had a couple of vertebrae, if not a full spine.

Trump kept complaining, looking for someone to blame. "I am waiting right now for so many people," he said on Fox Business a week after the dismissal of some of the original beachhead teams. "Hundreds and hundreds of people. And then they'll say 'why isn't Trump doing this faster?' You can't do it faster because they're obstructing. They're obstructionists." This was an attack on congressional Democrats, who lacked the necessary power in the Senate to "obstruct" his nominees. Trump also blamed the "lousy process," by which he meant the legal and legislative procedures involved in hiring people for prominent federal positions.

If anyone could be directly blamed for the chronic staffing problems of the Trump administration—which continued well into 2019—then it was the Presidential Personnel Office, which oversaw hiring for executive branch jobs. The office was miserably understaffed from the beginning, a *Washington Post* investigation in early 2018 found, "with only about 30 employees on hand." Documents obtained by the *Post* showed that Chris Christie had wanted Presidential Personnel to be staffed by some hundred people.

Most of these gatekeepers to the Trump administration were young and content to act their age. As the *Post* reported, PPO's quarters "became something of a social hub, where young staffers from throughout the administration stopped by to hang out on couches and smoke electronic cigarettes," as well as to play drinking games of the sort one generally left behind halfway through a college career.

The office was headed by John "Johnny" DeStefano, an amiable former staffer to House Speaker John A. Boehner, the wine-loving Republican from Ohio. DeStefano was a typical Trump hire: well liked, but not well suited. His experience in high-level management was nonexistent. A person who also worked on campus said that DeStefano's defining characteristic was an ability to come out of any situation, no matter how politically fraught, without any visible scars. He did not mean this as a compliment.

DeStefano did not fill PPO with capable Capitol Hill staffers, as few skilled congressional aides saw such a move helping their career ambitions. Sean E. Doocey, DeStefano's top deputy, was twenty-eight years old, a veteran of the Trump campaign. Another hire from the Trump campaign was thirty-year-old Caroline Wiles, who the *Post* found falsified the extent of her education at Flagler College in her native Florida. She had been apprehended twice for drunken driving. Max Miller, a twenty-nine-year-old whose arrest record included violence and alcohol abuse, had similarly misrepresented his educational history.

Katja Bullock, a veteran of previous Republican administrations was, at seventy-five, three times older than many of her peers. As the *Post* reported, four of her family members had gotten jobs in the Trump administration, which Bullock claimed, rather incredibly, had nothing to do with her own position.

A West Winger who observed the PPO at work was left with the impression of a "totally disorganized" and "totally haphazard" agency. Like a virus, its disorder wafted from the Eisenhower Executive Office Building into the White House and the rest of the executive branch. DeStefano and his staffers were obsessed with loyalty, to Trump but also to the RNC. That resulted in them hiring what the West Winger derisively referred to as "RNC kids." They were ambitious but inexperienced, mercenary with their fealty, ready to profess loyalty to anyone who might help with their political assent.

After the unflattering *Post* report was published, the Trump administration did what it always did when confronted with its own shortcomings. Instead of acknowledging mistakes and trying to correct them, it argued that there had been no mistakes at all, as if an admission of error was itself the most unpardonable sin. Raj Shah, the deputy White House press secretary, stayed true to form, blaming "historic obstruction from Democrats in Congress" and praising PPO for helping hire "the best and brightest appointees." He did not seem to realize where "the best and the brightest" came from, or what it meant.

As spring turned to summer, the Trump administration remained an archipelago of empty offices. Between the agency heads and career staffers, there was an enormous gap that should have been filled by deputies and assistant secretaries.

Some noticed, and were troubled. William "Bill" J. McGinley was a Republican lawyer who had worked for Jones Day and Patton Boggs before joining the administration. Affable and without pretense, he loved to annoy his staffers with sports metaphors. Among his favorite was that the administration was fielding only pitchers and catchers. There was no outfield, no infield. That left some department heads with the impression that nobody was watching and that they could do as they pleased. By the time McGinley understood what an enormous problem that was turning out to be, it was too late.

The Senate was more dilatory with Trump nominees (forty-three days) than it had been with Obama's (thirty-five days). Democratic intransigence may have been responsible, but not to any significant extent. The nominees were often poorly vetted or failed to submit the proper financial disclosure forms, making the delay a procedural necessity. Some seemed so spectacularly unsuited for federal employ, one wondered if they had been submitted by Trump solely to irritate Democrats.

Monica Crowley, a Fox News pundit, had to withdraw her nomination to the National Security Council after it was found that she plagiarized parts of her 2000 doctoral dissertation at Columbia, as well as parts of her 2012 book *What the (Bleep) Just Happened?*; Mark

E. Green was not to be the secretary of the army, as he had made hateful comments about transgender people (he also was not a fan of evolution); Samuel H. Clovis Jr., a Trump campaign veteran named the chief scientist at the U.S. Department of Agriculture, withdrew because he had encouraged a campaign aide to reach out to Russian officials in 2016; Tom Marino, who was to administer the Office of National Drug Control Policy at the White House, once helped pass legislation that made it more difficult to prosecute companies that were profiting from the opioid crisis; Kathleen Hartnett White ended her bid to become head of the Council on Environmental Quality after it came to light that the former beef industry lobbyist and Koch-funded think-tanker praised carbon dioxide as "a necessary nutrient for plant life" while lambasting climate change as "the Left's secular religion."

By late 2018, Senate records included the names of sixty-one nominees who had withdrawn their nominations from the Trump administration. Not all of them did so because of unflattering revelations made during the nominating process, but that was the case for many, and it did slow the pace of hiring, as well as the pace of governing.

There was one key respect in which the president did succeed in installing people who shared his vision of a smaller, weaker federal government. During the presidential campaign, Trump had promised to remake the federal judiciary in the image of the Federalist Society and Heritage Foundation, which had happily supplied him with a list of palatable Supreme Court justices.

Even more important, he had Don McGahn. If McGahn was deficient as a White House counsel in other respects, he compensated for his shortcomings by ensuring that whatever else Trump did or did not accomplish, his legacy on the federal bench would last for at least a generation.

There were the two Supreme Court justices—Neil Gorsuch and

Brett Kavanaugh, the latter practically resuscitated by McGahn after credible allegations of sexual assault—but they were almost beside the point in the project conservatives had envisioned. Supreme Court nominations inevitably attracted the vast majority of media attention, but lower-court appointments tended to be of greater consequence, as these judges would prove either the keepers or, more likely, destroyers of the administrative state. The Supreme Court took few cases each year: about one percent of the seven or eight thousand cases submitted to the court were granted certiorari status, meaning that the nine justices would hear the arguments. The rest were fated to remain in the lower courts, which were increasingly coming to look just as Trump promised they would.

Unsparingly critical as he could be of many former West Wing colleagues, Bannon would grow effusive in praising McGahn, whom he called "the most significant White House counsel in the history of the republic" but for Samuel I. Rosenman, the influential consigliere to Franklin Roosevelt and later Truman (he was the first to hold the position, under Roosevelt, though it was known as "special counsel" at that time). Rosenman, Bannon explained, was responsible for helping Roosevelt build the administrative state through the New Deal. Trump's conservative judges would undo Rosenman's work. "McGahn was like the bookend," Bannon gushed. "The alpha and the omega."

McGahn looked for judges who shared his view on the Chevron deference, a stature key to deconstructionists like him and Bannon. Stemming from a 1984 case, the Chevron deference became "a central pillar of the modern administrative state," a Hoover Institution scholar wrote, because it dictated that regulatory agencies—in the 1984 suit, the EPA—had primacy over the courts in determining how their rules were interpreted. That, in conservatives' view, was what endowed "unelected bureaucrats" with such terrific power.

Both of Trump's nominees to the Supreme Court were opposed

to the Chevron deference. Kavanaugh—an unoriginal, unimpressive thinker but an able predictor of what conservative activists would want from him—had criticized the Chevron deference in a Notre Dame speech just months before he was nominated to the high bench.

The lower-court nominees shared this view. Sent in tranches to Capitol Hill, where they faced a generally friendly Republican-led Senate Judiciary Committee, the vast majority of these nominees were confirmed.

There were a few exceptions. Among these was Matthew S. Petersen, of the Federal Election Commission, who under questioning from Senator John N. Kennedy, a Republican from Louisiana, admitted he had never tried a case, in a brutally uncomfortable four-minute exchange that became an unlikely social media sensation. Brett J. Talley, a Harvard Law graduate, was rated "not qualified" by the American Bar Association. He had written several horror novels, yet had failed to try a single case; Jeff Mateer had branded transgender youth as instruments of "Satan's plan" while also condemning same-sex marriage.

These three jurists withdrew their nominations, but most did not. By the end of 2018, Trump had confirmed 85 judges across the federal judiciary, providing what Garrett Ventry, a former adviser to the Senate Judiciary Committee on judicial nominations, called "a unifying theme for all Republicans." Those judges were young: the youngest, Allison Jones Rushing, was only thirty-six at the time of her nomination to a federal appellate court (she had not yet been confirmed as of early 2019, but would almost certainly get there in time). With their youth and ideological zeal, these judges would continue to wage Trump's war long after it had been conceded on other fronts.

Chapter 7

......

THE SHITSHOW STRATEGY

Trump's was the first intentionally nonlinear presidency, lurching several times each day between policy objectives that could have been dictated by a Fox News anchor, a friend from Mar-a-Lago, or the prime minister of Norway. This was especially true in the first six months, when a paranoid Priebus concluded that the best way to save his job was to not do it. He neglected his most basic responsibility, which was to regulate the flow of people and information into the Oval Office. Michael Wolff skulked around the campus, Sean Spicer hid in the bushes, and Priebus did nothing about any of it. Later, after he had been expelled from the White House, Priebus would complain about the White House under Trump, with seemingly no awareness of how much he had done to contribute to the disorder of the place.

The first several weeks under Trump were a genuine "shitshow," as one West Winger put it. This was the presidency as envisioned by Steve Bannon and Stephen Miller. This was Trump sitting at the *Resolute* desk, happily signing executive orders: on the Muslim ban, on funding for groups that did abortion-related work abroad, on the Trans-Pacific Partnership, which he and his supporters hated, on the Dakota Access Pipeline, which he and his supporters loved. The war on domestic regulation, a new approach to international trade:

these came with relentless speed during the winter and spring of 2017.

Priebus was too busy fending off attacks about his incompetence to do something, *anything*, to prove those attacks untrue. Trump had disdained process and procedure as a private businessman, and that disdain carried over into the Oval Office. Priebus's inability to foist anything like order on the West Wing worked to the advantage of those who had no business making anything approaching decisions of national import, but saw an opening to do just that. It was, for example, Representative Mark Meadows, a revanchist from North Carolina, who prevailed on Trump to declare a ban on transgender troops in the military that summer. There was no planning for the announcement, merely a tweet from the president that left Meadows thrilled but the Pentagon aghast.

"It was hopeless," one veteran of that time remembered.

The disorder was also exaggerated, agreed many of those who worked in senior West Wing positions. Many of them saw the press as grossly overplaying the disorder, the extent to which Trump trampled the norms of his office. Uniformly unreadable though they were, books by Trump veterans and surrogates to the last included an episode from Trump's first day in office. A capable young reporter for the Associated Press, Zeke Miller, wrote that a bust of Martin Luther King Jr. had been removed from the Oval Office. This was a perfectly innocent mistake, committed because a Secret Service agent was standing in front of the bust. Miller apologized and corrected his reporting, but memory of the incident lingered. For Trump and his supporters, it was irrefutable evidence that no matter what he did, the press had already concluded he was a grotesquely inept impostor. They would give him no quarter. He would return the favor.

Some in the White House grasped that such reports were to their advantage, that the press could—and should—be baited into reporting of this kind. A shitshow strategy thus emerged. If the public was arguing about the King bust or discussing reports of Trump wandering the West Wing in his bathrobe, it was almost certainly not paying attention to work being done across the federal government. "We never gave you time," the ex–White House staffer said of the press, a savage little smile playing on his lips. "We kept the foot on the gas. There was no chaos, only method."

And work was being done, even if Trump was spending an inordinate amount of time playing golf at Mar-a-Lago and watching Fox News. If his presidency had a North Star, it was deregulation, the conviction that we had too many laws, and consequently too many rules stemming from the interpretations of those laws. According to conservative dogma, those rules straitjacketed ordinary Americans, depriving them of God-given liberties, sullying the Jeffersonian ideal. The various constituents of the modern-day Republican Party—paleoconservatives, neoconservatives, libertarians, evangelicals—could not agree on gay marriage or taxation, but they definitely agreed that fewer rules were preferable to more rules. It may have been all they agreed on.

And if Trump disappointed on other fronts, he did not disappoint on this one. Even as some of its top nominees struggled to articulate the basics of governing before Senate committees, the Trump administration launched an aggressive, and generally successful, assault on the regulatory framework that had undergirded the U.S. government since the Great Depression.

Conservative convictions about regulation stemmed in good part from the writings of Milton Friedman, the libertarian thinker who "didn't make a distinction between the big government of the People's Republic of China and the big government of the United States," as the economist James K. Galbraith would later say of him.

In 1962, Friedman—then at the University of Chicago—published *Capitalism and Freedom*, an answer to the big-government liberalism ascendant under John F. Kennedy. "To the free man, the country is the collection of individuals who compose it, not something over and above them," Friedman wrote. All government, he argued, tends toward paternalism, toward dictating and prescribing, as well as proscribing. Government, in this conception, was the enemy of freedom, not freedom's enabler. "A major source of objection to a free economy is precisely that it gives people what they want instead of what a particular group thinks they ought to want," Friedman wrote. "Underlying most arguments against the free market is a lack of belief in freedom itself."

The year after *Capitalism and Freedom* was published, Kennedy was assassinated, and Lyndon Johnson became president. The five years that followed saw the most dramatic peacetime expansion of the federal government since the Great Depression. Johnson's Great Society, with its invocation of "creative federalism," included everything from Head Start to the Highway Beautification Act, as well as the Civil Rights Act, the Economic Opportunity Act, and the Voting Rights Act. The historian Paul K. Conkin wrote in 1986 that during the Johnson administration, "the American government approximately doubled its regulatory role and at least doubled the scope of transfer payments," which is to say, the money available through welfare programs.

As far as conservatives were concerned, those welfare programs created a permanent class of dependents who would always vote Democratic in order to keep those programs sufficiently funded.

By the 1970s, the hopeful mood of the early Johnson years had curdled into recrimination and regret. The good he had done at home paled beside his disastrous decision to turn the Vietnam conflict into a full-blown war. And the civil unrest of the late 1960s— Newark in flames, troops in Detroit—made skeptics of some of the very same people who believed that a Great Society was possible, perhaps even inevitable. As American cities smoldered and Southeast Asian jungles burned, notions of collective greatness seemed to recede, and many Americans retreated from the aspiration that marked the opening of the decade.

Upon assuming the presidency in 1969, Nixon brought Friedman, who had advised his campaign, to the White House. Friedman was a philosopher, not an ideologue, willing to go where the rigors of thinking would take him. One of those places was a resistance to the military draft, which he had announced in a magazine article in 1967, as the Vietnam War was reaching its bloody nadir. Once in the White House, Friedman worked with the Gates Commission on its 1970 report, which led to the eventual return to an all-volunteer army. It would prove one of the greatest achievements in a career punctuated by the Nobel Prize for Economics, which Friedman won in 1976.

Friedman was as opposed to regulation as he was to conscription. His fierce advocacy for free markets would render Friedman, who stood all of five feet two inches tall, a giant who loomed over the federal government well into the 21st century.

Nixon's successor, Gerald Ford, signaled his own intentions in a 1975 address to the National Federation of Independent Business: "We must free the business community from regulatory bondage so that it can produce." Among his prime targets was the Civil Aeronautics Board, which had controlled the operation of commercial airlines for four decades. He found an unlikely ally in Edward M. Kennedy, the liberal senator from Massachusetts. Ford also tried to deregulate the trucking industry with the Motor Carrier Reform Act, a proposal that met with strident opposition from organized labor, with the head of the Teamsters declaring "the end of Western civilization." Neither effort succeeded during Ford's single term in office, and Western civilization held on for a little while longer.

Jimmy Carter may have been a liberal, but he was also a deregulator, declaring that "the American people are sick of the bureaucratic confusion here in Washington," in a line that could have come from the mouth of Donald Trump, if not for the mellifluous Georgia accent. He succeeded where Ford had not, signing the Airline Deregulation Act in 1978 and, some two and a half years later, a new Motor Carrier Act (the original law was from 1935). He also deregulated home brewing, making the pious teetotaler a founding father of the craft beer movement.

It was not especially surprising that the Republican presidents who followed Carter—Reagan and the two Bushes—were avid deregulators. What *was* surprising, however, is how eagerly Bill Clinton, the first Democrat in the Oval Office since Carter, followed the lead of Reagan and the elder Bush. In 1996, as he prepared for reelection, Clinton famously declared at the State of the Union address that "the era of big government is over." Just a few days later, Clinton signed the Telecommunications Act, which he said would help promote competition, including in the new World Wide Web, while offering a "roadmap for deregulation in the future." It was under Clinton that Congress repealed the Glass-Steagall Act, a Depression-era law that placed constraints on the activities banks could conduct. With those limits effaced, the nation's financial system hurtled toward the banking and foreclosure crisis of 2008.

That crisis made the American public amenable to new regulation under Barack Obama, on the financial industry in particular. He created the Consumer Financial Protection Bureau, a brainchild of Senator Elizabeth Warren, the progressive Democrat from Massachusetts, and instituted the Volcker Rule, which prevented banks from engaging in a potentially destructive kind of trading (both measures were part of the Dodd–Frank Wall Street Reform and Consumer Protection Act, which passed in 2010).

In the final year of the Obama presidency, the administrative state embarked on a growth spurt, with 3,853 new regulations issued. There were new regulations regarding disclosures on nutritional labels, of sugar content in particular. There was a regulation that would have financial advisers working with retirement accounts to place the customer's interest before their own profit. There were new regulations on workplace exposure to silica, new rules for residential furnaces.

Conservatives issued many dire reports on the effects of the Obama administration's rules. James L. Gattuso of the Heritage Foundation found that the Obama administration enshrined a total of 20,642 regulations during his eight years in office, which, by his calculation, added $22 billion per year in federal outlays. The Competitive Enterprise Institute declared that "the total cost of the regulatory state" was $1.963 trillion by the time Obama left office. He hadn't erected that state all on his own, but these critics charged that he grew it much too eagerly.

Republicans running for president in 2016 were uniformly dismayed by all the new Obama rules, none more so than Donald Trump. Campaigning in New Hampshire during the Republican primary, Trump said that the gun industry was overregulated, even though the United States had the most lax gun laws in the industrialized world. "We have tremendous regulations already, a lot of people don't even realize," he said. During the general election campaign, Trump charged that Clinton would offer nothing but "more taxes, more regulations, more bureaucrats, more restrictions on American energy and American production."

A little more than a week after he took office—and two days after he signed his executive order on ethics—Trump signed Executive Order 13771, titled "Reducing Regulation and Controlling Regulatory Costs." The directive instructed the future members of his cabinet that "for every one new regulation issued, at least two prior regulations be identified for elimination."

Never one for modesty, Trump declared that "the American dream is back."

Conservatives had been waiting—and planning—for this moment

for years. During the 2012 presidential campaign, Mitt Romney had hired a young policy expert named Andrew P. Bremberg to compile a list of Obama regulations to be reversed once Romney took office. "When Romney lost, the project did not die," said one veteran of the Trump administration familiar with those efforts. During the second Obama term, conservative lawyers around Washington fantasized about how they would go about undoing Obama's regulatory legacy after 2016. "You can't just get that shit out of your head," said the White House alumnus.

With Trump in power, Republicans saw three ways to "whack" regulations, as the former White House official put it. They could use executive orders. In some cases, they could have agencies delay the implementation of certain rules, a method that Scott Pruitt's EPA would pioneer. They could also use an immensely effective but largely unknown instrument called the Congressional Review Act.

The Congressional Review Act was the brainchild of Newt Gingrich, the spiky conservative from Georgia who led the 1994 Republican takeover of the House. Passed in 1996, the law gave Congress sixty legislative days to review any new rules. If it did not like a rule, Congress could vote to nullify it.

Clinton himself did not use the CRA a single time. George W. Bush used it once, to cancel a Clinton workplace ergonomic program. Congress attempted to use the CRA against Obama on five separate occasions, but he leaned on his presidential veto powers to block each of these efforts.

The Trump administration would not be reluctant about using the CRA, and it would not wait around for the cabinet to be confirmed before starting to dismantle Obama's regulatory legacy. More than two weeks before his inauguration, Trump announced that the onetime Romney operative Andrew Bremberg would head his Domestic Policy Council. Bremberg worked with deputy chief of staff Rick Dearborn and Marc Short, the White House director of legislative affairs, to coordinate with Ryan and McConnell on how they would use the CRA. Trump was on board, remembered the White House official involved in the effort. "I love it," the president said. "Show me which ones we're talking about." Here was the moment conservatives had been dreaming of and plotting for during the Obama years.

The CRA proved a perfect tool for Trump, since it was effective and easy to wield. Both chambers of Congress were controlled by Republicans, effectively allowing Trump to nullify extant regulations with a few pen strokes. And that's exactly what Trump did, with Bremberg working like "a machine," according to colleagues, to cancel as many Obama rules as the sixty-day window would allow. In his first several months in office, he used the CRA more than a dozen times.

The first Obama regulation Trump did away with stipulated that energy companies had "to disclose payments made to governments for the commercial development of oil, natural gas or minerals." The rule, issued by the Securities and Exchange Commission in 2016, was supposed to align corporate interests with diplomatic ones. Trump got rid of it on February 14, 2017.

Trump's CRA tactics did not receive nearly as much attention as reports of bedlam in the Oval. Those reports, explained a former White House official, "were our greatest advantage," the shitshow strategy at work. Here was Steve Bannon's long-promised deconstruction of the administrative state, and it was largely ignored in favor of furious debate over the latest Trump tweet.

Trump was happy to avoid having to answer potentially uncomfortable questions about his use of the CRA. Back in the spring of 2016, Trump the candidate had criticized Obama for using executive orders to govern, which he did, in Trump's estimation, "because he couldn't get anybody to agree with him." The CRA wasn't exactly the same as an executive order, since it required congressional approval, but that was little more than a fait accompli on a Capitol Hill controlled entirely by Republicans, who were either genuinely in thrall of Trump or far too frightened of his Twitter feed to say much of anything.

The deregulatory push continued into the spring of 2017. That April, Trump repealed a rule that prevented Internet companies from selling individuals' data without explicit consent. Given the newfound worries of many Americans about online security, this seemed like a thoroughly reasonable rule that both Republicans and Democrats could support. And many did. Not among them, however, was Ajit Pai, the new regulation-averse Federal Communications Commission chairman. So the seemingly sensible restriction went. The telecommunications lobby praised Trump for getting rid of "a confusing and conflicting consumer privacy framework."

When this author offered a former White House official who worked on the CRA that actions like these had the appearance of a corporate giveaway—especially when lobbying groups showed their hand by loudly cheering those rollbacks—the official grew vehement. "I could give a shit about the industry," he said. "We took the political question out of it. We kept thinking of small town and exurban America." For him, at least, there was a direct correlation between fewer rules and more jobs. And, yes, he added, of course he cared about workplace safety and the environment. But liberals had assumed "agendas that push the realm of crazy." Republicans had no choice but to push back.

In his conception, and in Trump's, regulations were holding back American businesses. That was not accurate, though it was also not accurate to claim that regulations were somehow helpful to the economy. Regulation scholars Cary Coglianese and Christopher Carrigan found that "what we know about the relationship between regulation and employment contrasts strikingly with the grandiose claims found in contemporary political debate about either dramatic job-killing or job-creating effects of regulation. The empirical evidence actually provides little reason to expect that U.S. economic woes can be solved by reforming the regulatory process." That meant that regulations were, in themselves, neither good nor evil. They were either celebrated or vilified by people in power, sometimes out of genuine conviction, more often to suit political ends.

Whether intentionally or not, corporate interests did stand to gain from Trump's aggressive use of the CRA. Industry groups poured money into the presidential transition, which received $6.5 million from "private sources," including those tied to American Resort Development Association, Caesars Entertainment, Philip Morris International, Uranium Producers of America, and the Pipe Line Contractors Association. A spokesman for one of those groups, Associated Builders and Contractors, explained to the Center for Public Integrity that his group's members were looking for "a regulatory environment that will encourage greater business investment in the economy." In other words, they were engaging in the most basic of transactional politics, paying into Trump's fund in hopes that Trump would pay them back by undoing Obama's legacy.

The new president did not disappoint. With the help of a friendly Congress, Trump used the CRA to kill an Obama rule that mandated employers to report workplace injuries. That rule would have been helpful to construction workers, who might well have wanted to know whether a builder had a poor safety record. Among those seeking repeal of the worker safety rule was Associated Builders and Contractors, the lobbying group that had donated to the Trump transition with the stated expectation of gaining something in return. Now, that wish was granted. "Just because you have an injury in the workplace doesn't mean you have the [sic] bad employer," reassured an official from the U.S. Chamber of Commerce, a pro-business group.

Trump undid the Stream Protection Rule, which was intended

to keep surface coal mines from polluting waterways with the potential toxic by-products of their activities. "This is one very, very important step to get coal back on its feet," said a spokesman for the National Mining Association, a lobbying group loyal to the Republican Party.

During the campaign, Trump had railed against Goldman Sachs and "hedge-fund guys." But as president, he used the CRA to repeal a rule issued by the Consumer Financial Protection Bureau that prevented discriminatory lending in the automotive industry. "A good day for American consumers," declared Representative Jeb Hensarling, the Texas Republican who chaired the House Financial Services Committee and who thought the CFPB was a "rogue bureau." It was certainly a good day for Hensarling, who received hundreds of thousands of dollars in campaign funds from banks and financial institutions. That proved money well spent. And despite his own penchant for suing adversaries and critics, Trump did away with a CFPB rule that had made it easier for individuals to join class-action lawsuits against credit card companies and banks.

Among the rules jettisoned by the Trump administration were some that seemed to bear little connection to his broader policy program. Trump rescinded a rule that pertained to hunting in sixteen federal wildlife refuges in Alaska. The rule, issued by the National Park Service and relevant only in that state, forbade inhumane and unsportsmanlike practices, including hunting from airplanes and motorboats, using steel-jaw traps, and killing bears in hibernation. Representative Don Young, a crusty Republican from Alaska announced that he was "pleased by this decision to correct an illegal Obama-era power grab." Others saw only cruelty at work. The president of the Humane Society complained to Politico: "The drama in the White House sucked up all the oxygen in the press room. This should be a national embarrassment, but it got no attention."

Trump used the CRA sixteen times in his first two years in office, far more than any other president. Though he would use it once in the fall of 2017 and once more the following May, both times on the aforementioned Consumer Financial Protection Bureau rules, the vast majority of his CRA rollbacks came that first winter and spring, the last of them on May 17, 2017, regarding a Department of Labor rule about pensions.

The shitshow strategy could only achieve so much, but in those first months of the Trump administration, it achieved plenty. And then an unlikely concept visited the White House: order.

Chapter 8

••••••

BETTER PEOPLE

On July 28, 2017, President Trump flew to Long Island to give a speech to law enforcement officers, whom he encouraged to be "rough" with suspected gang members. After the speech, Trump flew back to Washington, landing at Andrews Air Force Base a little before 2 p.m.

Reince Priebus walked out of the plane and into a waiting car with several colleagues. They sat there, waiting for the president to emerge from Air Force One. Suddenly, there was a commotion, the telltale consulting of smartphones, an indication that something was amiss.

Still aboard Air Force One, the president had just sent a tweet that announced that John F. Kelly, the marine general, would be his new chief of staff. This was news to everyone, including Priebus. Everyone knew it was coming, they just didn't know it was coming like this. The other staffers got out of the car. It drove away with Priebus alone, newly out of a job, humiliated by the president before the entire nation.

Exactly a week before Priebus was fired, Sean Spicer resigned his position as White House spokesman in protest over the hiring of slick New York hedge fund manager Anthony Scaramucci, who would famously last ten days as Trump's communications director

(Scaramucci delighted in arguing that it was actually eleven days). By this time, Katie Walsh had already left the White House. Many of the junior RNC-linked aides in "lower press" (the ones who sat in a narrow suite separated by a sliding blue door from the Brady Briefing Room, while their more senior colleagues in "upper press" were on the first floor of the White House, much closer to the Oval Office) had also been pushed out of the building.

Priebus's replacement, Kelly, had been serving as the secretary of the Department of Homeland Security since the beginning of the Trump presidency. He had retired from the U.S. Marine Corps in early 2016, having risen from a grunt in 1970 to a four-star general in charge of the military's Southern Command, which oversaw operations in Latin and South America. Tom Cotton, the ambitious young Republican senator from Arkansas, initially suggested Kelly to Bannon as a potential secretary of state during the presidential transition. Bannon knew of Kelly; he also knew that Kelly had lost a son serving in Afghanistan and was eager to get on with civilian life. When he called Kelly, the retired general did not seem especially enthusiastic about joining the administration, though he did agree to meet with Trump out of a sense of duty.

Not a year later, he was being celebrated as the disciplinarian who would finally bring Trump to heel.

The hope would not prove entirely unfounded. For one, there were "a lot fewer on the fly meetings," said one of his closest aides in the West Wing. The door Priebus kept open, Kelly closed. Priebus had been obsessed with the building's power politics; Kelly happily delegated responsibility to trusted subordinates. Unlike the subordinates Priebus brought to the White House, Kelly's deputies did not care if they were liked.

Kelly's top staffers made the trip with him from the secluded DHS headquarters at a former girls' seminary on Nebraska Avenue, in upper Northwest Washington, to an office suite five doors from the Oval

Office. Joining Kelly in the White House was Zachary D. Fuentes, an aide of such imperious manner, he came to be known as Zachary of the United States. An even more influential aide was Kirstjen M. Nielsen, whom Kelly trusted above all others. She was in her mid-forties, her only experience in the White House having come when she spent five years as an assistant to George W. Bush. Seen as arrogant and abrasive by some, Nielsen let it be known that the level of disarray in the White House was unacceptable.

After grueling days of putting out fires, Kelly, Nielsen, and Fuentes would retreat to their quarters and complain about Trump with open disdain. When, in September 2018, an anonymous Trump administration official published an op-ed in the *New York Times* claiming that they were doing everything possible to subvert Trump's destructive impulses, some thought Fuentes was the author. (Asked over email if he wrote the op-ed, Fuentes responded to me with the following message: "NOT TRUE!!")

Bannon's influence would never be as great as during the first month of the Trump presidency. As time went on, he became concerned that congressional Republicans were distracting the president from the populist and nationalist agenda that had distinguished Trump from every other Republican candidate for president. A conventional Trump would be no better than Marco Rubio come 2020.

In his office, Bannon had a whiteboard on which he listed presidential agenda items: "Pledges on Infrastructure," "Pledges on Immigration," "Pledges on Obamacare." To Bannon, this was a daily reminder of what he and Trump promised the American people. It was cluttered and ambitious, maybe even delusive, but it was what they said they were going to do, and now they had better do it. Others saw it as hopelessly unrealistic, even naïve, premised on a faulty understanding of the political perils Trump faced. "Ivanka hated it," Bannon would later recall with something approaching relish. "She didn't want to build the wall. She didn't want to drain the swamp. She doesn't want to do that. She's a progressive Democrat."

Walking into Bannon's office, the president's daughter touted her own priorities. "This is the program," she would say, "not your program. *This* is the program." She and her husband Jared Kushner wanted to work on prison reform and paid family leave. They wanted the United States to stay in the Paris climate accord. Bannon thought it was all insanity, but his own allies in the White House were few and growing fewer. And he was growing frustrated, exhausted. By the time Kelly dismissed Bannon in mid-August, both men knew it was time for him to go.

That left Stephen Miller as the "keeper of the president's commitments," as one person who worked with him in the West Wing put it. Miller surprised many by showing himself a deft navigator of the building's treacherous political currents. Though he was a Bannon protégé, he saw that it was more expedient to align himself with Kushner. He poached staffers from the Domestic Policy Council, which was headed by Bremberg, for his own outfit, which was focused on speechwriting and immigration.

Despite his almost singular focus on immigration, Miller saw himself as a free agent who could capably insert himself into any high-level policy discussion. This confidence was not widely shared. Miller would sometimes offer his opinions on economic matters, which would earn scorn from Gary D. Cohn, head of the National Economic Council.

The fight over who would steer policymaking in the White House did not receive nearly as much attention as personality clashes involving figures like Conway and Bannon. Those clashes were enormously entertaining, but they were also largely irrelevant because they involved characters who were either losing influence (Bannon) or never had influence to begin with (Conway).

When the Trump presidency began, Bremberg was touted as

Trump's "details man," as Amie Parnes of *The Hill* wrote. "There aren't too many people in Trump's senior circle who have done this before," an unnamed former Bremberg colleague told Parnes. Bremberg was to be one of the quiet, efficient men who pushed Trump's agenda through Congress.

At first, this seemed true enough. He did engineer use of the Congressional Review Act, even if this ultimately involved little more than taking instruction from Paul Ryan and Mitch McConnell about which Obama rules they wanted to abrogate. But over time, Bremberg would see his influence in the West Wing curbed. Miller vitiated the Domestic Policy Council, though he was by no means the only one. Kushner took on criminal justice, an issue in which he was profoundly invested. Cohn considered the economy his own domain. H. R. McMaster may not have been Trump's favorite person, but he was not going to let anyone intrude on the National Security Council.

Bremberg further harmed his reputation during the failed effort to repeal and replace the Affordable Care Act. Healthcare policy was supposed to be Bremberg's expertise; most media autopsies of the anti-ACA push made little or no mention of his role, but his colleagues in the West Wing knew that he bore at least some of the responsibility for Trump's biggest domestic policy failure during his first year in office.

Bremberg and Miller were among the most promising of Trump's advisers. But by becoming embroiled in battles of their own, they never quite rose above the daily struggles of the administration. They retained significant influence, but that influence would remain circumscribed. Neither could play the role of the indispensable younger man who could win the president's confidence by curbing his passions instead of inflaming them.

That role would instead be filled by an unlikely candidate.

After serving as a congressional sherpa for Scott Pruitt during the transition, Rob Porter was appointed Trump's staff secretary, a position whose title did no justice to its importance. If the chief of staff managed the flow of people, the staff secretary managed the flow of counsel and information. Frequently, the position was held by someone young and ambitious whose career was clearly on the ascent. John D. Podesta, guardian of the Democratic establishment, had been "staff sec" to Bill Clinton in his first years as president before ultimately becoming his chief of staff. Brett Kavanaugh, the future Supreme Court justice, had served in the same role for George W. Bush before being appointed to the immensely influential D.C. Circuit court of appeals.

Porter had been steeped in presidential politics from youth. He was the son of Roger B. Porter, a Mormon who served in the White House for Ford, Reagan, and Bush. One photo showed Porter with his wife Ann and their three children in the Oval Office with Reagan. Profiling him in 1990 for the *New York Times*, Maureen Dowd called Porter "amiable, meticulous and tenacious," adding that in the George H. W. Bush administration, he was "regarded as the perfect person to run the domestic policy shop at a time when the President is focusing on the more heady foreign policy agenda." To underscore Porter's influence, Dowd reported that he played tennis with the president.

Roger Porter also taught at Harvard, where he would come to hold an endowed chair at the Kennedy School of Government. Rob took his undergraduate degree at Harvard, where he overlapped with Jared Kushner. He was the center of the school's tight conservative circle: a 2000 article in the *Harvard Crimson* was headlined "The Zealot," identifying Porter as the leader of campus Republicans and describing him as above obsessing over the trivialities of electoral politics, more interested in substantive policy matters.

Rob won a Rhodes Scholarship to study political theory at Oxford, then went to Harvard Law before moving to Washington and beginning a career in politics. His last job before joining the Trump transition was as chief of staff to Orrin G. Hatch, the U.S. senator from Utah who cast himself as a principled conservative but could be craftily transactional in his politics. His junior Republican colleague from Utah, Senator Mike Lee, was frank in his abhorrence for Trump during the presidential campaign. Hatch, a practicing Mormon, stood by Trump even after the *Access Hollywood* tape. Having his own chief of staff named a high-ranking West Winger could be seen as a sign of confidence from Trump. It was also a potential means to influence the Oval that few of Hatch's colleagues would enjoy.

Porter was not one of the disturbingly colorful Trump characters who ordinary Americans came to know in the winter and spring of 2017. Porter did not tweet or make appearances on Fox News. His hair brushed back meticulously in the Princeton style, his voice fine but not fragile, he seemed to belong to another Washington. He radiated a cold intelligence that could be an affront to those who did not have his Harvard and Oxford pedigree. Imperious in bearing and manner, he recalled McGeorge Bundy, the haughtily brilliant adviser to Kennedy and Johnson. It was not Porter's lot, however, to work in the White House of Kennedy or Johnson.

Many of Trump's top aides were students of politics, the tactics of how campaigns were won or lost; Porter was a student of policy and governing institutions, of how political promises annealed into something real. He was particularly interested in how a president wielded his power: what kind of organization would allow him to be an effective manager, what kind of approach was bound to frustrate. He read scholars like Pfiffner and Kamarck, who were among the best thinkers on the presidency. He was also an admirer of Fred I. Greenstein, whose 1982 book *The Hidden-Hand Presidency* was a favorable study of Eisenhower's leadership and a kind of guidebook to presidential politics, and Richard E. Neustadt, whose 1960 *Presidential Power* was another classic of the genre.

As he prepared to join the White House in January 2017, Porter reached out to previous staff secretaries. He had a two-hour lunch with John Podesta. Porter was among those who saw the several similarities between early Clinton and early Trump. The question was whether Trump would be able to transcend his federal government inexperience, as Clinton did.

The signs were not encouraging. Porter told friends he was dismayed by the lack of organizational capacity in the new administration. He thought his colleagues—Bannon, Kelly, Kushner, Miller—were intelligent, but it was impossible not to notice that most of them had no history whatsoever of government service. This was an administration not out of its element but out of its galaxy.

Because Don McGahn was often absent from the Oval Office, Porter was left to explain to Trump why he lacked legal authority for a proposed executive order or why, even if signed, it would be met with a quick and probably successful court challenge.

"You're always telling me 'no,'" Trump would grumble. But he also started to take notice of the tall, impressively educated, meticulously mannered aide who seemed unconcerned by the skirmishes that broke out daily in the West Wing.

After Michael Flynn resigned from his role as the national security advisor in mid-February, Trump gave the post to Lieutenant General H. R. McMaster, a choice many cheered because the scholarly McMaster was seen as an antidote to Flynn, with his wild conspiratorial flights and troubling allegiances. Trump took a visceral dislike to McMaster. He hated the way McMaster looked, the way McMaster spoke. And *how long* McMaster spoke when he was invited to brief the president. One briefing lasted over an hour. Trump begged for relief.

About four months into the new presidency, Porter approached Priebus with the idea of giving Trump condensed briefing materials—"decision memos"—that Porter would present to the president each day. These decision memoranda would encapsulate all the arguments and counterarguments Trump would have otherwise heard from the people who had taken to walking unannounced into the Oval Office. Once Trump made a decision by signing the memorandum, the decision would be implemented by the appropriate agency or office.

Priebus liked the idea, but he was not around long enough to see it through. Yet he did show his own confidence in Porter by naming him assistant to the president for policy coordination in addition to his staff secretary role. If this was not technically a promotion, it was a significant expansion of Porter's portfolio, one that cemented his growing influence on policy. (Priebus did not publicize the upgrade of Porter's title because he feared that he would be accused of trying to consolidate power within the West Wing.)

Kelly was enthusiastic about Porter's efforts to organize information flow in the West Wing and helped him turn it into reality. On August 21, 2017, Kelly and Porter sent a memorandum to all cabinet officials and senior White House officials. "Securing Presidential Decisions" was its subject.

"The President will make all decisions on public-facing policy matters by signature and on the basis of decision memoranda (DMs) that have been vetted through the White House Staff Secretary," the memorandum read. "Decisions are not final—and therefore may not be implemented—until the Staff Secretary secures a cleared DM that has been signed by the President."

Anticipating resistance from those who benefited from disorder, Kelly and Porter called the new system a "required process" that would help "avoid unforced legal, policy, and political errors." They warned of any decision Trump made without a signed memo: "such decisions are provisional only."

Another memorandum sent that day by Kelly and Porter, this one on "paper flow to and from the president," clarified Porter's role for those who were apt to question it: "The White House Staff Secretary serves as both the inbox and the outbox for all Presidential materials." The memorandum also said that news articles had to "first

be submitted to the Staff Secretary." This would make it more difficult to influence Trump by slipping him an item from Fox News or
Breitbart.

Porter, who was Trump's opposite in every way imaginable,
now became the president's daily cheat sheet to the business of
presidential decision-making. Each day, Porter would brief the
president, bringing into the Oval Office memos that would com-
press a complex debate on an issue into a single page, with
accompanying materials. Sometimes, Trump would read the memorandum. More often, he would say to Porter, "Tell me about this,"
after which Porter would do his best to summarize the alternatives
and the arguments on each side. Trump would listen, then make
his decision and sign.

Not everyone trusted Porter, suspecting that he was not the "policy neutral" adviser he made himself out to be. Critics charged that
he was "picking winners and losers," not dispassionately presenting
different options to the president.

But to a certain extent the process worked, and it worked especially
well when Trump was confronted with a decision too significant to
make without presidential input but not significant enough to require
extensive consultation with congressional allies or other advisers. And
Porter knew, just as Kelly did, that he could never change the president. He would never be Eisenhower or Reagan. What advisers could
do was shape how the president was informed and how issues were
presented to him, largely by insisting that no decision reached the
Oval without Porter's approval.

The clampdown enraged those who liked the old, informal way of
doing things, which was the way Trump had done things as a businessman. Wilbur Ross, used to being an executive, bristled at being
subjected to a process that put a layer of bureaucracy between him
and the president. He continued to try to sneak his own memos to
Trump. It did not work.

Scott Pruitt, who lusted for power shamelessly, tried his own runaround. As a decision on the Paris climate change accords loomed, Pruitt—nobody's idea of a deep thinker—tried to present an amateurish memo to the president. Bannon had a memo of his own. Porter told them what he told everyone: this has to go through the required process.

Throughout the spring and summer of 2017, Porter also convened a high-level weekly meeting on trade. At 9:30 a.m. every Tuesday, Porter gathered the principals—Ross, Mnuchin, Cohn, Kushner, China hawk Peter Navarro, U.S. Trade Representative Robert E. Lighthizer, and others—in the Roosevelt Room, to work together on an issue that was central to the administration but which, until then, had suffered from a total lack of coordination.

Porter later told friends that that time—between September 2017 and February 2018—was a kind of brief golden age for the Trump West Wing. The historical lessons of presidential power were finally being put to use. Process snuck into the Oval Office. Some days, it even managed to linger there for a while, if never for all that long.

It would be an overstatement to say that the process Porter sought to implement was alone responsible for steadying the West Wing during the summer and fall of 2017. But he did use his knowledge of White House organization and presidential power to carve out channels through which decisions could flow more efficiently and effectively than they had before.

Porter had his detractors, in particular among Bannon and his allies. "Obsequious," one of those allies said. "Not my kind of guy" came the verdict from Bannon, who called people he was fond of "shipmates." He did not see Porter as a shipmate and refused to attend his meetings on trade, not wanting to legitimize a process he disapproved of. Most others, however, approved of the monumental task he had decided to take on.

"He tried," one person who worked with him said.

In the end, Porter was undone by his own past. Back in April 2017, just as his own influence in the White House was increasing the second of Porter's two former wives, Jennifer Willoughby, published a post on her personal blog in which she alleged that a former husband had been abusive. She did not name him, but as her only ex-husband, Porter asked her to take the post down. She refused.

Porter remained virtually unknown to the public until February 1, 2018, when the *Daily Mail*, a British tabloid with an established presence in the United States, revealed that he was dating Hope Hicks, the White House communications director. The article included photographs of Porter and Hicks out for dinner in Washington, apparently unaware that they were being tracked.

Five days later came another *Daily Mail* story, this one as disturbing as the first had been trivial. It included a recounting of domestic abuse allegations made against Porter by Willoughby and his first wife, Colbie Holderness. Soon there were pictures, too, namely a photograph of Holderness with a black eye, which she said Porter gave her on a vacation in Italy.

Several other men in the Trump administration had either been accused of sexual misconduct, as Trump was, or domestic abuse, as Bannon had once been. But Porter was younger, and he was more obviously the child of privilege—white privilege, in the parlance of social justice—a beneficiary of seemingly every boost the power elite could offer one of its own most promising scions.

Porter strenuously denied the allegations, and would continue to do so in the months to come. But it was largely fruitless, made worse by the bungled White House response. Nobody in the West Wing could explain definitively the status of Porter's security clearance, when Kelly learned about the allegations, who else knew about those allegations, when they had come to know, what they did with that knowledge.

Among those who believed that Porter should keep his job was Willoughby, his second wife. She made clear that she found Porter abusive. She also said he belonged in the White House. "I don't want to be married to him," she told the *Daily Mail*. "But I definitely want him in the White House and the position he is in. I think his integrity and ability to do his job is impeccable."

It was a striking statement, one that like Porter himself seemed to belong to another time. But it didn't help. Shortly after the *Daily Mail* story was published, Rob Porter elected to leave the White House.

This cheered the enemies of process. Peter Navarro and Wilbur Ross once again enjoyed access to the Oval Office, and just days later prevailed on Trump to launch steel and aluminum tariffs, the boldest salvo yet in the trade war on China. A White House official told Politico that the tariffs "never would have happened" if Porter, who had been closely coordinating the administration's trade policy, were still there.

Seeing his own influence wane, Gary Cohn also left the administration. Chaos, which had been barely held at bay, returned to the West Wing.

PART TWO: THE OCCUPATION

Chapter 9

······

TURBULENCE

They left Washington early and headed west, through Fairfax County, Virginia, where office towers rose like mountain peaks above the tree line, the highway whisking them past some of the wealthiest suburbs in the nation. The two reporters, Dan Diamond and Rachana Pradhan of Politico, were going to Dulles International Airport. They were not, however, planning to take a trip.

About four months earlier, in May 2017, someone had told Diamond and Pradhan something that was more than a rumor but less than a story: Tom Price, the health and human services secretary, was traveling around the nation—and on some occasions, internationally—on private and government jets. While government officials were sometimes allowed to use chartered or military aircraft, rules tightly circumscribed when they were able to do so. Politico's tipster suggested that Price, who had been confirmed by the Senate just three months earlier, had been using this privilege in ways that were way outside the limits.

Until that moment, Price had not emerged as an especially worrying member of the cabinet, if only because there were so many cabinet members to worry about. Suddenly, the silver-haired doctor with the wavering smile was the main character in a play that was bound to not have a happy ending.

During his twelve years in Washington as a Republican congressman representing Georgia's sixth district, Price had been a classic party man, one who was confident that his ambition would eventually be rewarded, not because of his brilliance as a politician—brilliance was more likely to be an impediment—but because he had staying power. He would say what party leaders wanted him to say until he could best those leaders, scramble over them somehow. Both parties were full of such men, loyal until loyalty no longer suited their ends.

By the time he came to be a national figure, Price was completely associated with Georgia. When he spoke, you heard the South. But he was actually a native of Michigan, one who earned his undergraduate and medical degrees from that state's prestigious flagship public university. In the early 1980s, he went to Atlanta for a residency at Emory; he would stay in the burgeoning Atlanta suburbs, devoting himself to his orthopedic practice.

In 1993, President Clinton implored Congress to pass his plan for "universal, comprehensive health care." Conservatives called this Hillarycare, because the First Lady took charge in crafting the proposal. They hated her, and they hated the plan she presented that November. Among those radicalized by opposition to Hillarycare was a thirty-nine-year-old orthopedic surgeon from the Atlanta suburbs. Price campaigned stridently against the Clinton proposal, which he argued would limit patients' freedom to make choices about the medical attention they received. The specter of "socialized medicine" would not return for another fifteen years, but in conservatives' successful fight against the Clinton health plan, the milquetoast surgeon got his first taste of politics. He was the college kid in a bar for the first time, putting his virginal lips to a frothy pint of beer. He loved it.

The following year, another creature of the Atlanta suburbs became the most prominent Republican on the national scene. He was round, with boyish cheeks, and his smile was also boyish, though with a touch of the malicious, the smile of someone who knew he was getting away with something. He had a doctorate in history from Tulane—his dissertation was titled "Belgian Education Policy in the Congo: 1945–1960"—but since the late 1970s, the would-be historian had served in Congress. His aim there was to rescue Republicans from the minority status they had been relegated to in the House for decades. Salvation was coming for the GOP, and it was named Newt Gingrich.

Gingrich capped an ambitious political ascent by becoming the House speaker in 1994. He did so by leveling withering attacks on the Clintons and congressional Democrats, the sort of attacks that would have been unbecoming only a few years before, back when Speaker Tip O'Neill, the Massachusetts liberal, and President Reagan, the conservative from California, could be genuine friends even as they remained political rivals. That had been a time time when Democrats and Republicans did not disagree on everything but the days of the week, when how you voted did not always depend on where you sat.

More than any other political figure of the late twentieth century, Gingrich realized that the era of political comity was increasingly the stuff of the past, to be venerated by wistful historians and self-righteous pundits. You could govern still, but only in monochrome: all red, or all blue. "People like me are what stand between us and Auschwitz," he said in 1994. "I see evil all around me every day."

Though his political career had begun in 1993, with opposition to the Clinton healthcare law, Price did not seek elected office until 1996, when he won a seat from the Atlanta suburbs to the Georgia Senate. The seat was easy to defend, and so Price defended it easily. Even as he became the state senate's minority whip, he seemed to retain a gentle demeanor. Because he had a mustache, some staffers nicknamed him "Ned Flanders," after the mustachioed, religious, totally harmless next-door neighbor on *The Simpsons*.

125

Price was transparently ambitious, but he was also serious and smart. In 2002, Price became majority leader in the Georgia Senate. In 2004, he announced that he was running for the U.S. House of Representatives from Georgia's sixth congressional district. It was the seat Gingrich held for twenty years before resigning from the House over ethics violations. Price won once again. Now, he was on his way to Washington. Airport security would not allow him to travel with his favored mustache trimmer in those anxious post-9/11 days, so the mustache went. Soon enough, the Ned Flanders image would go, too.

The congressional seat was as safe as the one he had held in the Georgia State Senate, and Price kept winning reelection by casting himself as a reliable conservative. As one Republican from the district told the *Atlanta Journal-Constitution,* in 2009 "We don't think Tom Price is being too conservative. We think some of the more moderate Republicans are being way too liberal."

Opposition to the Affordable Care Act, which Obama signed into law in 2009, was the bond that held the Republican conference together. And it was an issue on which Price, as a doctor, could credibly cast himself as an expert. Only this was expertise in the service of GOP dogma, not health policy. Shortly after the bill became law, Price called it "a costly and misguided encroachment of government that will destroy jobs and drive our nation further toward a fiscal crisis," a hyperbolic assertion that time would prove to be inaccurate. In a 2012 op-ed for the *Atlanta Journal-Constitution*, Price predicted that "we will see health care costs rise while diminishing quality and accessibility," once again proving himself a poor clairvoyant.

In 2015, Price introduced the Empowering Patients First Act, among the more serious of the mostly unserious Republican efforts to repeal the Affordable Care Act. Its primary feature was the health savings account, a class of tax-exempt fund that tended to benefit people of higher income. The bill also created high-risk pools for people who required more healthcare than average healthy persons.

The bill went nowhere, as Price had to know it would. The House was on its way to passing seventy ACA repeals, political gestures that stood no chance of becoming law under Obama. Still, Price's halfway credible plan did bolster the conviction that the surgeon from Georgia was a deep thinker on the GOP's most pressing issue.

In the spring of 2016, Price became one of nine House committee chairmen (he chaired the House Budget Committee, a powerful post that reflected how much his stock had risen) to sign a letter endorsing Donald Trump, who the week before had become the presumptive Republican nominee for president. In their endorsement of Trump, Price and his colleagues warned that the nation stood "on the precipice of one of the most important elections of our lifetime. This great nation cannot endure eight more years of Democrat-control of the White House." A Clinton victory, the signers warned, "enshrines ObamaCare as the law of the land," while a Republican one would finally bring about the ACA coup de grâce the GOP had been promising for years.

Price deftly positioned himself as the man who would help Trump do just that. Trump announced him as the new health and human services secretary on the Tuesday after Thanksgiving. Among those offering praise for the selection was Newt Gingrich, who said on Twitter that Price would be the "right leader to help Congress replace Obamacare." There was little pretense that he had been picked to do anything else.

During the confirmation process came the first hint that Price was not quite the morally upright, hardworking doctor-politician of soft-focus media reports. As a member of the House Ways and Means Committee, he had made legislative decisions that seemed to benefit biomedical companies in which he had rather enthusiastically invested. The Securities and Exchange Commission began investigating Ways and Means in 2013. Five years later, Representative Christopher Collins, a Republican from New York, was charged with insider trading related to stock he had purchased in Innate Immunotherapeutics, an Australian biotechnology company. While still in Congress, Price allegedly bought Innate stock on advice from Collins. The advice was good, if not exactly legal, and Price made $225,000 on the investment.

In his confirmation hearing, Price denied that he had done anything wrong while depicting himself as a doctor immune to Washington's partisanship. "One of my physician colleagues used to tell me that he never operated on a Democrat patient or a Republican patient, he operated on a patient," Price said at one point during his testimony. "And that's the way that I view this system. It's not a Republican system, it's not a Democrat system." His refusal to use the proper possessive, "Democratic," in favor of the pejorative "Democrat" favored by many of his conservative colleagues, was a small revelation about what he truly believed.

Democrats on the Senate Finance Committee boycotted the vote over Price's nomination (as well as Mnuchin's), but committee chair Orrin Hatch changed the rules so that the vote could proceed without any Democrats present. The full Senate confirmed Price along party lines, with 52 members voting for him and 47 against.

Now it was time for Price and his former colleagues in Congress to do what they had been promising for nearly a decade. McConnell and Ryan prevailed on Trump to make repeal of the Affordable Care Act his top legislative priority, even though a bipartisan package on infrastructure repair would have been a smarter move on both the political and policy fronts. Smarter, that is, for Trump. McConnell and Ryan needed to justify to their members the years they had devoted to railing against the ACA. Handing over billions to mend highways and bridges was nowhere in the congressional Republican agenda.

When I asked Trump about his decision not to lead with infrastructure, he gave one of his classically bombastic answers.

Infrastructure, he said, "is easy to get. I wanted to get the tax plan done," referencing the package of tax cuts Congress passed and he signed into law in late 2017. "I'm very much in line with infrastructure," he added, without offering any evidence to that effect.

House Republicans introduced the American Health Care Act on March 6, 2017. The next day, Price was trotted out at a White House press briefing. With Press Secretary Sean Spicer watching, Price pointed to a table on which two piles of paper lay, one taller than the other. "Notice how thick that is," he said of the taller stack, which represented the full text of the Affordable Care Act. The leaner AHCA was evidence, Price argued, that Republicans were "making certain that the process, that the decisions that are gonna be made, are not gonna be made by the federal government. They're gonna be made by patients, and families and doctors."

Price said nothing of how insurance companies would be free to raise premiums or refuse coverage altogether once the protections of the ACA for people with preexisting medical conditions were lifted. But others did. Six days later, the nonpartisan Congressional Budget Office estimated that 23 million Americans would lose their healthcare over a decade if AHCA became law. Republicans discounted these findings as either inaccurate or biased, though the dispassionate analysts of the CBO were neither.

Even as some Republicans voiced reservations, the AHCA hurtled out of committee and onto the House floor in late March. On March 23, Ryan desperately scrounged for "yeas," as Trump impatiently waited in the Oval Office for news of impending victory.

That same evening, Price was at Bullfeathers, the unadorned Capitol Hill bar ("bullfeathers" was Teddy Roosevelt's sanitized version of "bullshit"), enjoying drinks, as a brief but revealing video posted on social media by an observant citizen showed.

That a veteran of Congress like Price was not in the Rayburn or Longworth buildings where U.S. representatives were quartered, making a final push, was proof that either he lacked influence or the will to exert it. Either way, Trump would come to see the episode as indicative of Price's low standing.

The next day, Ryan pulled the bill.

Many months later, when the final act of the Price drama was through, a member of the transition expressed regret that he and his colleagues had not "kicked the tires" on Price more thoroughly. To some, he came across as self-regarding yet uninformed. He was supposed to have exerted influence on his former colleagues in Congress, only it turned out there was no influence to exert.

Not everyone thought he was to blame. Andrew Bremberg, director of the Domestic Policy Council, had worked in Health and Human Services under George W. Bush before becoming an adviser to McConnell. He could have done more, his critics charged, to master the policy details, to sharpen the administration's arguments while blunting fully predictable congressional opposition. Price, in this view, was not the only one at fault.

The debacle had several more acts. Frustrated by the House, Senate Republicans started writing their own healthcare bill, a task undertaken by McConnell largely in secret. The bill he released in June, the Better Care Reconciliation Act, was quickly determined by the CBO to imperil the healthcare of twenty-two million Americans.

If Tom Price's reputation were a stock, Tom Price would have been selling. In July, right before another ACA vote, President Trump unleashed a weird, unnerving stem-winder on a convention of Boy Scouts in West Virginia. At one point, he summoned onto the stage members of his cabinet who had been Scouts themselves: Ryan Zinke of Interior, goofily dressed in full Scout regalia, Rick Perry of the Department of Energy, and Price.

As Price came onto the stage, Trump said he hoped that Congress was on its way to "killing this horrible thing known as Obamacare."

Perry came over and grabbed Price by the shoulders, then walked away.

"U-S-A," the crowd began to chant.

Price began to clap. Then Trump started clapping, too. Then they were all clapping, while the crowd continued to chant. Everyone was cheering, only nobody seemed to know what they were cheering for.

The chanting stopped. Trump demanded of Price if he had the requisite votes. "He better get them. He better get them. Oh, he better. Otherwise, I'll say, 'Tom, you're fired,'" Trump growled, reprising his famous *Apprentice* slogan and gesture. "I'll get somebody."

The threat did little to lift Republican prospects. The McConnell-led repeal effort failed four days later, sunk by Senator John McCain's dramatic thumbs-down on the Senate floor.

Two months after the ACA repeal effort collapsed in the Senate, Diamond and Pradhan of Politico published their big scoop on Price: "Price's private-jet travel breaks precedent." The report noted that in the previous week alone, Price had taken five separate flights on private jets. The secretary was not jetting to hard-to-reach locales. One of his private flights was from Washington to Philadelphia. This cost, the Politico writers estimated, about $25,000, an expense billed to the American taxpayer. A seat on a regular civilian commercial aircraft would have cost about $400.

For someone who decried government waste, Price evidently had little compunction about burning through money. He took a trip to Nashville, where he owned a condominium, to spend time with his son. The trip would have cost perhaps $200 on a commercial flight, but Price used a Learjet instead. That left the American people with a $17,760 bill.

Later, an HHS spokeswoman would offer one of the more preposterous excuses tendered in this age of preposterous excuses for preposterous behavior: "This is Secretary Price, getting outside of D.C., making sure he is connected with the real American people."

Other political leaders found the capital region's three airports sufficient for such purposes. But this was a billionaire president, presiding over a billionaires' cabinet. Flying coach was for liberals and rubes.

Not only did Price abuse the power of his office, but he taunted his own employees back home with chronicles of his exploits, apparently unaware of just how much ire he was inciting. In his "Week in Review" newsletter, he boasted of his travels to the deskbound employees back in Washington whom he and President Trump were threatening with enormous budget cuts. There were dispatches from Liberia and Switzerland. "Hello from Alaska" came an email on an August day that had Washington slogging and sweating through punishing humidity.

These revelations rattled people who had known Price on Capitol Hill, who once worked with him or for him, who now saw him become a cable news staple for the worst possible reason. Nothing could have predicted this. "I knew Tom when he still had a mustache," one former congressional staffer who knew Price well said. That was the Price who was closer to Ned Flanders than Donald Trump. Who hosted "family dinners" for junior aides on Capitol Hill. Who believed that government was profligate, and should not be. Where had that Price gone? The former staffer professed confusion. Perhaps he had been enabled. Or maybe he was seduced.

Whoever Tom Price had been, he was that person no more. In the months he spent trying to take healthcare away from millions of Americans, Price more or less stole $341,000 of taxpayer money (according to a calculation by his own agency's inspector general) to spend on his lavish travel habits. As the embarrassing stories kept coming, he promised to write a check to the U.S. Treasury for about $51,000. In an interview with Fox News, he said he hoped "to not only regain the trust of the American people, but gain the trust of the administration and the president," a slavish appeal to Trump that, like all such appeals, was sure to fail.

The Fox News interview was on Thursday. On Friday, Price was pushed out, the interview having clearly failed to appease Trump, who disliked bad publicity far more than he disliked poor judgment. In his resignation letter, Price assumed a self-righteous tone, describing how he had spent four decades "putting people first," without mentioning the fortune he'd made in his dubious stock trades. He characterized the ethical questions over his penchant for private jets as nothing more than a "distraction." He showed no contrition or reflection. Nor would any of the Trump cabinet members who resigned after him.

Much like his fellow Georgian Newt Gingrich, Tom Price would leave official Washington in disgrace. Whether he returned to Atlanta in first class or coach could not be determined, nor whether decency compelled him to pay for the flight out of his own pocket.

Chapter 10

······

FELLOW TRAVELERS

If there was any comfort Tom Price could take from his plight, it was that he was not alone. Far from it.

The best politicians understood that voters were swayed by story, not argument. Trump's most potent, most vivid story was that of draining the swamp. The story was powerful and cathartic, only it suffered from a defect common to political stories, in that it was fiction. Many suspected this from the start, even as others held out hope that Trump would prove the incorruptible iconoclast he played on the campaign trail.

The counter-narrative of the private jet presidency put an end to all such hopes. It was a story first attached to Price, though like an airborne virus, it quickly spread. The story made people wonder just how deep the swamp in Washington was. If Trump couldn't drain it, then who could? Unless he'd never truly tried. Unless the whole promise had been little more than a feint, one accompanied by a wink that let his best people act out their worst impulses.

There were some in the White House who understood this, who did their best to bring Trump's cabinet into compliance with rules so basic, they should have needed no explaining. But as one person who witnessed those efforts put it, "nobody wanted to be the bad guy." By the time they finally took decisive action, the narrative of administration-wide corruption dominated the public discourse. It coupled with the narrative of a chaotic West Wing, which Kelly and Porter and others had desperately tried to suppress. This made for great cable television. It did not make for great governing.

Trump was by no means the first president forced to confront scandals caused by his cabinet members. George H. W. Bush's chief of staff, John H. Sununu, used military jets seventy-seven times in a period of about two years, a luxury that cost the federal government about half a million dollars. Apparently dissatisfied with the level of dentistry in Washington, he flew twice to see his own dentist in Boston. He flew to a ski resort in Colorado, and to his native New Hampshire. The press deemed him "Air Sununu," with *Newsweek* offering the following advice to the combative chief of staff, who had alienated many members of his own party: "If you're going to make such armies of enemies inside the Beltway, you'd better be sure there are no chinks in your armor." He did not listen, of course. Nor would many Trump officials, discovering that the self-righteous were rarely afforded an easy path down the road of contrition.

Bill Clinton tried to head off ethical crises with a memorandum on February 10, 1993, that warned, "taxpayers should pay no more than absolutely necessary to transport Government officials. The public should only be asked to fund necessities, not luxuries, for its public servants."

Within just three months of taking office, Clinton was embroiled in his first travel-related scandal, which came to be known as Travelgate. On May 19, 1993, the White House announced that all seven members of its travel office were being fired. When Press Secretary Dee Dee Myers took the podium in the Brady Briefing Room that day and explained that there had been "gross mismanagement," the White House press corps exploded with indignation.

As media critic David Shaw of the *Los Angeles Times* later explained, their anger may not have made sense to the ordinary American, but it made perfect sense to most people in that room. "The travel office smoothed the way for reporters traveling with the President—not only making reservations but arranging for hot meals, communications and overnight laundry service, finding missing baggage, doing the 1,001 small chores that can make the difference between an enjoyable trip and a disastrous one," Shaw wrote. There were, in other words, legitimate concerns about the travel office firings, which were exacerbated by the grievances of the press.

Hairgate arrived before Travelgate had a chance to depart the national consciousness. The principal actors in Hairgate were the celebrated hairstylist Cristophe Schatteman and Clinton's thick, increasingly silver mane. Cristophe—he went by one name, which by 2018 graced an outlet of his salon just a few blocks from the White House—charged $200 for a haircut (it would be $340 by the time Trump took office). This was a presumably fair price, as Cristophe was one of the best-regarded practitioners of his craft in Los Angeles. The only problem was that on May 18, 1993, Cristophe had to practice that craft as Air Force One was sitting on a tarmac at Los Angeles International Airport.

"It may have been the most expensive haircut in history," began a *New York Times* report on the incident. "Two of Los Angeles International Airport's four runways were shut down for nearly an hour on Tuesday, some incoming flights were delayed and Air Force One sat on the tarmac with engines running." Back in Washington, the White House was forced "to explain why the populist President tied up one of the country's busiest airports to have his hair trimmed."

In due time, airline records would show this to have been fake news. There were no delays, no crammed jets forced to circle above Los Angeles. There had been a couple of planes routed to other runways, but that was the extent of the inconvenience Clinton caused his fellow Americans as Cristophe snipped away at the president's locks. But that did not erase the memory of Hairgate, of a sitting president receiving an expensive haircut—from a first-name-only Belgian, no less—while commoners stewed in coach. Story won over facts. Didn't it always?

Shaw of the *Los Angeles Times* explained that Hairgate and Travelgate had become "gates" because members of the media were frustrated with how Clinton was treating them. That frustration seeped into their reporting, making them more likely to inflate minor offenses into flagrant violations.

But also, the transgressions kept happening. In 1994, David Watkins—a hometown friend whom Clinton brought to the White House, and who was involved in the Travelgate dismissals—decided to commandeer the presidential helicopter Marine One to ferry himself to a golf course in rural Maryland. This was a terrifically bad idea, and Watkins was fired from his job. Clinton managed to make things worse by paying him a $3,000-a-month retainer, taken out of campaign funds, for most of the next year. No amount of goodwill from the press could smooth over a debacle like that.

George W. Bush had travel troubles, too. In 2006, Representative Henry A. Waxman, the powerful Democrat from Southern California, sent a letter to the Office of Management and Budget alleging that during the campaign season two years before, Bush administration officials had taken to traveling around the country in private jets for transparently political purposes. "It is apparent that cabinet secretaries and agency heads are using private aircraft for trips that could more economically occur on commercial aircraft," Waxman wrote, pointing to "at least 125 trips to more than 300 locations" since 2001, "at a cost to the taxpayer of over $1.5 million."

Not all of it may have been improper, but none of it looked good. Rod Paige, the education secretary, had spent $50,290 to fly around the country touting No Child Left Behind, the Bush education reform law. Ann M. Veneman, the agriculture secretary, spent nearly $12,000 to fly on a private plane to Iowa to shill for the Bush tax cuts.

The greatest offender was Michael O. Leavitt, then the health and human services secretary. As head of the EPA, he had spent about $42,000 on private flights in October 2004, right before the presidential election. One of those trips was to Nevada, where he celebrated a "middle school for its response to a jar of spilled mercury." Later, as head of HHS, Leavitt took to jetting around the country in a Gulfstream owned by the Centers for Disease Control and Prevention. He flew on the craft nineteen times, charging the federal government $726,048.

Trump had cast Hillary Clinton as hopelessly corrupt, while arguing that his own wealth insulated him from influence. And maybe it did, or could. But there were men and women in his cabinet who, while rich by any normal standard, did not have his wealth. How were they to play the part of government officials in a government headed by a billionaire? Tom Price's plight hinted at how difficult that would prove, how the seductive perfume of luxury would float through the halls of government buildings.

Trump's cabinet had a lone Obama holdover: Secretary of Veterans Affairs David J. Shulkin. Shulkin was, like Price, a doctor; unlike Price, he was neither an ideologue nor someone who harbored any political ambitions. Appointed by Obama in 2015 to serve as the department's undersecretary for health, he took over a department that one high-ranking official said was "a mess." There was "no strategic direction" for improving care for the men and women returning from Afghanistan and Iraq. The year before Shulkin joined the department, investigators found that officials at the Phoenix VA were reporting false wait times for veterans to receive care. In reality, receiving medical attention took an average of four months, as evidenced by a secret list that chronicled the grim reality. Perhaps as many as forty people died as a result of these delays. And this in a department whose Washington headquarters bore a quote from Lincoln engraved near the entrance: "To care for him who shall have borne the battle and for his widow, and his orphan."

Shulkin's efforts at the VA were encouraging, and though he was not Trump's top choice to lead the department, the Senate confirmed Shulkin 100 to 0. He was the only Trump cabinet nominee to receive unanimous support from the Senate.

The beachhead team arrived at the VA on the third week of November. "They really didn't want to have a lot of input or interaction" with political appointees of the previous administration, one Obama-appointed official recalled. As at EPA, there was a complete ideological rupture at work. Democrats wanted to improve the VA system, while Republicans argued that the only way to improve the VA was to privatize it.

The beachhead team had no interest in healing this rift. The former VA official, who was part of and supported the Obama reform efforts, remembered that one of the beachhead team members inadvertently left a memorandum on a public printer. The memo, which was supposed to be private, instructed the Trump people not to have any interaction with the Obama people.

This wasn't a transition, but a standoff. "There really weren't a lot of openings for us to engage," the former top VA administrator complained. "We weren't invited to meetings." Things got worse when members of the transition became political appointees, which gave them a permanent power base from which to assail Shulkin, who advocated for reform but not privatization. Among those most intent on undermining Shulkin were Darin Selnick, who had been a senior official at Concerned Veterans for America, a group funded by the Koch brothers that wanted to circumvent the VA and make veterans' care a matter of the private marketplace; Peter O'Rourke, who was nominally Shulkin's chief of staff but who routinely communicated about privatization efforts with Trump allies at Mar-a-Lago; Thomas "Jake" Leinenkugel, the scion of a Wisconsin beer family who looked for ways to undermine Shulkin; Camilo J. Sandoval, who while working on the Trump campaign had allegedly harassed and bullied a female staffer.

Most people could not be expected to grasp the byzantine rivalries of the Trump administration, of the battles between beachhead teams and career staffers, lifers, and politicals. What the public saw was the bloodied corpses of those who were on those rivalries' losing ends. Shulkin was one of these.

On June 29, 2017, Shulkin sent a memorandum to top managers in his department. In the memo, "Essential Employee Travel," Shulkin outlined a new process by which travel would be approved and documented. "I expect this will result in decreased employee travel and generate savings," he wrote.

Two weeks later, Shulkin and his wife, Merle Bari, got on a plane and flew from New York's John F. Kennedy International Airport to Copenhagen. With them were three VA staffers and one staffer's husband. There was also a six-person security detail. "The 10-day trip was not entirely a vacation," the *Washington Post* would report several months later, when details of the trip first became public. There were some who believed that the story was leaked to the *Post* as part of a "deliberate strategy" to discredit Shulkin. Whether he deserved to be discredited or not, the strategy worked.

Shulkin planned the trip so that it began with meetings in Denmark and ended about a week later with meetings in London. In between, there was watching tennis at Wimbledon, visiting medieval castles, dining, and shopping. A tourist from Madison, Wisconsin, told the *Post* she spotted Shulkin and company "whisked to the front of the line" at an attraction in Copenhagen. One of Shulkin's taxpayer-funded security guards, she said, was hauling a "large number of shopping bags."

Shulkin called this "poor reporting," though no significant errors of fact came to light. The true error, as he saw it, was not in fact but in focus. After his ouster, there continued to be dispute over whether Shulkin really did use security guards as shopping sherpas. And his supporters said that Shulkin and his wife did not enjoy an expensive jaunt on the taxpayers' dime, that the costs were exaggerated and misrepresented, to make decent people look indecent, to push the last of the Obama people out of the Trump administration.

The *Washington Post* broke the story of Shulkin's trip on September 29. That same day, Tom Price resigned for having spent his tenure at HHS on luxurious travel, and little else. Shulkin lasted through the winter of 2018, his firing announced by a tweet from Trump on March 28. As he departed the Trump administration, he wrote an op-ed for the *New York Times* arguing that he had been forced out for opposing the privatization of veterans' healthcare services. There was compelling evidence to support Shulkin's charge. Yet the wounds of scandal never fully healed.

Shulkin did have some accomplishments during his three years at the VA, including offering same-day urgent-care services, starting to integrate medical records with the Department of Defense and allowing veterans who had "bad paper" (that is, other than honorable discharge) to receive mental health services from the VA. In the summer of 2017, Shulkin stood next to Trump as the president signed the Department of Veterans Affairs Accountability and Whistleblower Protection Act of 2017, which made it easier to root out malefactors while protecting those who reported wrongdoing to the government.

Ultimately, however, Shulkin could not escape the ethical morass of becoming a Trump official. John Kelly, the president's chief of staff, strongly decried the decision to let Shulkin go, according to a person familiar with (and sympathetic to) Shulkin's situation.

"He took his own agenda off the tracks" that person said of Trump. This was an assessment particular to the VA, but it was true of most other agencies in the federal government. If the forces working on an ordinary presidential cabinet were centrifugal, as James Pfiffner of George Mason argued in his influential paper, the forces working on the Trump administration looked like a Jackson Pollock action painting. In that confusion, the selfish thrived.

Things were not looking good for the president who promised the most ethical and competent administration in history. His supporters began to downplay the promise. "I don't think it's like they wake up in the morning and say, 'How can we drain the swamp today?'" conceded Christopher Ruddy, the publisher of conservative site Newsmax and a close friend of the president, in the fall of 2017. "At the end of the day, the swamp rules," added Ruddy with a measure of resignation. Like most of Trump's closest associates, he tended to stay far from Washington; they feared the swamp's malarial rot, not realizing how many of their own were carriers of the disease.

The disease was spreading. By November 2017, several of Trump's cabinet members were under investigation, whether by the inspectors general of their own agencies, the Office of Management and Budget, or the rare congressional committee that discovered its conscience in the age of Trump.

Shulkin's abuse of government funds, whether minor or not, was inexplicable because he had never been known as a grifter. Steve Mnuchin was another matter. Having amassed a fortune of $400 million, in part through foreclosing on homeowners, Trump's treasury secretary was not known as a man of scruples. Nor was he regarded as a serious thinker by the serious people in Washington and New York. He became treasury secretary by sticking with Trump as national finance chairman throughout the presidential campaign. "Mnuchin won the Treasury on the getting the money into the campaign," Bannon said. He had told Mnuchin, "When we win, you are Secretary of Treasury."

He may not have been Nobel material, but he also was not an utter clown. Career staffers praised Mnuchin for dismissing members of the beachhead teams, who he understood were supposed to watch over the department and report anything untoward to Trump. "He had a very serious approach," one top treasury staffer remembered. "He was a very self-confident guy. Not a lot of patience." If he was

THE BEST PEOPLE

short on patience, the staffer said, he was long on haughtiness. Yet he did command respect from career staff who saw that he was "somebody who obviously understood markets" and was not, like other Trump cabinet members, intent on destroying the agency he was charged with leading.

Mnuchin was on his third wife, like Trump. His was the Scottish actress Louise Linton, an eternally pouting blonde. She had attracted attention—not the good kind—for a memoir she self-published about a trip to Africa at the age of eighteen. The book, *In Congo's Shadow* described a continent "rife with hidden danger" and relied on crude, outdated stereotypes of Africa and its people. Linton's vanity and indiscretion would help bring shame on her husband, and herself.

After the Republican effort to repeal the Affordable Care Act failed, the White House turned to its second-most important priority, which was cutting taxes. Mnuchin was expected to be central to this effort. But then the motion of the planets got in the way.

On August 21, 2017, Mnuchin and Linton traveled to Louisville, Kentucky. There, he and Senate Majority Leader McConnell, the senior senator from that state, addressed a local chamber of commerce. Mnuchin touted Trump's proposed tax cuts as benefiting ordinary workers, though virtually all macroeconomists agreed they would do the exact opposite. After the luncheon with McConnell, Mnuchin and Linton toured Fort Knox, where the U.S. government held 4,600 metric tons of gold.

There was another reason for the trip, what many suspected later was the main reason for Mnuchin to travel to sweltering Kentucky in late August. The day that Mnuchin and Linton visited Kentucky, the rare spectacle of a total solar eclipse was to take place. The eclipse would only be visible in certain locations. The western tip of Kentucky happened to be one of these. (As for the risible notion that Mnuchin was legitimately pushing the president's tax cuts: if that were really the case, he would have been better off trying to influence sometimes-renegade Republicans like Bob Corker of Tennessee or Jeff Flake of Arizona. The two votes from Kentucky were as secure as the gold in Fort Knox.)

The public may never have learned about the trip—or about the couple's broader penchant for military jets—if not for Linton's fabulous Instagram account. For the enlightenment of the social network's 700 million users, Linton posted an image of herself descending the steps of an aircraft clearly marked as belonging to the U.S. government. There was something resplendent and glamorous about Linton, dressed in white, her rich, golden hair falling below her shoulders. She was a first lady, not a cabinet secretary's wife. She knew it, and she wanted others to know too: "Great #daytrip to #Kentucky!" the Instagram post said. This was amended with a grating cavalcade of fashion-label hashtags: "#rolandmouret pants, #tomford sunnies, #hermesscarf, #valentinorockstudheels #valentino." The post concluded with a self-righteous "#usa."

Linton may not have known that most in the #usa could not afford $445 sunglasses by Tom Ford, or the rest of her outfit, which *Vanity Fair* calculated to have cost $13,775 (a "low estimate," according to the fashion-savvy magazine). It was just as likely that she knew but did not care.

Among those infuriated by Linton's post was Jennifer Miller, a forty-four-year-old mother of three from Lake Oswego, Oregon. Miller had this to say: "Glad we could pay for your little getaway. #deplorable." The whole episode could have been just another forgettable Internet skirmish, except that Linton decided to respond to Miller in a lengthy post packed with sarcasm and grandiloquence. "I'm pretty sure we paid more taxes toward our day 'trip' than you did," the post said in part. "Pretty sure the amount we sacrifice per year is a lot more than you'd be willing to sacrifice if the choice was yours." She ended the post by suggesting that Miller relax by watching the latest episode of *Game of Thrones*.

Linton and Mnuchin were pilloried as clueless kleptocrats, but there was nothing new about that charge, nor any sense that its validity would shame the shameless couple. The more observant of her critics deduced from public reports, and the Instagram post, that Mnuchin and Linton had used flimsy pretenses—the luncheon with McConnell—to travel to see the eclipse. They could have done that, of course, without using military aircraft, which cost the American taxpayer $33,000.

When there was smoke in the Trump administration, there was usually a nuclear meltdown. It soon came to light that Mnuchin had taken another flight from Washington to New York and back for $15,000. An ordinary person might have paid about $200 for the flight. To this category of spendthrifts belonged Mnuchin's predecessor Tim Geithner, who regularly flew between Washington and New York in coach. This did not hamper his efforts in helping the Obama administration successfully rescue the economy from the housing crisis of 2008.

On October 5, after Price had been fired and Shulkin thoroughly embarrassed, the Treasury's inspector general revealed that Mnuchin had already used military craft seven times during his brief time as a federal employee, for a total cost of $800,000, about fourteen times what the average American family made in a year. And this was supposed to be the presidency of average Americans.

It was now just about a year since Trump had first made his drain-the-swamp promise in the final lap of the 2016 presidential campaign, and the swamp was taking on historic proportions. In addition to Price, Shulkin, and Mnuchin, there was Scott Pruitt, the administrator of the Environmental Protection Agency, who had built himself a $43,000 private communications booth and pulled high-ranking EPA agents off assignment to serve as his personal bodyguards, in addition to incurring what was reported at the time to be $58,000 in travel costs (and his troubles were only beginning);

Ryan Zinke, the interior secretary, was being investigated for travel expenses that included a $12,375 chartered flight to Montana from Las Vegas, where he had attended an event for a hockey team owned by one of his benefactors. "A little B.S. over travel," Zinke said, before things got much more serious, ending with his departure from the Trump cabinet in late 2018.

Elaine Chao, who headed the Transportation Department, had used government planes on at least seven occasions, according to the *Washington Post.* She was also facing questions about her ownership of stock in Vulcan Materials, a building company that would likely benefit from a $1 trillion infrastructure plan Trump touted but never came close to implementing; Rick Perry, the energy secretary, took a private plane to visit "a uranium facility in Piketon, Ohio," in late September 2017, according to Reuters. He once also, the same outlet reported, flew into "a private airport in Kansas that was within a 45-minute drive of Kansas City International Airport."

The Trump administration was not yet a year old, and already several of its top cabinet officials were the subjects of multiple investigations. And many more were about to come, now that the extent of the cabinet's selfishness and corruption were becoming known. Representative Elijah E. Cummings of Maryland, then the ranking Democrat on the House Committee on Oversight and Reform, put the matter bluntly: "I've never seen anything like this."

Neither had some of the Republican old-timers in the White House, many of whom had last worked for George W. Bush and remembered a competent operation overseen by Dick Cheney. Among these was Joseph "Joe" W. Hagin, who had worked for both Bush the father and Bush the son. Hagin, who was a deputy chief of staff for operations in the White House, tried to run things as he knew them, but some bristled, finding him too much a "43 guy" who didn't understand the way 45—Trump—wanted to do things. Still, Hagin garnered respect from most of his colleagues. And he was among the first to notice that cabinet members were plainly not listening to the directives they had been given.

Those directives were coming from Bill McGinley, a veteran Washington lawyer with expertise in compliance. He was also in that class of administration officials who shunned self-promotion and approached his work with a genuine sense of duty. Only he had no idea what he had signed up for.

McGinley's initial approach was to invite the chiefs of staff of the executive departments to his office in the Eisenhower Executive Office Building for a weekly seminar. Each week, the seminar would offer instruction on the finer points of public service. The main problem was that it was one thing to tell something to Ryan Jackson, quite another to say it to the man he worked for, Scott Pruitt. Not all the chiefs of staff had the influence with their department heads to keep them out of trouble (Jackson was among those who did not). And not all the chiefs took McGinley's seminars seriously, further undermining their intent.

McGinley's strongest critics said he was too much the "concierge," a go-between for the cabinet members and the White House, as opposed to a White House enforcer who made sure the cabinet chiefs did not stray. Hagin had similar critics, though his broad portfolio would have made it difficult for him to provide the tough oversight that the best people desperately demanded.

The scandals over private flights broke throughout the fall of 2017, just as Kelly and Porter were laboring to get the West Wing in order. It fell to Kelly to play bad cop with the cabinet, too. On September 29, 2017, the same day that Tom Price resigned, a memorandum from the White House said that "all travel on Government-owned, rented, leased, or chartered aircraft…shall require prior approval" from Kelly.

McGinley also toughened his approach, though what that really meant was that he had to simplify it. He was accustomed to working with corporate executives; now he was working with children. "I can't babysit the cabinet," he would complain. But that was exactly what he was being asked to do. That winter, he drafted a memorandum titled "Creating a Culture of Compliance" that was shared with the most troublesome of the cabinet members, including Zinke and Pruitt. Its main points were astonishingly basic but inarguably necessary:

- You are the best guardian of your reputation.
- Work closely with your ethics officer.
- Be critical of your schedule.
- Remember, an ethics opinion matters only if the ethics officer reviewed all of the information.
- Even if legal, that does not mean you should do it.

By spring, this became a speech, which McGinley would give to different agencies, traveling like Paul the Apostle across the federal bureaucracy, preaching the gospel of compliance. If the messages in McGinley's speech were heartening—here was somebody in the Trump administration who clearly cared about doing right—it was disheartening that the points in the speech had to be made in the first place, especially this late in a presidential term:

"We work for the American people.... Be good stewards of taxpayers' money." What business did anyone who didn't already know as much have working in the federal government?

In his speech, McGinley touched at length on the plight of David H. Safavian, an official in the George W. Bush administration who was sent to prison for lying about his association with lobbyist Jack Abramoff (a frequent visitor to Abramoff's eatery Signatures, Safavian was trying to help Abramoff buy two government properties, one of which was the Old Post Office, which would in time become the Trump International Hotel).

The pressure from Kelly and McGinley, not to mention the unrelenting media coverage, did help. It scared Ben Carson and Steve

Mnuchin straight (at least for a little while: in January 2019, the *New York Times* reported that Mnuchin had flown to California on the private plane of disgraced banker Michael R. Milken, who had long sought a presidential pardon for his financial crimes). Rick Perry, too. And some never caused any trouble to begin with. But there were a few cabinet members, McGinley knew, who were beyond redemption. They were the ones who were desperate to impress Trump, and also to emulate him. They were the ones who would not listen to anyone else. They would bring down the whole teetering edifice. And they would call it victory.

Chapter 11

·······

THE POSSUM

Scott Pruitt's career as a federal public servant ended on the afternoon of July 5, 2018. On that day, three officials from the EPA inspector general's office were meeting with this author. The meeting itself was off the record. It lasted about an hour. As the three officials were leaving the Yahoo News newsroom, less than a block from the White House, one of the officials looked up at a flat-screen television in the front lobby, which was tuned to CNN.

"Oh my God," she cried.

Everyone looked up. Though the television was silent, the chyron at the bottom of the screen said that Trump had finally cut Pruitt loose.

Notably, none of the EPA officials seemed especially bothered. They were far too professional to show joy, but their lack of disappointment or surprise would have been difficult to miss. There was little mystery, after all, about what career EPA officials thought of the man who did his best to destroy the agency where they worked.

Two things were surprising about the Pruitt firing. The first was how long it took, and how resistant Trump had been to letting the guillotine fall on the chubby Oklahoman's neck. Just a month before—when many, though not all, of Pruitt's ethical shortcomings had been uncovered—Trump praised Pruitt at a Federal Emergency

Management Agency meeting where both men were present. "EPA is doing really, really well," Trump said, in one of his shows of awkward and edgy praise. "Somebody has to say that about you a little bit, you know that, Scott." Before that, he had called Pruitt the victim of media bias and zeal.

That was thin cover. Trump's own chief of staff had concluded that Pruitt was an irredeemable pestilence on the Trump administration, one that had to be extirpated as quickly as possible. It took him several months, but in early July 2018, John Kelly succeeded, helped along by tweets from Fox News primetime host Laura Ingraham and the complaints of other conservatives grown exhausted by the damage Pruitt managed to daily inflict on their cause. No number of vanquished Obama regulations was worth quite this much trouble.

The second notable aspect of Pruitt's demise was just how much harm he did manage to inflict on the nation's environmental policy, even as it became clear that he was on his way out. On his final day in office, Pruitt removed the cap on the number of glider trucks that could be manufactured in the United States. Because they used antiquated engines, gliders released a far greater number of pollutants than newer, more efficient trucks. There was no reason to grant this exemption, except that the glider lobby wanted it. And as had been the case for decades, Scott Pruitt gladly did what an industry lobby asked of him. He had no reason to deviate from that practice, which had served him remarkably well.

Short and stolid, Pruitt carried himself with a rancher's confidence. His white hair was closely cropped, and though he wore glasses, there was nothing scholarly or bureaucratic about Edward Scott Pruitt. At forty-eight, he was the second-youngest member of Trump's original cabinet (Nikki Haley was his junior by four years) and frequently wore a boyish smile that made him look even younger.

Pruitt grew up in Lexington, Kentucky. His father ran restaurants, while his mother stayed home, tending to the three Pruitt children.

On the strength of his skill as a baseball player, Pruitt entered the University of Kentucky in 1986. "The Possum," as he was known, did not distinguish himself as a ballplayer. In 1987, he transferred from Kentucky to Georgetown College, a small Baptist school outside of Lexington. He continued to play baseball, eventually earning a try-out with the Cincinnati Reds. But once it became clear that a career in the major leagues was unlikely, Pruitt turned to law, entering the University of Tulsa's law school in 1990. He would stay in Oklahoma for the next two-and-a-half decades.

After graduating from law school in 1993, Pruitt started Christian Legal Services, Inc., a law practice that represented clients seeking religious liberty protections under the First Amendment. Among these was a state employee who had supposedly been prevented from holding a Bible study group in her home. Subsequent reporting found that, in fact, Pruitt's client "had been instructed to avoid prose-lytizing to agency clients." The case demonstrated Pruitt's conviction that Christianity had been pushed out of the public square, a belief that would bring him into alignment with the culture warriors then ascendant in the Republican Party.

Pruitt's political career began in 1998, when he successfully challenged a sixteen-year incumbent for his seat on the Oklahoma State Senate. Although he'd never run for office, Pruitt announced his arrival in electoral politics with breathtaking confidence: "This race has little to do with Ged Wright," he said of his opponent as the primary neared. "He simply holds the seat I'm seeking." Pruitt won.

Pruitt was not interested in the backbencher's sleepy, comfortable existence. He was elected the Republican whip in 2001 and the assistant Republican floor leader in 2003, giving him increasing prominence within a Republican caucus whose clout was growing in Oklahoma. His religious conservatism earned him the nickname "Pastor Pruitt" from the *Tulsa World*. He tried to curb the teaching of evolution in public schools and proposed a restrictive new abortion measure. Both measures failed. Aside from those efforts, Pruitt could boast few legislative accomplishments. Accomplishment on behalf of the people of Oklahoma was not what he was after.

In 2007, Pruitt left the State Senate for the RedHawks, a minor league baseball team in Oklahoma City, of which he had purchased a share four years before. When he decided to run for the attorney general's office three years after that, he did so with a new strategy. Rigidity and recalcitrance became his main selling point. Oklahoma would be as stubborn as Scott Pruitt, who, if he were elected as attorney general, would no longer have forty-seven other state senators to contend with. As the state's top law enforcement officer, he would have complete control over how to focus the energies of a staff of about 150.

Pruitt was not going to prosecute wrongdoers within Oklahoma, but rather those he saw as threatening the state's sovereignty. This was in keeping with the rise of the Tea Party movement, which saw in President Obama the first signs of incipient socialism. Pruitt's job, accordingly, was to be less law enforcement than constitutional defense. "As attorney general," Pruitt pledged in a 2010 campaign advertisement, "day one, I would file a lawsuit against President Obama to stop the application of healthcare in the state of Oklahoma," a reference to the Affordable Care Act. In a refrain similar to the one he would strike some seven years later, he vowed to institute an "office of federalism," whose staff lawyers would "wake up each day, and go to bed each night, thinking about the ways they can push back against Washington."

For that election, he took a $5,000 contribution from Koch Industries, whose owners, the brothers Koch, were busy funding candidates and causes that would resist Obama's vision of a more expansive federal government. Other contributors included Bank of America, Chevron, and the National Rifle Association, but it was the Koch contribution that provided the clearest evidence of a marriage between

Pruitt's longstanding conservative convictions and a reinvigorated national movement of anti-government activism couched in the language of individual liberty, free markets and states' rights.

"It was a perfect timing of his personal philosophy matching up with what the people of Oklahoma wanted," explained former Pruitt campaign adviser Tyler Laughlin many years later.

One of Pruitt's first steps as attorney general was to file suit against Kathleen Sebelius, the Health and Human Services chief, in an attempt to stop the federal government from giving tax credits for health insurance. He also shuttered his office's Environmental Protection Unit and, as promised, opened a new branch of the attorney general's office, the Federalism Unit, whose mission was to fend off the federal government as if it were a criminal gang creeping across the borders of Oklahoma.

Since 2005, the Oklahoma attorney general's office had been working on a lawsuit against Arkansas-based poultry producers who, he alleged, had polluted the Illinois River. Pruitt had taken $40,000 from poultry executives during his run for that office. Pruitt halted the lawsuit. In this, and other actions Pruitt took, it was impossible to tell where his own convictions ended and the concerns of donors began. Like the very craftiest politicians, he made the two indistinguishable.

Pruitt also began to shift his attention away from the Affordable Care Act to the EPA, which he sued fourteen times during his nearly two terms in office, often in concert with other attorneys general—but also with the participation of energy companies that had been among his most loyal supporters. In some instances, the *New York Times* found, Pruitt simply cut-and-pasted language sent him by energy companies into correspondences with the EPA.

In 2012, Pruitt was elected the head of the Republican Attorneys General Association, or RAGA, which coordinated anti-Obama legal actions on a variety of fronts. RAGA's creed was best summarized by Texas attorney general Greg Abbott, who filed forty-four suits against the Obama administration before becoming that state's governor: "I go into the office, I sue the federal government and I go home." RAGA, to which Abbott belonged with twenty-six other attorneys general around the nation, received $353,250 from Koch Industries during the 2016 election cycle.

In early 2013, Pruitt convened a Summit on Federalism and the Future of Fossil Fuels, held in Oklahoma City. The sponsoring institution was the Law and Economics Center at the George Mason University School of Law, which had deep ties to the Koch network. Among the speakers were William F. Whitsitt, a vice president at Devon Energy who had drafted the language Pruitt later sent to the EPA, and Harold G. Hamm, an Oklahoma-based energy executive who was crucial to Pruitt's political rise (and who later became a close adviser of President Trump). There were also lawyers who worked for firms involved in Pruitt's lawsuits against the EPA.

"These days, whenever states go to court against the Obama administration, the chances are that Pruitt is somehow involved," *Governing* magazine said in a 2015 profile of Pruitt.

Pruitt was not up for reelection in 2016, but his path forward seemed fairly clear. The governorship would be open in 2018, while senior Senator Inhofe, in his eighties, would likely retire in the next several years. Pruitt could do in Oklahoma City what Abbott had done in 2014 in Austin.

Then came November 8, 2016.

Nobody expected that President Trump would be a friend to the environment, given just how shamelessly—and dishonestly—he had pandered to the coal industry during his presidential campaign, all but promising to restore the halcyon days of 1920. But the president-elect loved to draw an audience with the possibility of surprise. On December 5, Trump met with Al Gore, the former vice president and environmental activist, in Trump Tower. On his way out, Gore told reporters the meeting was "a sincere search for areas of common ground."

That was a clever feint. Two days later, Pruitt walked through the same lobby. "Pruitt was a guy we had targeted for a long time," Bannon said later. The energy guys liked him; so did McGahn, a quiet but insistent adherent to conservative ideology.

Where Bannon saw an able soldier in his war on the administrative state, employees at EPA saw a smirking destroyer of everything they had been working to accomplish. "We were terrified when Scott Pruitt was nominated," an EPA employee later recalled to *New York* magazine. "He seemed to be somebody who understood the legal underpinnings of our work and the ways to legally unbind it. He's competent in the wrong ways."

That would prove an accurate assessment, but only to a point. Pruitt would not turn out to be quite as competent as he once seemed. And he was more dishonest and deranged than anyone could imagine, so that when it came time to pack up his things in July 2018, he managed to make Tom Price's grotesque abuse of government services seem like the theft of a pencil sharpener. But that was more than a year away, and the moment when Pruitt would became the butt of jokes on late-night television seemed unimaginable.

Democrats vociferously opposed Pruitt's nomination, but they were powerless to stop it; Rob Porter had done his due diligence in taking Pruitt around the Hill, making sure that nobody in the Republican conference suddenly developed an independent spirit. None would.

Pruitt greeted his new employees on February 21, 2017, at an address at EPA headquarters just down the block from the White House. "I believe that we as an agency, and we as a nation, can be both pro-energy and jobs and pro-environment," Pruitt said. "But we don't have to choose between the two." He then added a sentiment that was jarring for someone who was to lead an agency tasked with protecting the environment against humanity's encroachments: "I don't believe," Pruitt said, "we can be better as a country."

The very notion of environmentalism, with its language of re-mediation and redemption, presumed the exact opposite. Pruitt's religious faith—he was a Southern Baptist, a deacon at his suburban Tulsa church—explained this unfounded optimism regarding the effects of human activity on the natural world. A feature of Pruitt's faith was premillennialism, a conviction that the return of Jesus Christ was imminent. If that was the case, worrying about sea levels and ozone layers was pointless. In this way, Pruitt harkened back to James G. Watt, the Reagan-era interior secretary who once answered a question about the custodianship of the nation's natural resources by telling a congressional committee, "I do not know how many future generations we can count on before the Lord returns."

No federal department suffered as much under Trump as EPA. A climate scientist who came to EPA in September 2016 was thrilled to be working on the vanguard of her field. "It felt really amazing," she remembered more than two years later. Recent achievements included the Paris accords and the Clean Power Plan, on which President Hillary Clinton was expected to build. The transition documents were written with her in mind. But these had to be rewritten, and simplified, come November 9.

The transition was slow and ominous. The most trenchant impression for the climate scientist was of Myron Ebell, the global warming denier, lurking in the halls. Once, as she came off an elevator, Ebell waved at her. "It was creepy," she recalled. How did he know who she was? And if he did know, was it because she worked on climate change? Unfamiliar faces were greeted at the Pennsylvania Avenue headquarters with suspicious glances from career staffers. The strangers could have been colleagues from another part of the building, but many feared that the new administration was sending in political operatives to root out opposition to its pro-energy agenda.

There was good reason to worry about Scott Pruitt and the people he was bringing with him. The new administrator's chief of staff would be Ryan Jackson, who had been chief of staff to Senator Inhofe, who brought a snowball to the Senate floor in 2015 to show that global warming was not taking place. In time, several other Inhofe alumni would come to fill out Pruitt's team, even as Inhofe himself gradually lost faith in his fellow Oklahoman.

Oklahomans came to form a retinue around Pruitt, including several who had worked with him back home. The most prominent among these were the sisters Millan and Sydney M. Hupp, who had done political work for Pruitt and would serve as two of his closest advisers at EPA headquarters. Sarah A. Greenwalt, a lawyer who worked in the Oklahoma attorney general's office under Pruitt, joined EPA as a high-ranking adviser.

Pruitt also attracted an astonishing number of officials who migrated from lobbying groups that had business before the EPA, that business being the eradication of EPA regulations. Samantha Dravis—Pruitt's closest adviser, who earned a reputation from career staffers as a screamer—had worked for the Republican Attorneys General Association. Dr. Nancy B. Beck, named a high-ranking official in the EPA's Office of Chemical Safety and Pollution Prevention, came, like several other Pruitt hires, from the American Chemistry Council, an industry lobbying group that worked to lessen the already not-too-tight regulations on the eighty thousand chemicals used in one form or another in the United States. Sure enough, Beck set about calling into question what had been considered settled science. Under her direction, the EPA moved to lift bans on chlorpyrifos, a harmful pesticide, and perfluorooctanoic acid, or PFOA, a carcinogen.

William L. Wehrum, who headed the Office of Air and Radiation, sued the EPA thirty-one times on behest of private industry. Robert Phalen, appointed to lead an EPA science advisory board, once expressed disappointment that "modern air is a little too clean for optimum health."

Pruitt and his political appointees were sequestered on the third floor, the administrator himself in the lavish, wood-paneled office that had once been the refuge of the postmaster general. Not that most career employees got anywhere near Pruitt's inner sanctum. They knew that they did not belong on the third floor, where everyone was always pecking away on a smartphone, and where young women in high heels looked like clones of Ivanka Trump (it was hard not to notice that Pruitt, who came to Washington without his wife, surrounded himself with young and attractive women). The hallways were decorated with framed photographs of Pruitt posing with ordinary Americans, carefully curated to showcase people of different races and occupations. There were also photographs of Pruitt and Trump. These were paid for by the American taxpayer.

White House officials were annoyed when they learned of Pruitt's taste for expensive interior design. "He wanted the Palace of Versailles for his office," one of those officials would complain. But there was nothing to be done about it, because Pruitt indicated plainly that he would not take instructions unless they came from Trump himself.

There was little communication between Pruitt and career staffers. To learn what he had in mind for the EPA, they watched Fox News. The network, for its part, was eager to have Pruitt, and to treat him gently on air. Before several 2017 appearances on *Fox & Friends*—a program so popular with Trump that it amounted to a daily presidential briefing—producers allowed Pruitt to scrutinize and sign off on the script, a privilege rarely afforded to government officials outside of dictatorships.

By the late spring of 2017, Pruitt had assembled a formidable shock force of oil-and-gas lobbyists, climate-change deniers, and conservative ideologues. If the work of deconstructing the administrative state were a competition among cabinet members, Pruitt would have easily had the lead. He thought himself immensely good at the task. In public appearances, he often wore a smirk, which seemed to annoy his liberal adversaries to no end. At EPA headquarters, career staffers who had served Republicans and Democrats but had never served anyone like Trump opted for a strategy of "hunker down and survive," as senior EPA staffer Christopher Zarba put it.

The work itself was miserable, *made* so by Pruitt and his appointees. In the spring of 2017, letters poured in from around the country from children of all ages, asking Pruitt about his position on climate change, begging him to do something about this visibly worsening crisis. Career staffers were not allowed to answer letters until responses were vetted by political appointees, who were intent on not making even the slightest concession on global warming. The review could take months. Even then, the result was often an insulting, nonsensical "Thank you." It pained career staffers to lie to children. Short of resigning, there was nothing they could do.

"A lot of things had to go through headquarters that didn't have to go through headquarters before," said Loreen Targos, a shop steward with the American Federation of Government Employees who worked as a physical scientist in the EPA's regional office in Chicago. One colleague working on air pollution was constantly bullied with invocations of "cooperative federalism," a favorite Pruitt phrase that amounted to nothing more than code for the loosening of environmental regulations.

Some of the political appointees at least tried to make an effort. At briefings with career staffers, Bill Wehrum liked to call himself "the adult in the room," which everyone understood to be a dig at the increasingly unhinged Pruitt. But his adulthood only went so far. At one briefing, he took umbrage at a report on soil science. "I thought this was supposed to be a neutral report," he complained. The career staffers were stunned. Scientific findings were apolitical, even if they demanded a political response, and that Wehrum failed to grasp this point was downright chilling. His briefers were also told to stop using the collective plural "we" when discussing such reports. Wehrum found that usage passive-aggressive because it implied that EPA staffers were aligned with scientists. He wanted them aligned with Pruitt.

On June 1, 2017, the president indicated that he would withdraw the United States from the Paris climate accords, a nonbinding agreement on the reduction of carbon emissions. Pruitt sat in the audience as Trump spoke in the Rose Garden. The next day, Pruitt appeared in the White House briefing room to praise Trump for his "very courageous decision." Pruitt reminded everyone that "we have nothing to be apologetic about as a country."

It would turn out that the most revealing thing said in the briefing room that afternoon would come from Sean Spicer, not Scott Pruitt. In introducing the EPA administrator, Spicer asked reporters to be considerate of Pruitt's time, since he had "a flight to get to" that Friday afternoon.

Pruitt was, in fact, flying quite a bit, as later investigations would reveal. Almost every weekend, he flew back home, the trips subsidized by the federal government. One day of pseudo-campaigning around Oklahoma by Pruitt and his staff cost the American taxpayer $14,434. In the first six months of the Trump administration, Pruitt, who had decried the wanton spending of Washington bureaucrats, accrued a travel bill of $107,441.

Some of this perambulation involved Pruitt meeting with farmers, ranchers, and energy company representatives who wanted a repeal of the Obama-era Waters of the United States rule, which expanded on the regulations of the Clean Water Act. Willing, as always, to play the corporate handmaiden, Pruitt supported the rule's repeal, crowing about the need for "regulatory certainty," a nonsensical Orwellianism he especially liked. He even made an advertisement against the rule for the National Cattlemen's Beef Association, a lobbying group. Pruitt may not have been especially astute, but he had chutzpah to spare.

Back in Oklahoma, when he was the attorney general, Pruitt had spent extravagantly on a Tulsa outpost in the Bank of America Center skyscraper, though much cheaper options—such as keeping the Tulsa branch of the attorney general's office in the Sun Building— were readily available, according to records obtained by E&E News. Pruitt similarly made the most of Washington, too. His office at EPA headquarters was spacious and paneled in dark wood, a monument to public service. Pruitt wanted more, seeing his own importance as only a truly inconsequential man could. Even as he bemoaned the cost of government regulations, he saw no problem with spending nearly $10,000 on decorating his own office, including $2,963 for a standing desk. He spent $1,560 on pens from a high-end Washington jeweler. These, EPA spokesman Jahan Wilcox would later explain, were intended for "foreign counterparts and dignitaries."

Career staffers saw through Pruitt's pompous façade, and rumors of Pruitt's excesses began circulating among EPA employees. In one story that made the rounds, Pruitt traveled to an EPA site in a western state. He was supposed to exit his van so that an agency photographer could snap a few pictures, but then someone casually mentioned to Pruitt that there were rattlesnakes around. This news spooked Pruitt, and he stayed in the van the rest of his time on the ground. (What a striking contrast this was to Lyndon Johnson, who, when taking a CBS crew around his ranch in the Hill Country of Texas, got out of the car to urinate. This alarmed one member of the crew. "Aren't you afraid a rattlesnake might bite it?" No, the president was not afraid. "Hell, it *is* part rattlesnake," he answered.)

"We questioned his psychological health," said career staffer Zarba. There was good reason to. Laughably paranoid about being undermined by EPA officials, Pruitt had a part of his office torn out so that a steel-lined private communication booth, sitting on a floor of concrete, could be installed. Pruitt was later asked, in congressional testimony, why he needed such a booth when one was already available in EPA headquarters. He had no good answer. He also had his office swept for listening devices and outfitted with biometric locks. This madness had a considerable price tag: $43,000.

At the same time, Pruitt had no compunction about mistreating the people who worked for him. He was known to yell at both senior career employees and political appointees. "His staff was coaching me on how to be yelled at" ahead of a meeting with the administrator, Zarba remembered: "Don't make a face. Don't ask questions." He disregarded the advice. Zarba left EPA on his own terms. In retirement, he would spend his days in Annapolis, sailing. He was one of seven hundred employees who fled the EPA in Pruitt's first year, nearly a third of them scientists. If there was any true Bannonite deconstruction happening in the federal government, it was at the EPA on Pruitt's watch.

The feelings of career staffers were best represented by Michael Cox, a Seattle-area climate expert who had spent twenty-seven years at the EPA. On March 31, 2017, he sent a resignation letter to Pruitt. "I have worked under six Administrations with political appointees leading EPA from both parties," Cox wrote. "This is the first time I remember staff openly dismissing and mocking the environmental policies of an Administration and by extension you, the individual selected to implement the policies." The letter contained eight sections. "Please Step Back and Listen to EPA Career Staff," the last of them was titled.

This was not going to happen. Pruitt saw himself not as a servant, and certainly not as a bureaucrat, but as a world-historical figure who could take as he pleased because he was above the laws that constrained ordinary men. Just a week after Trump indicated his desire to withdraw the United States from the Paris accords (the withdrawal itself would take time, and Trump would sometimes hint at having second thoughts), Pruitt went to Rome, on a trip organized by Leonard A. Leo of the Federalist Society. Pruitt attended a private mass at the Vatican. He also dined at La Terrazza, the sumptuous rooftop restaurant of the Hotel Eden, with Cardinal George Pell, who stood accused of multiple acts of pedophilia in his native Australia. EPA staffers did their best to keep the meeting secret. In the end, they failed.

The combination of wanderlust and self-promotion was genuinely impressive. In December 2017, Pruitt went on a trip to Morocco, which was organized by the lobbyist Richard Smotkin. Pruitt pitched Moroccan authorities on American natural gas, an odd bit of salesmanship for the nation's top environmental regulator. He had also planned a trip to Israel in early 2018, a necessary visit for any American politician trying to make a play for the Jewish-American lobby ahead of a presidential run. But stories about Pruitt's abuse of power were starting to come out—though not at nearly the rate at which they would be landing come spring—and the preposterously vain and purposeless trip was canceled.

Within the EPA, there were small acts of resistance to Pruitt's agenda and excesses, most of which spoke to career staffers' loathing of Pruitt and also their inability to do much about it. They were powerless, and they knew it, and Pruitt knew it. Still, they tried. At the one-year anniversary of Trump's inauguration, a prankster graced EPA headquarters with a large poster that showed several photographs of Pruitt and Trump.

"A Year of Great Achievements for Coal, Gas, and Oil Billionaires," the poster said, with several bullet points below:

- Strict new "you want it, you got it" policy for corporate polluters.
- Science? Lollll no thanks.
- Super sweet luxury travel for the boss.
- Fired experts, hired sooo many fossil fuel lobbyists.
- I was expressly told not to mention "climate change" on this sign.

Just like Trump, Pruitt had abettors who encouraged his worst impulses because they figured the arrangement could benefit them.

Pruitt's grandiosity (and its attendant paranoia) was helped along by Pasquale "Nino" Perrotta, a longtime security agent at the EPA who had previously worked in law enforcement in New York City, helping to take down members of Italian organized crime. He later moved to federal security work, joining the U.S. Secret Service in 1995 and the EPA in 2004. Despite his employment in the federal government, in 2016 Perrotta decided to also provide security for David J. Pecker, the *National Enquirer* publisher who was a close ally of President Trump. This was about as kosher as a ham sandwich.

Perrotta became Pruitt's security chief after the previous EPA security official, Eric Weese, was dismissed from the position for raising questions about Pruitt's conduct. Perrotta had no such questions. He stoked Pruitt's vanity, and benefited in the process. It was the private firm he was running on the side that undertook the gratuitous "sweep" of Pruitt's office for listening devices. And it was Perrotta who suggested that Pruitt surround himself with an army of nineteen security officers. Interpreting the criticism of ordinary Americans as "threats," Perrotta urged Pruitt to fly first class, which Pruitt readily agreed to do. Perrotta also had Pruitt travel in an armored Chevy Suburban that leased for $10,200 per year and whose "armor" included bulletproof seats.

Taking on the trappings of a third-world dictator, Pruitt took his security staff along when his family visited Disneyland, and when he went to see the University of Oklahoma football team play in the Rose Bowl. He wanted his staff to look into a $100,000 per month private jet service. He wanted a bulletproof desk and high-end bulletproof vests, because he imagined himself the potential victim of an assassination attempt. He was that important, at least in his own mind.

And yes, ordinary people did hate Pruitt, but mostly because they saw him as a vainglorious fool. One of the "threats" against Pruitt used to justify his security expenses cited a *Newsweek* cover adorned with the administrator's face, only with a mustache appended. Someone pasted this doctored cover in an elevator at EPA's headquarters, evidently leading Pruitt to conclude that his life was in danger. Another threat was a tweet directed at Pruitt and Senate Majority Leader McConnell by a person in Paragould, Arkansas. Interviewed by federal agents, the suspect said that they had been "drinking while watching the Rachel Maddow show and posted the tweets as a flippant comment, not realizing at the time that they could be considered a threat."

The belief that he was under siege allowed Pruitt to justify any expense, no matter how unnecessary. In one email to other staffers, Perrotta wrote that Pruitt "encourages the use" of sirens when traveling in his SUV. What would have necessitated the deployment of emergency signals? A reservation at Le Diplomate, a favorite Pruitt restaurant in Logan Circle that could be difficult to reach from EPA headquarters during the evening rush. One of his visits to the restaurant came just hours after Trump indicated his intention to withdraw from the Paris accords. The restaurant's French cuisine had to have tasted especially rich that evening.

Lavish was the word all around for Scott Pruitt, even as he and Trump looked to cut funding for the agency. Needing a place to live, Pruitt rented a Capitol Hill condominium from Vicki Hart, a healthcare lobbyist whose husband, J. Steven Hart, worked for the corporate lobbying firm of Williams & Jensen (and who had been present at the Trump transition meeting at BakerHostetler's offices right before the election). The apartment, in a refurbished row house on a prime block, could have easily gone for $3,000 a month, but Pruitt paid only fifty dollars per night, and only on nights when he stayed there.

Even then, he proved a miserable tenant. He refused to take out the garbage. His daughter McKenna scratched the wooden floors with her luggage when she stayed with him, in violation of the lease (McKenna was a law school student at the University of Virginia; she interned over the summer of 2017 at the White House, and there were accusations that her father's influence helped her land both prestigious positions). One day, the large security force Pruitt had amassed around himself grew concerned because he wasn't responding to messages. They broke down the door of the Harts' condo, only to find Pruitt inside, apparently asleep (by the summer of 2018, unproven rumors about Pruitt's personal life had become as notorious as horseflies, giving rise to suspicions—some sinister, some silly—whenever a new report about his behavior appeared). The damage amounted to $2,640, to be paid by Pruitt's fellow Americans.

There was reason to believe the Harts did not rent to Pruitt out of pure munificence. Despite Pruitt's unconvincing assertions to the contrary, Steven Hart had business before the EPA pertaining to clients Coca-Cola and the pork purveyor Smithfield Foods. Then there was the Harts' attempt to pressure Pruitt into hiring a young man Jimmy Guiliano, who had recently graduated from the Naval Academy. "This kid who is important to us," Steven Hart said of Guiliano in one email to Pruitt's chief of staff. Despite his purported importance, Guiliano did not get a job at the EPA.

By early August 2017, Pruitt had apparently had enough of the Harts' condominium on Capitol Hill. He spent a month in Tulsa, then returned to Washington. He and his wife, Marlyn, moved to a U Street apartment, but as top EPA aide Millan Hupp later said in congressional testimony, "they were not comfortable in the area." As energy and environment reporter Miranda Green of *The Hill* noted on Twitter, U Street is "the historical African American district in DC." An EPA spokesperson told her the issue was actually a noisy Mexican restaurant.

The Pruitts subsequently moved to Eastern Market, near Capitol

Hill. They did so by enlisting Hupp's help as their real estate agent. As she later admitted, she conducted this search while ostensibly working for the EPA, meaning that the American taxpayer was subsidizing Pruitt's journey through the intricacies of the district's real estate market. Using a federal employee to conduct personal business was grossly illegal, a perfect example of the government corruption Trump had promised to eradicate.

That fall, Pruitt also dispatched Hupp to purchase a used mattress from the Trump International Hotel. The request was almost too bizarre for mockery. And though mockery did pour down on Pruitt yet again, the yearning remained unrealized: the hotel did not sell mattresses. Even great men sometimes had to settle for soiled bedding that was not the soiled bedding they had hoped for.

Much about Pruitt's strange and scandalous tenure at the EPA would not be known until the spring and summer of 2018, when every day seemed to bring news of a new scandal for Pruitt. For just about all of 2017, he had been a man on the ascent. The *Los Angeles Times* deemed him Trump's "most adept and dangerous hatchet man" in the summer of 2017, a month after the Paris withdrawal, when Pruitt's stock was as high as it would ever be. Even Pruitt's most vociferous critics were awed by his regulatory rollback. One senior official at the Environmental Defense Fund worried that he could become a mainstay of American political life—a U.S. senator, perhaps even president. Pruitt did visit Iowa that December.

In early January 2018—now just a few months before the tsunami of scandal would come crashing down on the pudgy, self-satisfied mandarin—the EPA published a list of sixty-seven environmental safeguards Pruitt had either fully rolled back or was in the process of undoing. These included the 2015 Waters of the United States rule and the Clean Power Plan, which established nationwide carbon emissions standards for power plants. Here was the regulatory equivalent of the German blitzkrieg across Poland: so extensive, and effective, that no front was safe. An Obama administration rule had curbed power plant emissions of mercury and arsenic, among the most destructive elements to human health. Despite scientific consensus about how harmful those emissions were, Pruitt ordered the rule under "review," thus indicating his intention to weaken it.

Pruitt could do little about the nation's environmental laws, but he had great say in how and when those laws were applied, if they were going to be applied at all. Using the complexity (and obscurity) of the federal rule-making process, Pruitt proposed to either overturn or arrest the implementation of Obama-era rules with remarkable efficiency. In April 2017, for example, he wrote a letter to energy executives announcing an administrative stay on a rule regarding air pollution by energy producers. He made other such decisions regarding rules about toxic wastewater effluents from energy plants, as well as a program designed to address chemical accidents and air quality standards for ground-level ozone, or smog.

Betsy Southerland, who spent thirty years as a scientist at the EPA but chose to retire shortly after Pruitt's arrival, was confident the courts would ultimately prevent Pruitt from entirely undoing Obama's legacy, just as the courts had almost entirely halted Pruitt's assault on Obama's regulations from Oklahoma. However, she also figured that given all the forthcoming legal challenges, plus the motions and countermotions they would involve, the nation would not return to the environmental regulatory structure that was in place when Obama left office until 2028.

Even with all the enemies Pruitt was making on the left, the man who eventually brought Pruitt down was not a rogue environmentalist or a creature of the Deep State lodged within the EPA. It was, instead, a young Trump political appointee named Kevin Chmielewski, a clean-cut Republican who became the unlikely hero of the environmental movement.

The nation first heard Chmielewski's name in April 2016, when then candidate Trump held a rally at Stephen Decatur High School in Berlin, a small coastal town in Maryland. In the midst of the speech, Trump wondered, "Where the hell is Kevin? Get him out here," Trump commanded. Chmielewski promptly took the stage.

Chmielewski was not one of those functionaries who had always lusted for a proximity to power. He was a lackadaisical student in his youth. "I was one of those knucklehead kids growing up who got straight C's and D's," he would remember in an interview with the *Dispatch*, a local newspaper. "I was on welfare, I never went to college and I should have been one of those kids that ends up in jail or doing dishes somewhere." He took up surfing, and after high school, went into the Coast Guard. In 2003, however, he got a taste of politics when he was given the chance to do advance work—the work done in advance of a dignitary's arrival at a given location—for Vice President Dick Cheney.

Coming into Washington often led to delusions of grandeur, but there was no sense that Chmielewski succumbed to that temptation. "I attribute my success to the people in our school system and our community who raised me," he told the *Dispatch* after his appearance on stage with Trump. Even in the midst of a presidential season marked by daily shows of grandiosity and indecency (and by no means only from Trump), Chmielewski maintained his plain, dignified composure. Later, pro-Pruitt propagandists in the conservative press would labor mightily to call his dignity into question. They would find laughably little success.

In February 2018, Vice President Mike Pence went to Asia, and Chmielewski went with him. When he returned stateside, he was told he no longer had a job at the EPA. The dismissal was not made public until April, when the *New York Times* reported that Chmielewski was one of five high-ranking EPA officials pushed out of the agency for trying to restrain Pruitt in his imitation of a mogul's lifestyle.

They included Eric Weese, the security official who spoke out against Pruitt's use of car sirens and lights, only to have Nino Perrotta gladly take his place.

Of the five, Chmielewski was the only political appointee, a Trump loyalist, who could not be dismissed as a disgruntled career staffer. Pruitt failed to understand this, to grasp that he was making an enemy who was determined to seek out revenge.

That would not prove especially difficult, given the intensifying focus on Pruitt. Chmielewski went to House Democrats, finding a receptive audience in Representative Cummings, the ranking member of the House Oversight Committee. A week after the *Times* published its report on Chmielewski's dismissal, Cummings and other Democrats sent a letter to Pruitt. It was clear that Chmielewski told them about everything: the insane security measures, the use of Millan Hupp as a taxpayer-funded real estate agent, improper raises to favored deputies. He even told the legislators that Pruitt demanded his flights be booked with Delta so that he could earn points from his airline of choice.

Finally, the letter said that Chmielewski and others were either fired or otherwise marginalized for trying to check Pruitt's deepening megalomania. In Chmielewski's case, there was a threatening call with Perrotta, who said he "didn't give a fuck" about who may have been listening in.

Pruitt was clearly afraid of Chmielewski, dispatching his press secretary, Wilcox, to place damaging news items in conservative publications like the *Washington Free Beacon* and the *Daily Caller*. Chmielewski's agenda was not anti-Trump, it was pro-decency. Some Trump loyalists did scoff at the favorable media depictions of Chmielewski, pointing to what they saw as self-aggrandizing behavior. There were rumors that he was staying with Corey Lewandowski, the former Trump campaign manager who was running a consultancy out of a bright and roomy Capitol Hill house. Nobody ever explained what the Chmielewski-Lewandowski connection meant, how deep it was, why it was relevant in this city of complexly inter-twined connections. The point was to damage Chmielewski, to blunt his claims through insinuation.

This campaign did not work. The media in Washington may have been a little too adept at turning a hangnail into a scandal, yet in the case of Pruitt, the alarm was commensurate with the administrator's behavior. And the alarm only got louder as some of Pruitt's top aides turned against him, resigning their EPA positions while also offering damning testimony about what those positions had entailed. Dravis testified before a House committee in late June about how Pruitt had her embark on the wildly unethical enterprise of helping his wife find a job with the Republican Attorneys General Association. That effort was not to be confused with Sydney Hupp's overtures to Chick-fil-A, the fast-food chain in which Marlyn Pruitt sought to become a franchisee.

The mattress story—which came from Millan Hupp's testimony—broke on June 4 and marked the final, depraved stage of Pruitt's brief but florid career as a federal employee. Now the stories came as relentlessly as a summer shower over Washington: He ordered his subordinates to drive him around Washington so he could find an overpriced Ritz-Carlton moisturizer he was fond of. Like a cut-rate potentate, he commanded underlings to fetch him protein bars. By the end of it all, there were sixteen separate investigations into Pruitt's transgressions, though that number did not do full justice to the hubris of a small, compact man who imagined himself bound for great things.

"Every fucking day this guy had a new story," a senior White House official later said. There was something impressively insistent about the corruption, as if Scott Pruitt genuinely thought himself invincible.

Some speculated that Pruitt was finally forced to resign after a report that he had openly lobbied before Trump for U.S. Attorney

General Jeff Sessions to be fired, so that he could take his job. "He was a little too aggressive," Bannon thought. He made the president uncomfortable with his clumsy displays of ambition, his desperate hanging around the White House mess hall, like a teenager yearning to sit at the cool kids' table.

Maybe it was just that Trump realized that Pruitt was a bargain-basement lackey, and that there were innumerable other lackeys who could do the job he did without generating a year's worth of headlines on a weekly basis. Laura Ingraham, the influential Fox News prime time host, had first called for Pruitt to be fired in June. She did it again on July 3, in a brutally compact message: "Pruitt is the swamp. Drain it." Two days later, Scott Pruitt joined the ranks of the unemployed.

Pruitt followed in the footsteps of Tom Price, leaving the EPA on an obsequious and self-righteous note, with a resignation letter that praised Trump's "courage, steadfastness and resolute commitment to get results for the American people." The tone indicated that Pruitt was already planning on a political comeback in his native Oklahoma. An endorsement from Trump would help, so Pruitt laid it on thick as lard. "I believe you are serving as President today because of God's providence," the letter continued. "I believe that same providence brought me into your service."

The victim ploy worked, to an extent. "The swamp came after him," Bannon later said, calling Pruitt "by far the most effective" cabinet member. "That's the reason he's gone," Bannon added. "If you're effective, they're going to come after you." It was comforting to think so, but was it true? Had the likes of Laura Ingraham really joined the Resistance?

Fearsome as he seemed during his tenure, Pruitt left with a legacy that was not likely to survive for long. That had been the case with his time as Oklahoma's attorney general. Not one of Pruitt's fourteen challenges to the EPA proved successful in fully getting rid of an EPA rule. Federal courts tossed six of the challenges, while seven others remained in litigation. His one partial victory, on a procedural matter, continued to be the subject of a legal dispute.

Even before Pruitt resigned, the courts were eroding his accomplishments as an anti-environmental crusader. Faced with a lawsuit by fifteen states, Pruitt dropped his objection to a smog rule issued by the Obama administration. And the D.C. Circuit court ruled that he could not stay the rule on air pollution from oil and gas production. After he left the EPA, the agency—facing a near-certain defeat in court—reinstated the glider rule he had undermined.

Pruitt's successor, Andrew Wheeler, was a former coal lobbyist whose policy aims were identical to Pruitt's. At least he showed less inclination to waste taxpayer funds. Wheeler had a few scandals of his own, including a fondness for racist social media posts, but these were relatively minor, given the enormity of Pruitt's corruption.

Zarba, the career EPA staffer, offered a droplet of praise: "He is not as stupid as Pruitt." That was promising. It was also dangerous. There was no telling what intelligence combined with maliciousness might do to the EPA.

Chapter 12

......

THE COWBOY

In early May 2018, as Scott Pruitt was on his way to becoming President Trump's most scandal-prone cabinet official, an EPA staffer named Michael Abboud reached out to reporters about a potential story. Abboud worked in the agency's communications staff, but his outreach had nothing to do with celebrating the latest EPA achievement. Instead, he wanted to talk about Ryan Zinke.

As the interior secretary, Zinke oversaw all federal lands. That included 58 national parks and 566 wildlife refuges, as well as 250 million acres of open space across the West under the control of the Bureau of Land Management, which also oversaw 700 million subsurface acres rich with minerals. This gave Zinke the power to regulate everything from entry fees at iconic parks like Yellowstone and Yosemite (which he wanted to raise) to drilling and mining claims on public lands (these, Zinke was happy to hand out practically for pennies).

Pitching stories about the heads of other agencies did not fall into the typical job responsibilities of an EPA press aide. And the stories Abboud allegedly offered, according to reporting by the *Atlantic*, would reflect poorly on Zinke, thus diverting some of the attention that had relentlessly focused on Pruitt. The EPA administrator was quickly becoming everyone's favorite government official, for all the wrong reasons. Days before, he had testified in front of two separate House committees on Capitol Hill. This had gone poorly, with Pruitt sounding evasive and dishonest, blaming career officials at the EPA for mistakes that were clearly his own. Abboud must have figured that if he could get reporters to chase after Zinke, Pruitt might be able to catch his breath.

The idea was not entirely harebrained. Zinke was nearly as expert as Pruitt at inviting investigations into his behavior. In February 2018, *New York Times* columnist Gail Collins had enjoined readers to pick Trump's "worst" cabinet member. Pruitt won, but Zinke came in second.

Pruitt's resignation in early July thrilled Trump's foes. They couldn't take down the president himself, but they could pick off his cabinet members. True, those cabinet members would simply be replaced by other conservative functionaries, and probably more competent ones at that, but those replacements would take time and political energy, especially if Senate confirmation were required. There was also the pleasure of watching Trump rage at his cabinet members, not because they did wrong but because they embarrassed him, called into question his ability to judge people and manage them. Taking out Pruitt did little to change the administration's environmental policy, but it did inflict a psychic wound on the White House.

The opposition was gleeful, and it wanted more. And nowhere was a better target than the Department of the Interior, which Ryan Zinke had turned into a combination of fiefdom and frat house. Downstairs, in the cafeteria, he installed the arcade game Big Buck Hunter, a gesture meant to "highlight #sportsmen contributions 2 conservation," as he explained in a tweet. Upstairs, in his sumptuous office, Zinke met with energy executives and energy lobbyists who were now interior political appointees. There, they worked out plans to turn public lands over to private industry.

"Dumb as a brick." That was how a former top White House official described Ryan Zinke in early December 2018, just weeks before Zinke's career as the secretary of the interior came to an end. This verdict was rendered lovingly, laughingly. He loved Zinke, a military man who looked the part of a military man. He was, like the very best of Trump's people, straight out of central casting. Only the casting call was for a comedy of errors.

"An absolute yahoo," is how former interior climate expert Joel Clement remembered Zinke. "All hat and no cattle." But as was the case at the EPA and so many other federal agencies, incompetence may well have been the purpose, if the deeper purpose was to make Americans cynical about government, to have their worst fears about government confirmed. In that case, Ryan Zinke proved a fine exemplar of Trump-era public service.

Ryan Zinke certainly had swagger, unlike the sclerotic Wilbur Ross or the irritating, unlikable Pruitt. "A huge piece of manpower Trump would love," Bannon called him. He knew Zinke from his time running Breitbart News and wanted to give him something related to the military or national security, like the VA. Only that was not to be, so he was handed Interior.

No member of Trump's cabinet tried harder to play the part of the Washington outsider. He was the boot-clad iconoclast who disdained political convention, the Montana cowboy chafing at Beltway rules. On his first day at work, March 2, 2017, Zinke rode a horse to the Department of Interior headquarters in downtown Washington, D.C., arriving like a conquering king, accompanied by a U.S. Park Police escort, also on horseback. He was attired in cowboy hat and jeans, a rodeo windbreaker instead of a suit jacket. At Interior's headquarters awaited a legion of uniformed officers, who received their new boss to the sounds of an honor song beaten out on a drum by a Bureau of Indian Affairs employee who also happened to be a member of the Northern Cheyenne tribe, based in Zinke's native Montana.

This entrance might have given the impression that Zinke was new to politics, that he was arriving in Washington in the only way he knew how. That was not the case. Prior to joining the Trump cabinet, Zinke had served for two years in the U.S. House of Representatives, Montana's sole delegate in the chamber. Before that, he'd spent four years in the Montana Senate. In 2012, he ran for lieutenant governor. A basic truth of politics held that no one ever ran for lieutenant governor, or lieutenant anything, unless he or she had much higher aspirations in mind. Zinke lost that race, but not the ambition that fueled it.

Zinke was not the front-runner to become interior secretary. The job was supposed to go to Cathy McMorris Rodgers, a U.S. representative from Washington State who was the sole Republican woman in a leadership position in Congress. Hunting enthusiasts were not happy with reports that McMorris Rodgers was about to be given the job, because she favored the sale of federal lands, which could potentially close them off to sportsmen. The hunters had an ally in Donald Trump Jr., the president's oldest son, who was fond of posting on social media photographs of himself with game he'd killed. Junior spoke on the phone and met with Zinke in early December. The two liked each other, and Zinke got the job.

Historically, secretary of the interior was a fraught position, because the department covered so much literal and jurisdictional ground. It included the Bureau of Indian Affairs, but also the National Park Service, and the U.S. Geological Survey, as well as the Fish and Wildlife Service. Its Office of Insular Affairs administered island territories including Samoa and Guam, while the Bureau of Reclamation was in charge of irrigation policies. Even Interior's own history cited the nickname that had long hounded this cobbled-together agency: the Department of Everything Else.

Because the department was in control of so many natural resources, its chiefs were frequently susceptible to corruption. The possibilities were near endless. The cabinet chief who presided over Interior's vast headquarters, which took up an entire block of downtown Washington, administered an astonishing array of wealth that ostensibly belonged to the American public. Energy companies had business before the interior secretary. So did hunters and fishermen, as well as loggers and conservationists, not to mention gaming companies wanting access to Native American territories. There were near-infinite opportunities for corruption. These were opportunities not a few of Zinke's predecessors happily explored.

The first to seriously experiment with blatant self-enrichment was Columbus Delano, a congressman from Ohio who was picked to lead the Interior Department by President Ulysses S. Grant in 1870. Unhappy that the Union Pacific Railroad had difficulty receiving land grants from the federal government, Delano intervened on the railroad's behalf and pressured Grant to dismiss Amos T. Akerman, the U.S. attorney general, who had opposed Union Pacific. Akerman had been the administration's most aggressive enforcer of civil rights for African Americans, having successfully secured convictions for six hundred members of the Ku Klux Klan; after he left the Grant administration, efforts to curb the Klan were greatly diminished.

In 1875, it became clear that Delano was issuing surveying contracts in a way that benefited his son, John. Faced with a burgeoning scandal, Grant gave a Trump-like reason for why Delano should be kept on: "If Delano were now to resign, it would be retreating under fire and be accepted as an admission of the charges." The fire only grew stronger, however, and Delano left that fall.

Richard A. Ballinger became interior secretary in 1909, appointed by William Howard Taft. Presaging Zinke and Pruitt, Ballinger peddled land to coal concerns and hydroelectric companies, reversing protections only recently put in place by Theodore Roosevelt. Confronted by a reporter about what amounted to a giveaway of nearly sixteen thousand acres of pristine land in Montana, Ballinger resorted to the fake news defense: "The dope you put out is all wrong and false." He resigned in 1911.

It would have been difficult to top Albert B. Fall, one of the chief actors in the Teapot Dome scandal, which marked the most inglorious episode of the generally inglorious presidency of Warren G. Harding. Teapot Dome was a petroleum reserve in Wyoming; the scandal that would bear its name involved Fall, and other administration members, illegally lease those reserves to oil companies. In 1929, Fall became the first-ever member of a presidential cabinet to also earn the distinction of being a convicted felon, though he had actually resigned the position six years before his corruption case came to trial.

Perhaps the most notorious modern-day interior secretary before Trump came along served in the Reagan administration. Even if conservatives were initially disappointed with Reagan's cabinet, the right would always have a friend in the Wyoming-born James Gaius Watt. The *Washington Post* called him "a brisk, self-certain and acerbic westerner who pronounced almost immediately that his task was to 'undo 50 years of bad government,'" a description that could have just as easily applied to Zinke in 2017.

Democrats despised Watt. "When a new administration comes in, you expect change. But you didn't expect them to go out and pick the most controversial, bombastic person they could find and put him in," said longtime Arizona congressman and famed conservationist Morris K. Udall.

Watt described his own views in a way that would not give opponents like Udall much comfort: "We will mine more, drill more, cut more timber." He spurned conservation, making lavish giveaways to energy concerns. In 1982, a congressional subcommittee asked him for information on his management of national parks. Watt refused to honor the basic congressional duty of oversight, vowing to "resist committees sending staff to ramble through our files and interrogate and question our staff."

Watt's demise came in 1983. That September, he spoke to the U.S. Chamber of Commerce, a group he had previously worked for. He used the occasion to mock affirmative action. "We have every mixture you can have. I have a black, a woman, two Jews and a cripple. And we have talent," Watt joked. Even in the Reagan years, this caused significant outrage, and Watt was forced to resign, which he did from the California ranch of Thomas Barrack, whose son Thomas Jr. would be a close Trump confidant.

Corruption was not at issue at the time, but Watt later managed some of that, too. After he left the federal government, he became a lobbyist. In that capacity, he was "paid more than $500,000," court records said, "and was promised additional sums" to pry from Housing and Urban Development administrators "funding and benefits for private landlords and developers." Asked about that activity in 1989, he lied to a congressional committee. That resulted, six years later, in an indictment on twenty-five counts.

Democrats were not free of ethical failures. Bruce Babbitt, the former Arizona governor, was an interior secretary for Bill Clinton, so admired by the president that he was considered for a Supreme Court nomination in both 1993 and 1994. In 1995, three bands of Chippewa peoples from Hudson, Wisconsin, sought to turn a dog-racing track, the St. Croix Meadows, into a casino. The Interior Department rejected the bid, which some charged was done at the behest of a dissenting Chippewa band that gave $230,000 to the Democratic National Committee. The ensuing scandal came to be known as Wampumgate.

One reason that Republican secretaries of the interior were more prone to corruption was that they were ideologically disposed to believe that public lands should be opened to energy companies, that the plight of the desert tortoise was less significant than the business of pumping oil out of the ground. That made them natural kin to corporate interests who held the same conviction.

Cliché has long had Washington exerting a corrupting influence on otherwise honest Americans, but no secret force fields have ever been discovered at work on the banks of the Potomac River. Arrival in Washington could magnify existing flaws, but the city lacked the power to invent new ones. This has always been an inconvenient, uncomfortable truth to admit; far easier to blame Washington itself, as opposed to the politicians who populated it, for every act of corruption and greed that took place within the city's confines.

The glorious landscape of Montana was at the center of Zinke's identity. He was a fifth-generation native of the state, born and raised in Whitefish, near the Canadian border, on the edge of Glacier National Park. Originally from Germany, the Zinkes came to what would later become North Dakota in the 1880s before moving to Montana in the 1930s. Zinke was born in 1961 and lived a "relatively privileged life," as he put it in his biography, *American Commander*, thanks to his maternal grandfather's Chevrolet dealership.

Zinke spent much of his childhood outside, exploring. Then came football. Zinke played strong safety for the Whitefish High School Bulldogs, who won the state title in 1979. Having grown to six foot four in height and 210 pounds in weight, Zinke received a full scholarship to play football at the University of Oregon. (Zinke wrote in *American Commander* how, some years after his college career was through, he was having a drink in a London military club when he met an Oregon football fan who informed him that, according to the man's wife, Zinke had "the best ass in the Pac-10.")

Zinke studied geology at Oregon, "a good fit for someone with a passion for the outdoors." Although he never pursued a graduate degree in the field, Zinke would routinely refer to himself as a geologist in debates over public lands. This was a misrepresentation of his expertise, but also a clue about how Zinke saw himself, as a rugged renaissance man, a scholar of the western steppe, equally adept with book and gun.

In 1985, Zinke finished college and went through Officer Candidate School. He then made it through the grueling training that allowed him to join the elite Navy SEALs. He would stay a SEAL until 2008.

Being a SEAL defined Zinke the way being a Chicago community organizer defined Obama. "As a former Navy SEAL," Trump said in nominating Zinke to head the Interior Department, "he has incredible leadership skills and an attitude of doing whatever it takes to win." But the picture Zinke presented of himself was riddled with falsehoods.

Zinke did perform admirably during deployments in Iraq and the restive republics formerly comprising Yugoslavia. But he also made an error that was highly damaging to his prospects as a career officer, an error that presaged some of the trouble he would bring upon himself at Interior. What happened, in short, was that Zinke used the pretense of SEAL-related business to expense trips back to Montana, where he was renovating a house. The Navy found out and Zinke had to pay back $211. The amount was piddling, but the damage to his military career was immense. Cited for "lapses of judgment" in a 1999 vice admiral's "fitness report," Zinke was branded as someone who lacked the character to lead other men into combat.

Zinke did not take the rebuke to heart, and as he turned to politics, he made sure that voters saw no reason to doubt his integrity. What they were to see instead was a warrior-scholar, a patriot who harkened back to an ancient ideal of public service. It was a powerful image, one that would have been even more powerful if it were grounded in truth.

In 2012, Zinke started a political action committee, Special Operations for America, aiming to stop President Obama from winning a second term in office. One of Obama's achievements had been the successful elimination of Osama bin Laden the year before. Zinke didn't buy it. Special Operations for America put out a press release that said that "Navy SEALs, special operations personnel and veterans across America have been outraged since Barack Obama conveniently took credit for killing Osama Bin Laden for political gain."

In the winter of 2014, Zinke announced that he would run for Montana's at-large seat in the U.S. House of Representatives. This bothered Captain Larry W. Bailey, who once commanded Zinke in the Navy SEALs and was familiar with Zinke's military career. The letter Bailey wrote that spring, which was circulated privately before seeing publication in the *Montana Post* and elsewhere, began by calling Zinke a friend. After that, things got less kind. He described Zinke as dishonest and egotistical. "Ryan's ambitions will not stop here," Bailey warned of Zinke's bid for the House. "He has shown by his dissimulation of facts regarding his career that he is willing to do whatever it takes to reach the next level—in his case, the US Senate. I cannot abide that prospect, because THEN he is representing ME and every citizen of this land as a member of one of the world's most prestigious deliberative bodies."

The rebuke had no effect on Zinke. On August 21, his campaign sent a fund-raising email. The subject line: "Who killed Osama bin Laden?" The ensuing message crowed about how Zinke "spent 23 years as a Navy SEAL and served as a Team Leader on SEAL Team Six—the team responsible for the mission to get Osama bin Laden." It was true, SEAL Team Six had done the job. Only, by that time, Zinke was safely back home. He had as much to do with that mission as he did with the invasion of Normandy.

Bailey was right about Zinke's desire to climb ever higher, wrong about where that climb would take him: not the U.S. Senate, but the cabinet of President Trump.

Zinke's confirmation hearings to become interior secretary were among the less contentious to take place in that contentious winter of 2017. He admitted that climate change was real—a true feat of courage for a Trump nominee—though he qualified the assertion by suggesting that "it's not proven science." He also said he was "absolutely against transfer or sale of public land," though he was not necessarily against *leasing* land to energy concerns. This would prove a crucial difference, one that Zinke exploited like a gap in the offensive line.

Leadership would be welcome at Interior, where the transition had not been so much chaotic as nonexistent. There had mostly been "radio silence" from the Trump administration, according to Joel Clement. "Everything was mystery." There had been rumors that Trump might hand the department over to former Alaska governor Sarah Palin, she of "drill, baby, drill," fame. At least that disaster was avoided. Other disasters loomed.

Clement was the kind of federal employee one rarely read or heard about, because one rarely heard of government workers unless they were caught in an act of fraud or abuse. And so one knew little of who they were, what they did. This made it easier for those who wanted to demonize the federal workforce. A faceless enemy was always easier to attack.

After earning his bachelor's degree from the University of Virginia in 1988, Clement moved to Seattle, where he worked as a canopy biologist, trying to understand the delicate dynamics that made a forest thrive. He later shifted his focus to climate change. Clement joined Interior in 2011 to direct its Office of Policy Analysis. One of his main initiatives was to help Alaska's indigenous people cope with climate change, the effects of which they were feeling more keenly than the rest of us because they live inside or close to the Arctic Circle.

"We were all waiting with bated breath for this guy," Clement recalled wistfully. "We had this sort of misconception that Zinke was the individual who testified to the Senate." That is, a man who truly loved the West and thus understood what was necessary to save it. How wrong any such confidence would prove, and how quickly.

At the very first, little changed. "He didn't really bring people with him," Clement remembered, and many members of the beachhead team stayed on. Most influential among these was James E. Cason, who had worked for several previous Republican administrations. In 1989, his nomination to head the U.S. Forest Service was pulled after he was deemed by one Democrat a "James Watt clone." Under Zinke, Cason would run many of Interior's day-to-day operations. Another figure who helped shape Interior—and who would, in fact, come to more or less head the entire department—was David L. Bernhardt, a powerful energy and water lobbyist whose many conflicts of interest did not keep him out of the federal government. Those conflicts were so numerous, he had them printed on a card he carried on his person.

Zinke's retinue did not think to interact with senior career staffers, the ones who knew the work of the department best, neither during the transition nor in the first weeks after Zinke's imperious arrival on horseback. "They were keeping things pretty close up there on the secretary's hallway," Clement remembered. Morale fell, then fell lower.

Senior career staffers wanted to brief Zinke on their work, but he wasn't especially interested. "They were huddling" on Interior's sixth-floor executive offices, "trying to figure out how they were going to kick through the Heritage Foundation's agenda," Clement later said. That included making it easier for energy companies to access oil and gas on public lands. Remembering this, Clement chuckled. "There was nothing we were doing that they cared about."

In late May, Zinke made a raft of hires that would shape the top ranks of Interior for the next two years. Joining Interior that day was

Lori Mashburn, an alumna of the Heritage Foundation and the Trump campaign; before attaining either of those posts, she had worked for the Institute on Religion and Democracy, a hectoring far-right group whose warped vision of Christianity advocated for foreign wars and retrograde cultural values but against helping the poor. Timothy G. Williams Jr. had worked for Americans for Prosperity, the Koch brothers' political organization. Scott J. Cameron was an exceptionally well-connected Republican operative who had lobbied for energy companies. Several of the new staffers were also young veterans of the Trump campaign, their hires suggesting that Zinke knew exactly where his horses would get their water.

Just like Pruitt, Zinke saw himself destined for greatness. He commanded that every time he entered Interior's headquarters in Washington, a special "secretarial flag" be raised above the building, then lowered again when he left. Sally Jewell, who headed the department during the Obama administration, expressed the amused astonishment of many: "I had no idea there was a secretarial flag. And if I had known there was a flag the last thing I would have done was to ever fly it." The *Washington Post* report that broke the story of his flag fixation noted that Zinke had commissioned "challenge coins," commemorative medallions customarily given by members of the military to visiting dignitaries. He also moved to have three sets of doors repaired for the Pruitt-esque sum of $139,000.

Clement briefed Zinke once, sometime in the spring of 2017 (he could not remember the exact date). Of the issues traditionally covered by Interior, the only one Zinke appeared to be curious about was invasive species. As it happened, a species of invasive mussel—the zebra mussel—had been discovered in Montana. Another senior staffer who was invited to brief Zinke asked Clement to attend.

It was widely known around Interior that Zinke, like Trump, was not fond of reading briefing materials. But Clement and the other staffer found Zinke in some land far beyond unprepared. At one point, Zinke interrupted the briefing to offer that the invasive species problem could not be solved until all ravens and coyotes were killed. The staffers were stunned. They thought their boss was not just uninformed but possibly insane. He was also graceless, mocking Clement for having attended the University of Virginia, one of the best public colleges in the country.

Like so many other members of the Trump administration, Zinke encountered his most formidable enemy in his own hubris. That hubris manifested itself in the way he traveled. In March 2017, Zinke used private planes to travel to the U.S. Virgin Islands, where he attended a fund-raiser. That June, he flew to Las Vegas to give a motivational speech to the city's professional hockey team, the Golden Knights. The team was owned by William P. Foley II, a major supporter of Zinke's political career. After the talk, Zinke and his staffers flew from Las Vegas to Montana. They did so on a private jet owned by energy-industry executives. The jet was not provided to Zinke free of charge: he left the federal government with a $12,000 bill.

Zinke liked helicopters. That same summer, he spent $8,000 on a helicopter flight to reach Shepherdstown, West Virginia, in time for an emergency management exercise. He could have easily driven, but then he would have missed the Washington swearing-in of fellow Montanan Greg Gianforte, a donor to Zinke's campaigns who, in the midst of his own House race, body-slammed a reporter for daring to ask a question. Zinke also took a helicopter ride from Virginia to Washington so that he would not miss a horse-riding session with Vice President Mike Pence in Rock Creek Park. That cost $6,250, half of what the U.S. spends on education per child per year.

As wildfires burned across the West in the summer of 2017, Zinke thought it a good idea to take a helicopter ride over Nevada. The tour cost $40,000, an expense paid for out of funds reserved for fighting wildfires. The trip did not take Zinke to areas that had been damaged by the fires. Confronted with this inconvenient detail by

Newsweek, Interior tried to lie about Zinke's intentions, then all but admitted that he had wasted valuable emergency funds in search of airborne amusement.

Like his fellow department chief Steve Mnuchin, Zinke enjoyed husband-and-wife travel at taxpayers' expense. When Zinke and his wife Lola went to Turkey and Greece to celebrate their twenty-fifth wedding anniversary, an interior security detail went along, though the trip had nothing to do with the agency or its business. Unwisely, Lola Zinke documented the trip on Twitter.

Lola Zinke took several other trips with her husband—to California, Alaska—the couple deftly erasing the line between official business and pleasure travel. This did not surprise interior staffers who had seen the Zinkes together. One employee of the National Park Service remembered how Zinke came to Yosemite National Park, in California, where she worked. During the visit, Zinke addressed employees in a large warehouse with a metal roof. It was storming outside, and his audience had trouble hearing him. Someone asked him to use the microphone. Zinke bristled at the suggestion: he would simply speak louder, so confident was he in the power of his masculine timbre. A few moments later, Lola told him to speak into a microphone. The cowboy quickly complied. Minor as the incident was, it stuck with the Yosemite staffer as one of those small moments that revealed something about a person's character.

Zinke took, and he also took away. Even though his rhetoric championed the ordinary American, his actions consistently favored corporate concerns. It was the latter that were going to fund future political ambitions, which Zinke harbored just as much as Pruitt. He turned the Interior Department into a reverse philanthropy, one that gave away to oil and gas companies natural treasures that belonged to the American people.

Only, the people who worked for him kept getting in the way. While Zinke could, and did, stock the upper reaches of the department with political appointees ready to do his bidding, he could do nothing about the seventy thousand employees who were tasked with protecting the nation's natural and cultural resources. Many of these employees worked in national parks or on Native American reservations. They rescued hikers from desert parks like Joshua Tree; they oversaw gaming operations that generated hundreds of millions of dollars. The people who did this work were not concerned with whether Zinke imagined himself as Montana's future governor or a Washington energy lobbyist. They had jobs to do.

Much like Trump, Zinke understood that federal employees were his enemy, if only because his own intentions were in such flagrant contravention to what public service entailed. "I got 30 percent of the crew that's not loyal to the flag," Zinke complained in a speech to the National Petroleum Council in September 2017. He said he was tired of his agenda being stalled in a "holding pattern" by interior employees. That agenda, as he explained in the speech, came from the White House, and involved effacing regulations that stood in industry's way. "The president wants it yesterday," Zinke warned.

Those who did not share this urgency were bullied out of the department. Clement left Interior that October. Several months earlier, he had been transferred to the Office of Natural Resources Revenue, where he was to audit payments to the federal government made by energy companies. This was not only a demotion but an insult, a reminder to Clement that his side had lost the political and ideological battle over global warming. In his resignation letter, Clement charged that Zinke "unlawfully retaliated" against him "for disclosing the perilous impacts of climate change upon Alaska Native communities."

Zinke continued to present himself as a conservationist in the mold of Theodore Roosevelt, despite the fact that his actions were in screaming opposition to everything Roosevelt stood for. That was never more apparent than in Zinke's approach to two national monuments in Utah: Grand Staircase–Escalante and Bears Ears.

In 1906, Roosevelt had signed the Antiquities Act, which allowed the president to protect land as a national monument, meaning it would be free from commercial exploitation. This was an "easier" designation than a national park, the creation of which required an act of Congress. Clinton had created Grand Staircase–Escalante, an archeological wonderland, in 1996; in 2016, Obama signed Bears Ears into existence to protect land spiritually significant to the Navajo, Hopi, and other Native American tribes in that area. In all, Obama used the Antiquities Act to create twenty-nine national monuments covering 553 million acres.

What was done by presidential decree could be undone by the same. In April 2017, Trump signed Executive Order 13792, which mandated that the Department of the Interior "review" twenty-seven national monuments designated in the previous twenty years. Eager to please the president, Zinke pushed for a report that praised Trump for ordering the review. The report argued that only the president "has the authority to make protective land designations outside of the narrow scope of the Act."

Zinke's report recommended that ten national monuments be reduced in size. The recommendation ignored overwhelming evidence that much of the land lacked commercial worth and was far more valuable as a conserved natural, cultural, and archeological resource. This became plain in the summer of 2018, when interior officials accidentally sent unredacted emails to journalists and environmental groups. Those emails showed that Zinke and his top aides minimized the benefits of keeping lands public while exaggerating the benefits of making those lands private.

By the time these emails came to light, the report in question had been submitted to Trump, and he had taken the action just about everyone expected him to take. In December 2017, he became the first president since Kennedy to shrink national monuments designated by his predecessors. Only two monuments were cut, but the cuts were drastic. Grand Staircase went from 1.9 million to 1 million acres. Bears Ears suffered an even greater diminution, from 1.3 million acres to just 228,000.

Zinke could do nothing to shrink national parks, which were the purview of Congress. But he did attempt to make them less accessible. In March 2018, Zinke proposed raising fees to enter seventeen of the nation's most popular national parks. The new cost of entry would be seventy dollars, and Zinke justified it by explaining that if "you give discounted or free passes to elderly, fourth graders, veterans, disabled and you do it by the carload, there's not a whole lot of people who actually pay at our front door." Trying to squeeze an extra buck from old people and war veterans did not square with Trump's populism, feigned as that populism may have been. A year later, the Interior Department finally ruled that it would raise the entrance fee to the seventeen national parks, but by all of five dollars.

Making public land inaccessible to the public seemed to constitute the whole of Zinke's vision for the Department of Interior. During his confirmation hearing, Zinke promised not to sell off public lands. In the narrowest sense, he kept his word. In reality, the promise was fiction.

In 2017, Zinke's Bureau of Land Management offered 10.3 million acres for leasing in Alaska's National Petroleum Reserve. Comprised of nine hundred separate lots, this was the biggest offering of land for leasing ever made by the BLM. Interest in the land was comparatively nonexistent, given the extremely low price of oil and the increasing dominance of both natural gas and renewable sources like wind and solar. In the end, only seven of the nine hundred lots were leased, for a total of 79,998 acres going to industry. Alaska, which was to benefit greatly from the sale—states split revenue with the Treasury—received all of $579,678.50, a fraction of what American taxpayers paid every time Trump decided to spend the weekend at Mar-a-Lago.

Zinke was not deterred by this poor showing. In 2018, he offered 2.4 million acres for leasing. This was less than what had been offered in 2017, but these were in far more accessible states in the intermountain West. About half, or 1.1 million acres, were in Wyoming, but there were also 535,000 acres offered in Utah, 295,000 in Nevada, and 236,000 in Colorado, along with smaller parcels in New Mexico, Montana, and Arizona. Some of the parcels were near national monuments and national parks, including Petrified Forest National Park in Arizona, Canyonlands National Park in Utah, and Dinosaur National Monument in Colorado.

Many of these lands were also in sage grouse habitat. The lordly, spike-tailed bird, which lived in the high desert of the West, had had its population so drastically diminished, that President Obama considered enacting protections under the Endangered Species Act. To avoid the kinds of restrictions federal action would bring, the Interior Department struck a deal with western states in 2015. The sage grouse remained off the endangered species list, but only as long as federal agencies working with states implemented management plans, ninety-eight of them in all, to protect the bird and the wild lands it relied on.

Zinke ordered those plans reviewed in June 2017, indicating that he was preparing to offer some of the land set aside for sage grouse to energy or mineral-extraction companies. "Zinke might as well have formed a shotgun posse to kill off the sage grouse directly," a conservationist quipped darkly to the *New York Times*. Zinke had no known personal animosity toward the bird. The sage grouse simply stood in the way of greater development of open lands across the West. Like the spotted owl of the Pacific Northwest or the desert tortoise of inland Southern California, the sage grouse represented interests that had conviction but lacked money, interests that loved the land, not only what could be taken from it.

Aware that leasing land across the West could prove highly

unpopular, BLM did what it could to silence the chorus of dissatisfied voices it rightly knew to expect. A thirty-day comment period on any proposed lease was canceled, and the time to file an administrative protest for a proposed lease already in the works was reduced to a mere ten days. During the Obama administration, the total time for both comment and protest had been sixty days.

Not only that, but interior officials who worked in parks and national monuments were pressured to make land available for leasing, even when it was clear that studding that land with oil derricks and mining equipment would not only tarnish the landscape but drive away the millions of tourists, both foreign and domestic, who came to see the unspoiled West each year.

"Why in the world, for a short-term gain, would you jeopardize those places by doing something stupid?" wondered Walt Dabney, who served as a park ranger for many decades. He lived in Moab, Utah, which periodically filled with tourists from the world over. The tourists brought millions to the local economy, and they did not "boom-and-bust like the oil and gas business." Energy-related development would lead them to vacation elsewhere. Dabney was certain. A true man of the West, he was not against energy extraction. He was only against doing things quickly, unthinkingly, maliciously. People who did things quickly and unthinkingly did not last long out in the sagebrush sea.

The Zinke plan proceeded apace, even as the opposition of conservationists, sportsmen, and other opposing parties grew louder. Their voices were joined by those of western governors, local officials, and representatives of Native American tribes. But the man who styled himself a modern-day Teddy Roosevelt would not be deterred from doing what he could to dismantle Roosevelt's legacy. In September 2018, the lease of federal lands garnered $972 million, in good part because the offerings were in New Mexico's oil-rich Permian Basin. Zinke touted this as an example of "American energy dominance."

Yet as 2019 approached, Zinke looked ever more like he was about to pull a Pruitt. The number of investigations into his behavior topped a dozen, never a good sign. There was also a touch of the bizarre, as if Pruitt had not provided enough of that. In early November, Zinke summoned the U.S. Park Police because a neighbor complained about an idling car that was taking up three parking spots. This wasn't exactly on par with looking for a used mattress from the Trump Hotel—though one of Zinke's associates did attempt to resolve the situation by pretending to be Zinke himself—but it was close.

There were more serious matters at hand. In August 2018, Politico reported that Zinke entered into what looked to be a wildly illegal arrangement with the chairman of Halliburton, who intended to build a brewery on land Zinke owned in Whitefish (operating a brewery was a longstanding Zinke goal; in fact, it may have been the most worthwhile goal he had).

Around Halloween, posters began to appear in downtown Washington, including near Interior's headquarters. They showed Zinke as "Count Corruption," outfitted like a vampire. Around him flew black bats whose bellies were sacks of cash. At the bottom of the poster was a hashtag: #FireZinke.

Reporters were now frequently asking about Zinke, just as months before they'd been asking about Pruitt. This irritated Trump. He was supposed to be the news, not his cabinet secretaries. And if cabinet secretaries were going to be in the news, why could they not make news for something other than corruption? "Certainly, I would not be happy with that at all," Trump said about the allegations that Zinke had improper dealings with the Halliburton chairman. "I'll take a look," the president added ominously.

Then, in a tweet that came on a raw December morning in Washington, Trump announced that Zinke was leaving his administration. It was a near certainty that he, like Pruitt, would be replaced by someone more capable, someone who could take apart and give away the Department of Interior without indulging his cowboy fantasies.

Ryan Zinke cast himself as the victim of "vicious and politically motivated attacks." Like Pruitt, he saw himself as a martyr, felled for his bravery in the face of conniving bureaucrats and conspiring liberals. His own shortcomings had nothing to do with it.

Chapter 13

......

ATTENDANT LORDS

If someone set your house on fire, you weren't likely to notice that they also trampled your vegetable garden. In the time of Trump, the fires came hot and fast. Daily, Americans woke to wonder if the president's early morning tweets had brought the nation closer to nuclear war with North Korea or Iran. Daily they debated if a vault deep in the Kremlin contained a tape of Trump consorting with Russian prostitutes. Nightly they marveled that somehow the rivets of the republic held, despite the tweetstorms hurled against its sides, the threats of impeachment, the shouted anxieties that the end of the American project was finally at hand.

And would it survive yet another day after that? You couldn't know a thing like that, not anymore, so you went to bed queasy with dread, already expecting the next morning's tweets, the crisis that would come on a Wednesday afternoon, which in another time, under another president, might have passed without a single breaking news alert.

But if this was all a crisis for some, it was an opening for others, namely those who considered public service a means to private enrichment. There were all too many such people in the Trump administration, who saw the daily firestorms engendered by the president as a perfect opportunity to engage in sustained campaigns of unbridled corruption, to plunder the house as it burned. There were such people in every presidential administration, because avarice never had a political lean. Only, never before had such people been so emboldened. Never before had they felt so free.

Three cabinet members stood out in this respect: Steve Mnuchin (Treasury), Ben Carson (Housing and Urban Development), and Wilbur Ross (Commerce). If history is to remember them at all, it will be only for the shame they brought on the offices they held. They were the "attendant lords" the poet T. S. Eliot savaged in his most widely known work, "The Love Song of J. Alfred Prufrock," men who were, in Eliot's perfectly cutting words, "Deferential, glad to be of use," even if they were faintly aware that they were "almost ridiculous."

All three were graduates of Yale College. Yearning to surround himself with men from "central casting," which often meant men with Ivy League degrees, Trump inadvertently exploded the notion of noblesse oblige, the idea that anyone who came to Washington from one of the preserves of eastern wealth would only do so to serve the American people. Thanks to the infelicitous trio from New Haven, the correlation between an elite education and a fitness for public service may be uncoupled for generations to come.

Trump represented a curious relationship to the power elite of the twenty-first century, which was a slightly more meritocratic version of the power elite that had ruled the twentieth. He claimed to speak for ordinary men, yet for his cabinet he hired men of high birth and great wealth. The very notion of expertise seemed to repulse Trump, most likely because he was threatened by people—women, minorities—who knew more than he did, who had chosen to accumulate knowledge and wisdom while he had chosen to accumulate money and fame.

Trump best liked men such as Ross and Mnuchin, whose wealth was either inherited or aggressively taken from others. This was in keeping with Trump's interest in genetics, in so far as that science, in his understanding, selectively conferred natural superiority. A sizable bank account was the best proof such superiority could have.

Wilbur Ross came to Yale the way many used to: in his father's footsteps. Wilbur L. Ross Sr., a Yale man, was a lawyer in the New Jersey suburbs. His son, a champion rifle-shooter at his Catholic school in Manhattan, arrived at Yale in 1955. Ross showed some inclination for the literary arts, but one English course he took demanded he write a thousand words per day. He dropped the class, which Ross later liked to smugly declare "probably saved me from a life of poverty." He took a summer internship on Wall Street and decided that finance was for him.

Mnuchin was also the son of a Yale graduate. He was among the wealthiest of Trump's cabinet members and, despite the fact that he was Jewish, closely resembled a traditional member of the Anglo-Saxon establishment. His father, Robert E. Mnuchin, was raised in the wealthy New York suburb of Scarsdale. He went to Yale, then to Goldman Sachs, paving the very road that his son would tread. Steve Mnuchin arrived at Yale in 1980. He joined Skull and Bones, the secret society, and drove a Porsche. He was not liked. When Mnuchin informed a classmate that he planned to go into finance, that classmate quipped, "You put the 'douche' in 'fiduciary.'"

Carson's story was the most compelling. He was raised in Detroit by a religious mother in a middle-class household, in a tidy house on South Deacon Street (though nothing lavish, it was hardly part of the inner-city hellscape of "poverty" and "mean streets" Carson would disingenuously evoke in a 2015 campaign ad). No one in his family had gone to Yale; Carson got to New Haven because of his stellar scores on standardized tests. He spent his time there in diligent study. In interviews with Yale student publication the *New Journal* in 2017, classmates described him as serious and well-meaning, if also pompous. "I had a distinct impression of him saying things that he thought were really brilliant, that other people didn't think were very good," one of those classmates recalled. After finishing his studies at Yale in 1973, Carson entered medical school at the University of Michigan, on his way to becoming a pediatric neurosurgeon at Johns Hopkins in Baltimore.

Decades after they had all left New Haven, this trio stood together in the Oval Office for a photo of Trump and eighteen of his cabinet members on March 13, 2017. One could have regarded them as evidence that an elite class remained intact, that power still traveled along secret swales, accessible only to those who went to the right schools, which were the same schools where the men in Kennedy's administration had gone. (The two other Ivies represented in Trump's cabinet were, as of mid-2018, Dartmouth and Harvard.)

Two years later, all that could be said about Carson, Mnuchin, and Ross is that they had managed to survive. The survival was not a function of achievement, or even loyalty. It was rather that there was always someone a little more incompetent, a little greedier, who demanded Trump's attention. They survived only because men like Pruitt and Price did not.

That survival came at a price.

Once celebrated as a resplendent example of the success America makes possible, Carson had his reputation irrevocably damaged by his service to Trump. That, however, was not the president's fault. Carson would have been better off remaining a private citizen, so that journalists and adversaries would never have reason to scrutinize his fraudulent self-mythology. Instead he entered politics as a conservative critic of President Obama and his health law. He became a Fox News contributor in 2013 and announced his presidential run two years later.

It quickly became apparent that the stories Carson told about himself in his autobiography *Gifted Hands*, at public events, and on television were at least partly fiction. He claimed that he had been a young man prone to violence, only to have mastered that impulse on the road to New Haven. It was a nice story, only the people who had known Carson in Detroit said it was untrue: there had never been any violent impulses to overcome. He said he had turned down admission "on full scholarship" to West Point. This, too, had never happened, and was a bad lie to begin with, since the military academy is basically free. And he claimed to have been named the "most honest" student at Yale. How ironic that he lied about this as well.

Trump did need diversity in his cabinet. And Bannon was a fan of the graying doctor, claiming that if Trump had not entered the Republican primary, "Carson was going to be the one" for the Breitbart crowd. But he proved a strikingly poor choice for Housing and Urban Development, which he quickly turned into one of the most incompetently managed agencies in the federal government, the administrative state not deconstructed so much as scrambled into incoherence.

The beachhead team at HUD, which preceded Carson, was the first ill omen for the agency. One senior HUD official remembered that the transition officials asked "very basic questions" and seemed to have only an "elementary understanding" of federal housing policy. "It wasn't clear what they were seeking to do," said the official, who left in September 2017.

Another high-ranking HUD official, who had joined the Obama administration in 2012, reported that he had "zero" interaction with Trump's beachhead team. As far as that official knew, Carson did not meet with the man he was succeeding, Julián Castro. Among career officials, there was the widespread belief that "Carson was not all qualified to run HUD."

Carson would do nothing to allay these fears. In his first address to HUD employees on March 6, 2017, Carson compared enslaved Africans to the immigrants who came willingly to America. "There were other immigrants," Carson said, "who came here in the bottom of slave ships, worked even longer, even harder, for less. But they too had a dream that one day their sons, daughters, grandsons, grand-daughters, great-grandsons, great-granddaughters, might pursue prosperity and happiness in this land." Not only did the remark stun many of those present, it earned a rebuke from the Anne Frank Center for Mutual Respect, which was not accustomed to chiding se-nior American statesmen.

The speech hinted at Carson's unique ability to play the malevolent incompetent, one who was equal parts mean-spirited and clueless. He often had the comportment of a man who no longer cared to hide the more unseemly aspects of his personality. His mouth would widen into the watery smile of an uncle sliding into senility. When those lips parted, out came a stream of sanctimony and self-regard, all of it de-livered in the somnolent drawl of someone who was not sure of what he was saying but was impelled to say it all the same.

Much as he offended his own staffers, much as he insulted the res-idents of public housing, Carson was terrified of Trump. That fear translated into institutional paralysis. "A lot of things stalled out," said the senior HUD official who left in September 2017. "They would just sit on things. They weren't empowered by the White House." During the Obama administration, that official worked on programs that would help protect public housing against the detri-mental effects of climate change. Now, her office "could not get anyone to give a crap."

It was not as if the new administration came in with a different vi-sion. There was no vision at all, which was a vision of its own. "There was just silence," the senior official said, which was "actually worse than being told 'no,' in some ways."

In the spring of 2017, Carson undertook a tour of the nation's pub-lic housing stock, the most memorable moment of which had Carson getting stuck in an elevator in a Miami housing project. That did not faze him, and some days later the secretary offered that public housing should not become "a comfortable setting that would make somebody want to say: 'I'll just stay here. They will take care of me.'"

Like many of his peers in the Trump cabinet, Carson seemed pathologically incapable of compassion. Empirical evidence was anathema as well, whether of poverty or climate change or racial injustice. In an interview that May with his adviser and enabler Armstrong Williams, the cabinet secretary responsible for providing shelter to the nation's indigent had this to say: "I think poverty to a large extent is also a state of mind. You take somebody that has the right mind-set, you can take everything from them and put them on the street, and I guarantee in a little while they'll be right back up there."

He was determined on punishing the 2 million Americans who lived in public housing, as well as the 4.7 million in subsidized Section 8 housing, for they did not conform to his narrative of personal redemption. In 2018, Carson proposed raising rent on people in subsidized housing from 30 to 35 percent of their income. As for the very poorest people, the ones living in the projects, they would see their rents triple, from $50 to $150 (he eventually scrapped that proposal).

Carson preached parsimony but did not practice it himself. To redecorate his office at HUD headquarters, Carson bought a $31,000 mahogany dining room set. A cabinet secretary was allowed $5,000 to redecorate, but as one of Carson's more forthright associates explained to a career HUD staffer, "$5,000 will not even buy a decent chair." And in true Pruitt fashion, responsibility was summarily deflected. Carson tried to blame his wife, Candy, even as email evidence showed that Carson himself authorized the exorbitant expenditure.

Carson's son Benjamin S. Carson Jr., known as B.J., presented another problem. B. J. Carson ran a private equity firm in Baltimore and remained a close adviser to his father once Carson became HUD secretary, despite the ethical issues this raised. Carson allowed B.J. to organize a "listening tour" of Baltimore, which had Carson the elder meet with business and civic leaders who were also associates of B.J. HUD staffers warned against the listening tour; Carson responded by calling his son "the largest employer in Maryland," which was not even remotely true.

People who once revered Carson were appalled. At the Archbishop Borders School in Baltimore—the city where Carson became famous as a Johns Hopkins surgeon—a portrait of the HUD secretary came down. "He was starting to become offensive," the principal explained. The Detroit school board voted to rename the Benjamin Carson High School of Science and Medicine because, as one of those board members said, Carson's name was "synonymous with having Trump's name on our school in blackface."

To his credit, Wilbur Ross never tried to be a role model to anyone. Ever since his graduation from Harvard Business School in 1961, he wanted to be rich. And by the time he entered the Trump cabinet, he had managed to satisfy that unwavering desire. Whereas Mnuchin was known as the "foreclosure king," for his role in the 2008 housing and financial crisis, Ross was called "the king of bankruptcy" for the vulpine form of capitalism he practiced, which involved buying troubled companies, restructuring them, and selling them at a great profit.

"I'm going to be the guy on trade," Ross declared upon becoming the commerce secretary, according to someone intimately involved in the presidential transition. But the best he could do was a trade deal that opened China to American beef, in exchange for China selling cooked chicken in the United States. Ross acted as if this were a monumental achievement, but nobody else saw it that way.

It did not help Ross's image that he was prone to napping during meetings. While sleeping, he drooled. When he woke, he wiped himself with whatever expensive tie he happened to be wearing that day. This was not the "killer" Trump once celebrated.

"You've got to be hard," Bannon would say in late 2018, as Ross was hanging on to his job by the thinnest of threads. "Wilbur comes back to that fucking beef deal and Trump goes nuts. He just got deals Trump doesn't like."

Ross's attempts to act as a pitchman and sell Trump's trade policies to the American public proved equally pathetic. In March 2018, as the president prepared to impose tariffs on some goods from China, Ross went on CNBC to make his case. He did so by displaying a can of soup. He explained that in a "can of Campbell's soup, there's about 2.6 cents', 2.6 pennies', worth of steel. So if that goes up by 25 percent, that's about six-tenths of one cent on the price of the can of Campbell's soup." Ross offered the soup can as proof that the brouhaha over tariffs was nonsensical. "So who in the world is going to be too bothered by six-tenths of a cent?" This was exactly the kind of bumbling media appearance to make Trump furious.

If there was a case to be made for a tough stance on trade—and there were Democrats making that case alongside Trump—Ross was the wrong person to make it. Everyone understood this, including the president. Throughout 2018, Ross saw his role on trade diminished, along with his White House influence. Mick Mulvaney, the Tea Party ideologue running the White House Office of Management and Budget, was said in the fall of 2018 to covet the title of commerce secretary (after John Kelly left, Mulvaney accepted the White House chief of staff position on an acting basis).

Much like Carson, Ross proved a victim of his own mythology. He'd claimed to be worth $3.7 billion, but Dan Alexander, a writer for *Forbes* who spent months unraveling Ross's deceptions, claimed that at least $2 billion of that worth was fictitious. And a good part of whatever wealth Ross did have was ill gotten, according to Alexander. He reported that Ross bilked his own financial partners out of as much as $120 million over the years, thus making him, in Alexander's estimation, "among the biggest grifters in American history." Once again, a cabinet member whose good work was to redound on Trump was embarrassing the president. At least Ross owned a private jet, so there were no travel-related scandals.

Even as his reputation and influence were both plummeting, Ross saw the potential to advance the Trump agenda—and curry favor with the White House—on another, lesser-known front: the census. Conducted every ten years, the count of the nation's population had been part of the Commerce Department since its creation at the turn of the twentieth century. Far more than just a nationwide headcount, the census had political implications because its findings about how populations have grown, shrunk, or shifted were used in subsequent congressional redistricting efforts, as well as in funding formulas for government programs.

Although the number of U.S. senators was fixed at two per state, states could lose or gain House seats based on population fluctuations. New York once had forty-five seats in the House, but its population had been shrinking, and after the 2020 census, it stood to lose one more seat, leaving it with only twenty-six. The census also helped determine who would hold those seats, because state legislators would use its demographic data to redraw congressional and state legislative districts. Unless a state used a bipartisan or nonpartisan redistricting commission, the party in power could—and likely would—gerrymander those district lines to squeeze out the maximum number of congressional representatives.

Ross seized on the census as a pet project. In March 2018, he announced that the 2020 census would ask respondents if they were citizens of the United States. Article 1, Section 2 of the U.S. Constitution called for an "enumeration," but made no mention of citizenship. The census had once asked about citizenship, but stopped having all Americans answer the question in 1950. A few Americans did see the citizenship question in subsequent iterations of the census, but only if they were among those selected to answer a longer list of questions, known as the long form. The long form was replaced in 2005 by the American Community Survey, which continues to ask the citizenship question.

The White House said that the citizenship question would help the federal government "better comply with the Voting Rights Act." But this was a cynical, flimsy excuse: the Voting Rights Act was passed to protect disenfranchised African Americans in the segregated South. Noncitizens were unable to vote in the first place, so questions of Voting Rights Act compliance would be entirely immaterial.

Asking the citizenship question would likely scare off immigrants, however, and that may have been the whole point. Immigrants, legal and otherwise, were already frightened by Trump's nativist rhetoric. Now, they might simply ignore the census altogether because of the new citizenship question. That would lead to a lower response rate than otherwise expected. Given where immigrants tended to live—big cities, for example—an undercount caused by the citizenship question would almost certainly lead to lower population results in Democratic areas. That would lead to blue states likely losing seats in Congress, and also to losing federal social program funding tied to population counts. Perhaps most important, state legislators could redraw—gerrymander—district lines in a way that favored their party. The party that would benefit both locally and nationally from an undercount would almost certainly be the GOP.

Ross was hot for the citizenship question from the moment he was sworn in, so that only four months into his time in the new administration, he was already getting impatient: "I am mystified," he wrote in May 2017, "why nothing has been done in response to my months old request that we include the citizenship question. Why not?" Ross worked on the citizenship question with Steve Bannon and Kris Kobach, the anti-immigration advocate who was then the Kansas secretary of state. He also consulted with John Gore, the voter suppression specialist who had been installed in the Civil Rights Division of the Department of Justice.

Nobody at the Census Bureau was fooled by what Ross was doing and why. His citizenship question ploy dismayed career employees who feared that they had become the tools of the Republican Party. "We are a data agency, a factual agency," said Johnny Zuagar, who headed the Census Bureau's chapter of the American Federation of Government Employees. People came into his office and told him bluntly, "I don't want to participate in this." For the first time, they were working for a department chief who was not merely incompetent but malicious.

"You have to talk people off the ledge a little bit," Zuagar said.

The Census Bureau had no permanent leadership after its head, John H. Thompson, left in May 2017. Many people worked from home. "They're not in the building like they used to be," Zuagar said. As across so much of the federal bureaucracy, there was silence at the Census Bureau.

A number of organizations—including one tied to Obama attorney general Eric H. Holder Jr.—filed suit over the citizenship question in 2018. Congress started asking questions. In the face of these questions, Ross showed the courage of a field mouse. He tried to blame Gore, but emails were made public clearly showing that he, not anyone else, was pushing for the citizenship question. In January 2019, federal judge Jesse M. Furman of New York issued a ruling that shredded every reason Ross had proffered. Furman wrote that Ross "failed to consider several important aspects of the problem; alternately ignored, cherry-picked, or badly misconstrued the evidence in the record before him; acted irrationally both in light of that evidence and his own stated decisional criteria; and failed to justify significant departures from past policies and practices." More than a mere loss, it was a humiliation.

This served to make Ross even more irrelevant to the Trump

administration than he had already become, though he had become mightily irrelevant in the preceding months. When the president went to the G20 in Buenos Aires in late November 2018, Ross was not with him. He was instead dispatched to Vandenberg Air Force Base, where he learned about the military's space programs. It was as clear a sign as could be that Wilbur Ross's short, unremarkable career as a public servant was coming to an end.

To his credit, Steve Mnuchin was not nearly as pernicious as Ross or Carson. He had few allies in the White House, but also few genuine enemies. "Just an errand boy for Steve Schwarzman," Bannon called him, referring to Stephen A. Schwarzman, a politically influential Manhattan billionaire who briefly served as a Trump economic adviser. Mnuchin was nobody's first choice, but since nobody's first choice was intent on joining the Trump administration, and Mnuchin had been a loyal (if not exactly effective) fund-raiser throughout the campaign, the job fell to him. "I thought Wall Street would go through fucking conniptions because he's not a heavyweight," Bannon acknowledged, "but he had been a good soldier." A good soldier, Mnuchin would remain, even if he would never be more than that.

He "played things well," one West Winger put it, content with remaining inconsequential. He appeared to enjoy his own irrelevance, for he was not forced to cede any of the trappings that came with power, even as he relinquished what power he had. It mattered little. A summer 2018 cover story on Mnuchin in *Bloomberg Businessweek* showed him in an unflattering profile, in front of a background composed of a mantra repeated eight times in large white print: "Everything Is Fine." And everything was fine, relatively speaking. In his rare public appearances, Mnuchin retained his wide, feline smile.

He was only marginally involved in the tax-cut effort that consumed much of the end of 2017 for the Trump administration, after the failed attempts to repeal and replace the Affordable Care Act.

That effort was led by Gary Cohn, the former Goldman Sachs chief executive, as well as allies outside the White House. Mnuchin had no connections to Congress, nor much of an ability to relate to ordinary people, to explain to them how cutting taxes for corporations and the wealthy could help those who were not titans of industry or born into wealth.

To explain the plan, Mnuchin had Treasury produce a single-page document. An expert with the right-leaning Tax Foundation dismissed it as a "thought experiment," while an official with the Committee for a Responsible Federal Budget called the analysis a "mockery." And those were among the more kind reviews of Mnuchin's plan.

The economy, though, was not Mnuchin's primary concern. He decided that he would act as Trump's public crisis manager, somehow imagining that he was the one to soothe Americans' inflamed feelings about the president. More likely, he just wanted to impress Trump with displays of loyalty. These led Lawrence H. Summers, the former Harvard president and economics professor—who regularly embarrassed Mnuchin by criticizing his expertise in public—to muse that "Steven Mnuchin may be the greatest sycophant in Cabinet history." There was good reason to believe that Summers was correct. For even if there was an especially high number of bootlickers in the Trump administration, no one licked boots quite like Steve Mnuchin.

In August 2017, many Americans were horrified by the shows of racism and anti-Semitism on display in Charlottesville, Virginia, during a white supremacist rally that left three dead. Their horror was compounded by Trump's assertion that among the frothing hate-mongers who descended on Charlottesville were "some very fine people." Mnuchin was not among the dismayed. When his Yale classmates asked him to resign in protest over the sanctioned ugliness in Charlottesville, Mnuchin lectured them haughtily: "As someone who is Jewish, I believe I understand the long history of violence and hatred against the Jews (and other minorities) and circumstances that give rise to these sentiments and actions," he wrote.

The following month, Trump tweeted angrily about the kneeling protests in the National Football League. Some thought the president was trying to exacerbate racial divisions. Mnuchin rushed to his defense, while criticizing the protesting athletes. "They can do free speech on their own time," he said.

That same September, Hurricane Maria devastated Puerto Rico, a crisis made worse by a slow federal response. Most everyone took issue with Trump's response, which vacillated from uninterested to annoyed. Mnuchin was right there to defend him. On television, the treasury secretary praised the federal government's response as "terrific," although much of the island lacked potable water and electricity, with the storm having come and gone many days before.

Mnuchin also defended Trump himself, who had gone on Twitter to attack Carmen Yulín Cruz, the mayor of Puerto Rico's capital city, San Juan. She had pleaded on CNN for more federal assistance and disputed Trump's optimistic description of the relief efforts. Trump responded exactly as one might predict: via Twitter. "Such poor leadership ability by the Mayor of San Juan, and others in Puerto Rico, who are not able to get their workers to help," the leader of the free world said in a two-part tweet sent from his golf club in New Jersey. "They want everything to be done for them when it should be a community effort." Several other tweets followed before some adult wrested the phone away and ushered the president back out onto the links.

Some were alarmed by Trump's approach to North Korea (the productive summit with Kim Jong-un in Singapore was at the time many months away). Mnuchin was not. "This is not about personalities; this is not personal," he said of Trump's taunts of the North Korean leader, whom he had taken to calling "Rocket Man."

Mnuchin grasped that his boss demanded public praise, that he needed it the way a whale needed plankton. That allowed him to survive even as other cabinet members succumbed to their own worst impulses. As 2018 came to its end, Mnuchin, Ross, and Carson remained in the administration, too, but that was only because Trump had simply forgotten about them. And that was no great over-sight, since they had done so little worth remembering.

Chapter 14

······

ADVANCING GOD'S KINGDOM

A week after his victory over Clinton, Trump met at Trump Tower with Eva Moskowitz, whose Success Academy charter school network achieved impressive results with children of color across New York City. The following weekend, he entertained Michelle A. Rhee, the former head of Washington, D.C.'s public schools, at his golf club in New Jersey. Despite her uneven results, Rhee had remained popular with those who thought incompetent teachers and the unions that protected them were holding back America's children.

The meetings suggested that Trump was serious about fixing American public education. If he could do that, and patch up the nation's highways, he might make a decent president after all. So, at least, some hoped.

Trump did not choose Moskowitz, or Rhee, or any of their accomplished peers in the school reform movement, to lead the Education Department, a federal agency with oversight over all of the nation's educational institutions, from dual-language preschools to vocational programs in aeronautics. He settled instead on Betsy DeVos, a virtual unknown to anyone working on education at any level outside of her native Michigan, where DeVos was known but not necessarily liked.

The choice mystified all those who had figured Trump was looking for a capable, forward-looking technocrat focused on student testing and teacher accountability. The choice horrified teachers unions, who knew DeVos only as a billionaire Republican who had labored to weaken the public schools in Michigan. Her nomination was, however, in keeping with Trump's apparent conviction that nothing fueled government work better than antipathy to the workings of government.

What nearly every holder of the office since the first education secretary—Shirley M. Hufstedler, appointed by Jimmy Carter to the new post in 1979—had in common was direct experience in teaching or educational administration (two were governors who'd enacted large reform measures). DeVos, by contrast, was a professional activist, one who had maintained a rigid set of simplistic views on schools and society for many years. It was a set of views shaped almost entirely by family and place, influenced little by her own experiences in adulthood. The most frightening thing about Betsy DeVos was not who she was, but what she had failed to become: a person whose views were enriched by observable reality.

Grand Rapids, Michigan, largely defined the life of the woman born in 1958 as Elisabeth Dee Prince. She grew up in nearby Holland, on the shores of Lake Michigan, where her father, Edgar D. Prince, ran an auto parts empire that he would eventually sell for $1.35 billion. The family belonged to the Reformed Church in America, which had its roots in a type of Protestantism known as Calvinism, the predominant faith of the Dutch who settled western Michigan.

Some fled their hometowns to attend college; Betsy Prince traveled just thirty miles to Grand Rapids, where in 1975 she enrolled in Calvin College, from which her mother, Elsa, had graduated. Any attempt to understand what DeVos would do as the nation's education secretary had to begin here, at this college of four thousand that bid its students to act as "Christ's agents of renewal in the world." The college was affiliated with the Christian Reformed Church and took its religious mission seriously. As of 2019, professors were still required to be "members in good standing of a congregation in the Christian Reformed Church," and to affirm their faith in the Belgic Confession, the Heidelberg Catechism, and the Canons of Dort, foundational aspects of the Reformed faith from the the sixteenth and seventeenth centuries.

The school was named after John Calvin, the sixteenth-century French thinker from whom Calvinism got its name. A branch of Protestantism that took root in Northern Europe, Calvinism hewed to its founder's doctrine of predestination, which held that God predestined all sinners to hell, and while he chose to save some as an act of grace, that salvation could not be earned. No amount of effort was sufficient to rescue the damned from damnation. It was also among the more intellectual of the various Protestant movements.

At Calvin College, Prince studied business and served on the student senate; she volunteered on Gerald Ford's losing presidential bid in 1976 and worked for other Republican campaigns. In 1980, she married Richard "Dick" DeVos Jr., a native of Grand Rapids and a student at nearby Northwood University. He stood to become the heir to the Amway fortune, the massive marketing company co-founded by his father that critics charged was a pyramid scheme. His family, like hers, was conservative, pious, and extremely rich.

The DeVoses had four children, whom they raised in Ada, a wealthy suburb of Grand Rapids. The town had superb public schools, but the DeVos children did not attend them. Two daughters were at least partly homeschooled, a fact that was happily noted after DeVos's nomination by homeschooling advocates, many of whom were religious conservatives elated to finally have a booster in Washington. Both sons attended the Grand Rapids Christian High School, which sported a DeVos Center for Arts and Worship.

DeVos rarely spoke to the press once she came to Washington, but there was a time when she was not so shy about expressing her convictions. In 2013, she told *Philanthropy* magazine that her desire to improve education began with a visit to the Potter's House Christian school in Grand Rapids, a private religious academy. "At the time, we had children who were school-age themselves. Well, that touched home," she said. "Dick and I became increasingly committed to helping other parents—parents from low-income families in particular. If we could choose the right school for our kids, it only seemed fair that they could do the same for theirs."

School choice sounded like an innocuous policy that sometimes was genuinely concerned with giving children better options. But it could also indicate a desire to weaken public education, which to some conservatives was teaching the wrong values and to other critics—not all of them from the right—was not teaching anything at all. In 2001, DeVos told a Christian group that her work on school choice was intended "to confront the culture in which we all live today in ways that will continue to help advance God's Kingdom, but not to stay in our own faith territory."

In 1990, Dick DeVos won election to Michigan's school board. Three years later, the couple led a successful push for legislation that would welcome charter schools to Michigan (the first charter school in the nation had opened in 1992 in St. Paul, Minnesota). But while charter schools multiplied, they did not prosper. As early as 1997, the state auditor found the state has shown "limited effectiveness and efficiency in monitoring" charters. Two years later, the Michigan Department of Education worried there was "no defined system of quality control in regard to charter schools," despite there being 138 institutions that enrolled 30,000 students across the state.

The DeVoses persisted in advocating for more choice, disregarding calls for oversight. In 2000, they pushed Michigan to adopt a voucher system, which proposed to give students about $3,300 to attend a private school of their choice, including a religious one. She began to establish groups like the Great Lakes Education Project, or GLEP, founded in 2001. The group's goal was "supporting qual- ity choices in public education for all Michigan students," in part by shaming public education. For example, one ad campaign, called Got Literacy?, featured misspelled school signs: "Welcome Back, Hope You Had a Good Break"; "15 Best Things about Our Pubic Schools." The campaign didn't mention that the first sign was from Arizona, and a student joke besides, while the second was made for an Indiana school district by an ad agency.

In 2011, GLEP and its conservative allies won a major victory when the Michigan legislature erased the charter school cap, creating what was close to an unrestrained market for charter school oper- ators. DeVos scored another victory in the summer of 2016, when she and her husband spent $1.45 million to stymie a legislative effort to provide more oversight to Michigan's charter schools. Choice, for DeVos, had come to mean something close to anarchy, with govern- ment's role not just diminished but actually eliminated.

The most effective argument against Betsy DeVos could be made with a single word: Detroit, where charter schools proliferated as a result of efforts by DeVos and other conservatives. On the National Assessment of Educational Progress, last administered in 2017, only 5 percent of Detroit children in the fourth grade were proficient in reading. The same percentage—5 percent—of eighth-graders were proficient in math. No big city in the United States performed worse on the exam.

Not all the worries about DeVos had to do with education. Fears also stemmed from association—and insinuation. Some were con- cerned about her stance on gay rights. Her parents helped start the far-right Family Research Council and were committed supporters of other conservative activist groups, like Focus on the Family (DeVos herself had shown some support for gay rights). Betsy's brother, Erik Prince, was the founder of private security firm Blackwater.

DeVos was confirmed by the narrowest margin of any Trump nominee, 50 to 51, requiring the tie-breaking vote of Vice President Mike Pence, who presided over the Senate. Given the brouhaha over her "potential grizzlies" response to Senator Chris Murphy's question about guns in schools, not to mention her general lack of knowledge about public education, it was somewhat astonishing that she was confirmed at all.

Just three days after her eye-of-the-needle confirmation, DeVos decided to pay a visit to the Jefferson Middle School Academy in the traditionally black and impoverished southwest quadrant of Washington, D.C. She was met by protesters, who booed the new secretary and attempted to block her entrance. "Betsy DeVos: Does Not Play with Others—Should Be Held Back," one of the placards they foisted said. Many educators, including liberal ones, condemned the protests as a show of incivility, but the point was made, however crudely.

Jeers were not likely to stop DeVos. Even as she became a bête noire for the left, she appointed an ever-growing number of deputies who shared her ideologically retrograde vision of education. More than any other cabinet member, DeVos demonstrated how perfectly bumbling but ultimately destructive the Trump administration could be.

Most of all, they wanted to undo what Obama had done. The right had taken issue with a number of Obama directives on education: his prosecution of for-profit colleges, his protections for transgender students, his insistence that colleges take students' allegations of sexual assault more seriously. As with so many other aspects of public policy, Republicans depicted Obama as moving too quickly, too far to the left for a country they insisted remained to the right of center.

Trump was so attractive because he promised to undo all that with chainsaw and sledgehammer. During the presidential campaign, he even promised to drastically diminish the Department of Education altogether. Most observers dismissed this as an unserious idea by an unserious candidate, an idea that did not need to be discussed because the man who came up with that idea was never going to be president. But in the summer of 2018, Trump proposed a plan to merge the departments of Education and Labor, curtailing the reach of both (that plan's prospects remained unclear as of early 2019).

DeVos did not have a tendency to graft the way Scott Pruitt and Ryan Zinke did. Nor did she treat herself to crass displays of self-importance. She didn't turn the department into a Blackwater headquarters, either. Instead, she went quietly about her work.

DeVos selected deputies—at unmistakable direction from conservative think tanks and the for-profit education industry—who showed open disdain for the Education Department and everything that it had most recently stood for. Some were culture warriors and some were profiteers. Few showed interest in using education as a means of helping the neglected communities that elected Trump, communities where education had atrophied beyond recognition.

Carlos G. Muñiz had worked in the office of Florida attorney general Pam Bondi, an unapologetic partisan who saw her office as little more than a stage for her coming-out as a Republican star. In 2013, New York State sued Trump's real estate seminar business, Trump University, for fraudulent practices, charging that students promised trade secrets were given low-quality instruction. Bondi could have joined the suit, but declined to do so. Right around that time, Trump's foundation contributed $25,000 to her reelection efforts (Bondi would steadfastly maintain the two events were utterly unrelated).

Muñiz schemed with Bondi about how to defend the decision not to join the Trump University suit. Later, he went on to represent Florida State University, which was being sued by a female student who had credibly claimed that star quarterback Jameis Winston raped her after a night of drinking in 2012. Investigation into the

Winston case revealed a culture in which football players were treated like gods, while sexual assault allegations were frequently diminished or dismissed. The case had been one of several that spurred Obama to make the issue of college sexual assault a priority for his Justice Department. It was a priority for Muñiz too, but only because of the hours he was able to bill as he and his co-counselors mounted a fantastical defense of a university corrupted by football.

In early 2016, Florida State settled with Winston's accuser for $950,000. A little more than a year later, Muñiz was made the top lawyer in the Education Department.

To head the Civil Rights Office, DeVos picked Candice E. Jackson, a smart young conservative activist. She had transferred from a Southern California community college to Stanford, where she wrote for the *Stanford Review*, the conservative publication cofounded by technology entrepreneur (and Trump supporter) Peter Thiel. Her articles included criticism of affirmative action, which Stanford and many other universities used to redress legacies of discrimination; Jackson said that the push for diversity resulted in discrimination of its own. In 2005, she published a book, *Their Lives: The Women Targeted by the Clinton Machine*, about the women who had accused Bill Clinton of sexual harassment. She also wrote Christian music.

Democrats were alarmed by Jackson's appointment. They were right to be. Several months after she joined the department, Jackson issued a directive mandating that investigations be conducted more quickly, with less energy devoted to trying to discover broader patterns of discrimination. She also told the *New York Times* that 90 percent of all sexual assault complaints on college campuses "fall into the category of 'we were both drunk.'" Jackson apologized for the preposterous assertion, but that did little to dispel suspicion about her aims.

DeVos did make a few surprising hires, including an unapologetic Democrat as a deputy assistant secretary in the Office of Elementary and Secondary Education and a former teacher of migrant workers in North Carolina to head the Office of English Language Acquisition. But she also struggled to fill the top ranks of her department, more so than any of her peers in the Trump cabinet. Nine months into the Trump administration, the Department of Education could boast "the highest vacancy rate of any Cabinet-level agency," according to education news site The 74, "with 12 of 15 positions open for which the White House has not announced a nominee or the Senate confirmed an officer." The situation did improve throughout 2018, so that by early 2019, 63 percent of the top positions in the department were filled. Still, it was a dismal place: in fact, the worst midsized federal agency at which to work, five notches below the Pruitt-ravaged EPA, according to a survey of federal employees conducted by the Partnership for Public Service late that year.

Governing by neglect was a trait DeVos shared with Trump. She said so herself, in a Republican summit in September 2017: "President Trump and I know our jobs: It's to get out of the way." There were other similarities, including an almost pathological inability to appreciate the experiences of others. Like the president, she saw lived experiences different from her own as a threat, because it might put into question what she'd always believed. So she praised historically black colleges, which arose during the era of lawful segregation, for being "real pioneers when it comes to school choice." The world had to conform to her worldview, not the other way around.

And despite her long-held Christian values, DeVos evidently regarded education as a Darwinian landscape, where the strong were to dominate the weak. Any barrier to that dominion had to be removed, so that the natural course of events could take place. School would be a place not for nurturing excellence but asserting brute superiority. Hers was an acutely heartless conservatism, made all the more so because it was applied to children and young people.

By the time the consequences of the financial and housing crises receded somewhat, many Americans realized that an even more per-ilous class of debt than subprime mortgages was threatening the nation: college loans. College was becoming more expensive, while wages remained flat, leading more families to borrow for higher ed-ucation. As a result, student debt reached $1.5 trillion by mid-2018. President Obama and his wife, Michelle, understood this problem from personal experience: between Columbia, Princeton, and Harvard Law, the Obamas owed a total of $120,000, which they did not fully pay off until 2004.

Obama instituted a loan forgiveness program, Pay As You Earn, that capped student loan payments for struggling young Americans to 10 percent of their income, and forgave those loans altogether after twenty years of diligent payment. He also greatly expanded the Public Service Loan Forgiveness Program, under which a loan could be forgiven in ten years, provided that the borrower was engaged in a socially beneficent career like teaching.

Most important, the Obama administration offered debt relief to students at for-profit colleges, who were routinely exploited by insti-tutions that promised to vault them into the middle class. A full 88 percent of students at for-profit colleges carried student loans. They owed an average of $39,950, about $7,000 more than at nonprofit private colleges and a full $14,000 more than at public universi-ties, according to the Institute for College Access and Success. After Corinthian Colleges, a group of ineffective, poorly run for-profit in-stitutions, collapsed in 2014, the Obama administration offered debt relief to its 350,000 students, an initiative that at its upper bound could end up costing $3.5 billion.

A week before the 2016 presidential election, the Obama adminis-tration published a new "borrower defense rule," which would allow students not to repay loans from what Education Secretary John B. King Jr. called "dodgy schools," a clear reference to for-profits. If stu-dents could show that a school had engaged in deceptive marketing or was responsible for poor educational outcomes—Corinthian appeared to have been guilty of both—they could have their loans forgiven.

DeVos made clear from the start that for-profit colleges finally had a friend in the federal government. The transition beachhead team included Taylor Hansen, a for-profit college lobbyist who would briefly work with DeVos's staff to weaken the Obama rules. Robert S. Eitel, who was also on the beachhead team, had been the chief counsel for Bridgepoint Education, a for-profit education company facing federal investigation. He became a top DeVos deputy.

To head the unit investigating for-profit colleges, DeVos hired Julian Schmoke Jr., who was previously a dean at DeVry University, a notorious operator in the industry that had paid a $100 million fine to the Federal Trade Commission. The move was akin to tasking Al Capone to investigate organized crime. In May 2018, the investigative unit was eliminated altogether as a result of Eitel's efforts.

DeVos raised from the dead the Accrediting Council for Independent Colleges and Schools, a body that had been eliminated by Obama after it became clear that it had sanctioned the corrupt behavior of Corinthian and other unscrupulous for-profit operators. DeVos temporarily reinstated the council despite the objections of Department of Education staff, which wrote her a 244-page report advising against the move.

She also delayed (and vowed to replace) Obama's borrower defense rule, explaining in the fall of 2017: "Under the previous rules, all one had to do was raise his or her hands to be entitled to so-called free money." But in October 2018, a judge ordered DeVos to stop stalling and implement the Obama rule. DeVos was still planning to write a rule of her own, one that would be a lot kinder to for-profit colleges and a lot less kind to the students they cheated.

DeVos also moved to eliminate the gainful employment rule, with which the Obama administration forced for-profit colleges and job-training programs to show that their students were trained to get jobs that would allow them to pay down loans. In the summer of 2018, DeVos indicated that she was going to rewrite the rule, but then fall came and there was nothing. That meant the Obama rule would stay until at least 2020.

On social matters, DeVos failed to show anything resembling compassion. Under the Obama administration, the Education Department moved to toughen the way schools dealt with sexual assault allegations; in the spring of 2011, the department issued a guidance that told schools to use a "preponderance of the evidence" standard to determine whether sexual misconduct had occurred. This was a lower standard than the "clear and convincing" bar that schools had been using until that time. The change would help accusers, who were becoming increasingly vocal about how prevalent rape had become on the American college campus. Sexual assault survivors found a champion on Capitol Hill in New York's junior senator, Kirsten E. Gillibrand, a Democrat, while the 2015 documentary film *The Hunting Ground* poignantly dramatized their plight. Pained and angry, the voices of college rape survivors were precursors to the #MeToo movement.

The Trump administration was no friend of #MeToo or its affiliated causes. In September 2017, DeVos made perhaps her most widely criticized move to date, rescinding the 2011 guidance, declaring that "the era of rule by letter is over," a suspect assertion given that the Trump administration was governing almost entirely by executive order, despite having control of both chambers of Congress. DeVos issued a directive of her own, one that counseled schools to raise the bar once more for what constituted a viable complaint: "When a school applies special procedures in sexual misconduct cases, it suggests a discriminatory purpose and should be avoided." The guidance also counseled schools to respect students' "free speech" rights, a favorite shibboleth of conservative campus activists.

So it went with the guidance Obama issued on transgender students. That guidance, from 2016, declared that "a school must not treat a transgender student differently from the way it treats other students of the same gender identity." Most coverage of the issue focused on the part of the guidance dealing with locker rooms and bathrooms: "A school may provide separate facilities on the basis of sex," the directive said, "but must allow transgender students access to such facilities consistent with their gender identity."

DeVos did away with these. Her own guidance, issued jointly with U.S. Attorney General Jeff Sessions in February 2017, said that "there must be due regard for the primary role of the States and local school districts in establishing educational policy" (in fairness to DeVos, it was Sessions who pushed for the guidance, while DeVos initially opposed the move). The appeal to states' rights was rooted in the segregated South's antipathy to integrating its school. Back then, too, the American government was accused of getting ahead of the American people.

As time went on, DeVos showed no sign of lessons learned, of compassion developed. In the spring of 2018, DeVos was asked during a House hearing by a congressman from upper Manhattan if she felt that school officials should report undocumented students to Immigration and Customs Enforcement, or ICE. There were many such students in New York and in large cities around the nation. If they feared ICE, they might stop coming to school. And if their children couldn't receive an education, why would parents stay in America?

DeVos answered that calling ICE should be "a school decision," betraying her ignorance of educational policy, as well as of legal precedent. A 1982 ruling by the Supreme Court in *Plyler v. Doe* said it was wrong to "deny a discrete group of innocent children the free public education that it offers to other children residing within its borders," which was subsequently interpreted to include immigration enforcement. The exchange was instructive only because it showed how little DeVos had learned, how much she failed to understand after two years as the nation's top education official. At a later hearing, she admitted in an exchange with Senator Murphy, he of "potential grizzlies" fame, that ICE could not enter a school.

Other than dismantling President Obama's legacy on education, how much of her own agenda had DeVos fulfilled? Not much, judging by how little progress she made on her signature issue of school choice. Trump had promised to devote $20 billion to such an initiative, just as he had promised that Mexico would pay for a border wall. It didn't help that DeVos had made few friends on Capitol Hill. Then there was the certain unruliness of a program potentially affecting all 98,300 of the country's public schools, and a check from Mexico for a border barrier started to seem more likely.

By the end of 2018, DeVos was reduced to a pathetic cheerleader for pointless causes. One had to do with allowing states to access federal grants to fund the arming of school employees. Out there, somewhere in the darkness, potential grizzlies roamed.

CONCLUSION: SOME PEOPLE

Once they wanted the best people. But now, two years into the Trump administration, they would take just about anyone. Having promised to drastically reduce the size of the federal government, perhaps by eliminating some agencies altogether, Trump discovered that even limited government needed legions of workers to carry out its functions. And so, with many federal agencies severely under-staffed, in June 2018, the White House turned to a job fair.

Announcement of the job fair, which was to be hosted by the Conservative Partnership Institute, was met with predictable glee. A functional White House shouldn't have needed a job fair, especially not this late into a presidential term. For critics of the administration, this was further proof that Trump was nothing like the capable chief executive portrayed on *The Apprentice*.

For job-seekers, however, this was an opportunity for advance-ment, perhaps a significant one given how many positions within the executive branch remained unfilled. The people who packed the Dirksen Senate Office Building on a hot Friday afternoon represent-ed the cross-section of what U.S. government service looks like: an elderly gentleman in an African-style kente-cloth hat, a young white guy in a white "Make America Great Again" baseball cap. Waiting for them behind rows of tables were mostly young employees of a num-ber of government agencies, from the Office of Presidential Personnel to the Peace Corps. They took résumés and chatted briefly with the applicants.

Given the rushed, unfiltered quality of the interactions, things could turn awkward, as when a woman at the Small Business Administration desk asked an applicant about his "background."

"You mean racial?" he wondered. The woman hastened to explain that she only wanted to know where he had worked.

Some tables offered swag, pencils from the Interior Department being perhaps the most attractive offering. At an Environmental Protection Agency desk, you could pick up a pamphlet titled *500 Days of American Greatness*, a final attempt by Pruitt (then just weeks away from dismissal) to ingratiate himself with Trump.

A woman at the White House Internship Program explained how "extraordinarily" competitive the application process was. Well, unless the EPA's Pruitt happened to be your father: earlier that day, the *New York Times* reported that Pruitt had leveraged the power of his office to seek a White House internship for his daughter McKenna.

Speaking from a podium, a staffer for Senator Mike Lee, a Utah Republican, praised the throng of job-seekers before him. "Most people in this town care only about their careers," he said. "I'm really encouraged to look around the room and see people who care about America, freedom, and"—here his voice took on a tenuous, interrogative tone, as if he wasn't entirely sure himself and needed his audience's affirmation—"making America great again?"

Next up was Sean Doocey, deputy assistant in the beleaguered Presidential Personnel Office. "We're looking to staff the president for the next six and a half years," he told the job-seekers. The prospect of a second Trump term garnered limited applause.

An hour into the three-hour event, the job fair became insufferably crowded, the Senate briefing room seemingly filled well beyond capacity. Lines grew long and melded into each other, so that an applicant to the Department of Commerce might suddenly find herself in line to join the ranks of the Treasury.

"I've only managed to get to one table so far," a young man

complained. He eyed the equally young man who stood behind the Department of Labor table, surmising that he was an intern: "Is he gonna give me a job?"

"This is a little bit of..." one attendee began, as he pushed through the increasingly thick crowd. He stopped himself. "I can't say the word."

Someone nearby offered to help: "Cluster?" There were four more letters, but there was no need to say them.

And yet things must be said about this administration, about the promises it has made but failed to keep, the people it promised to up-lift, only to forget them all over again. Much of this blame belongs to Trump, for the lackadaisical management style that kept him from evaluating cabinet members and political appointees with the dis-passionate analysis their respective jobs deserved. His refusal to take counsel, to listen to people who knew better than he did, led both his genuinely best and his most loyal—they were almost never the same—to either flee or fall.

Nikki Haley decided to leave her post at the United Nations in October; two months later, Trump announced that he would replace her with Heather Nauert, who until 2017—when she was appointed a spokesperson for the State Department—was a Fox News host. Though never destined for greatness, Attorney General Jeff Sessions engendered sympathy even from his political opponents for the months of abuse he withstood from Trump. That ended in November, when Trump finally fired him. Sessions was replaced by Matthew G. Whitaker, a thick-necked former University of Iowa tight end who once worked as an adviser for a Florida company that marketed a toilet for men who "measured" long in the pants.

Blaming Trump is always easy. Often, it is justified. But just as often, it obscures ailments of which he is the symptom, not the cause. If there is a moment when the sickness began, then it is probably October 27, 1964. On that evening, a B-movie actor who had formerly been a Democrat gave a speech to bolster Republican presidential candidate Barry Goldwater. Goldwater would lose the election to Lyndon B. Johnson, but the former actor would go on to become governor of California, before training his ambitions on the White House.

The speech Ronald Reagan delivered that day was called "A Time for Choosing," and in it outlined the principles that Trump's presidency represents, however luridly it does so. Goldwater, after all, was the godfather of the limited-government conservative, while Reagan was the most forceful—and convincing—messenger of that idea to the American public. That effort, which culminated in his eight-year presidency, began with the Goldwater speech, in which the former Hollywood unionist summoned the fear of socialism.

"Governments don't control things," Reagan lectured. "A government can't control the economy without controlling people." As evidence, he summoned the plight of the American farmer, and also alluded to "urban renewal" programs, a subtle reference to white fears and resentments of inner-city African Americans. "No government ever voluntarily reduces itself in size," Reagan warned. "Government programs, once launched, never disappear."

He would vividly echo that very same theme at his presidential inauguration in 1981: "Government is not the solution to our problem. Government is the problem." It was a problem he was all too happy to perpetuate. The national debt increased by $1.86 trillion during his eight years in office, while government spending increased by an annual average of 2.5 percent.

Nevertheless, the Reaganite philosophy of limited government is now one of the pillars of faith of the Republican Party. Nothing will shake it loose. In 2009, Louisiana governor Bobby Jindal delivered the response to President Obama's first State of the Union address. In his remarks, Jindal referenced the devastation of New Orleans by Hurricane Katrina. He told the story of an irate sheriff who was informed by "some bureaucrat" that private rescue boats had to show proof of insurance and registration.

From this, Jindal drew a lesson: "The strength of America is not found in our government." This is a popular conservative refrain, but also an ironic one, given the right's veneration for the U.S. Constitution, a document that guarantees liberty but also circumscribes liberty within a system of laws made and enforced by Washington. The conservative fantasy of limited government relies on an unrealistic conception of civil society, one that is more useful as a campaign slogan than an ideal to be devoutly wished for.

It has taken the Trump presidency for that much to become obvious. In many ways, he has been the most valuable argument liberals have had in at least a generation. By actually executing, however haltingly and crudely, on beloved conservative ideas—deregulation, limited government, judicial "originalism"—he has shown precisely how preposterous those ideas are, how much better they fare on Fox News than in the Oval Office. George W. Bush certainly understood as much, his "compassionate conservatism" a concession to conservatism's own failures.

It's not only that Trump didn't know what sort of president he wanted to be; he plainly didn't want to be president, at least not in the early, farcical days of his quixotic campaign. But then the farce became something more, to the consternation of millions, and to Trump himself. Still, even after he managed to wrest the presidency from Hillary Clinton, he had preciously few clues about what that presidency should look like. He rejected Chris Christie's transition plan, but also minimized the influence of Steve Bannon and his populist forces. The lack of a governing idea about how to govern, and where government should head, exposed Trump to competing influences from within a hopelessly fractured Republican Party that no longer knew what it stood for and no longer cared whom it stood with. Unaccustomed to managing anything larger than his relatively small marketing business, Trump succumbed to these influences, thus becoming a president held hostage by a political party to which he barely belonged.

The best people—Mnuchin, Kushner, Zinke, Pruitt, Ross drooling on himself at meetings, Carson offering bizarre homilies on people in housing projects, Price flying around the country like a Saudi prince—represent Reaganism gone metastatic. This is what selfishness elevated to a political philosophy looks like. For decades, the public was taught to fear "unelected bureaucrats," a clever phrase that subtly but unmistakably summoned the image of a black woman in a Washington office building, doing nothing as she collected a government paycheck. But the true grifters had degrees from Wharton and Yale. They lived on Capitol Hill, and they flew first class. They collected paychecks many times greater than anything the unelected bureaucrat would ever see in her lifetime.

It is difficult to feel sorry for Donald Trump, but there are moments when it is impossible not to. Here is a man who fashions himself a figure of historic importance, who openly compares himself to Roosevelt and Lincoln. And yet on a daily basis, he is undone by his own courtiers. And while the American people sent him to the White House, nobody sent Scott Pruitt to Washington in search of a used mattress. Nobody wanted to pay $31,000 for Ben Carson's office furniture.

But we did, because we were told they were the best people. And the best people must have the best things. Only we were supposed to get something in return, were we not? The best people were supposed to work for us, were they not? That was what the president promised. Some will say that, on the whole, Trump has kept the promises he made to the American people. Maybe so. But this one he has frequently and flagrantly broken.

Washington, D.C.
February 2019

ACKNOWLEDGMENTS

Many people took a significant risk in speaking to me for this book. I hope to have done their recollections and convictions justice.

I hope to have also reciprocated the confidence of those who envisioned this project and saw it through. They are truly some of the last best people in the publishing industry.

I first learned to be a journalist at the *New York Times Daily News*, then at *Newsweek* and Yahoo News. I hope that the above is a testament to the quality of that education, which not infrequently has come from men and women who may rightly be called journalistic legends.

My parents and brother have endured me far longer than anyone else. I don't quite know how, but I am grateful all the same. My in-laws have shown similar endurance, while having to countenance the fact of their daughter and granddaughter living 3,000 miles away.

Which brings me to the most important acknowledgment of all. Only one person left her native California and moved back east so I could report more thoroughly on the Trump administration; who chased after the children as I hunched over my laptop; who ate many a dinner alone because I was interviewing, reporting, editing, fact-checking. That was my wife Maia. Somehow my wife she remains, a model of fortitude and patience. Words cannot convey my gratitude to her.

For months, my six-year-old daughter would ask, "Daddy, is your book ever going to be done?" What a relief it was to finally answer the question in the affirmative. This is for you, Hannah, and for you, Ezra. May you find here, in due time, an honest chronicle of the strange land into which you were born, and the strange city called Washington where you live.

A NOTE ON SOURCES AND REPORTING METHODS

To write this book, I spoke to people who were friends of President Trump long before he'd entertained thoughts of the presidency; people who stoked those thoughts, then worked on his campaign to make those thoughts, once a seeming impossibility, a reality; people who stood and sat next to him on the evening of November 8, 2016; people who huddled with him in Trump Tower on those weird, cold November days after the impossible had transpired; people who managed his move from New York to Washington, from private citizen to public servant—and who helped prepare the federal government for his presidency. Several of the people I spoke to for this book spent significant time in the Oval Office. Some worked next door to the White House, in the Eisenhower Executive Office Building. The vast majority of these people continue to support President Trump, even as they harbor criticisms of how he managed the executive branch. Some bear resentment toward peers they saw as selfish, disloyal, or incompetent. Whatever the case, most of them asked that I not name them in this book. In return, they spoke honestly and at length about what they witnessed.

This seemed to me an entirely fair exchange. I hate to resort to anonymity because it has served, on occasion, as a refuge for the unscrupulous and the dishonest. At the same time, it is a tool that has allowed serious journalists to burrow into institutions that thrive on secrecy and silence, as well as the punishment and expulsion of those who dare speak the troubling truths they witnessed.

I also spoke to people who served in the federal government both under presidents Obama and Trump. Some witnessed the transition and left thereafter. Some left a few months into the Trump presidency. Some are still there. They were cabinet secretaries, deputy and assistant-level officials, and career staffers who'd spent decades working for the federal government. They did not want their professional or personal reputations harmed for having graciously offered me their views of the Trump administration. Again, this felt like a fair exchange.

I also relied on the excellent journalism of my peers at publications like the *New York Times*, the *Washington Post*, the *Wall Street Journal*, CNN, Yahoo News, ProPublica, Politico, the Center for Responsive Politics, and other outlets. What follows is as detailed and clear an acknowledgment of journalistic debts as I could muster. As this is not an academic book, I make no attempt at an academic bibliography. Nor did I think a jumble of URLs would prove especially enlightening. I do, however, hope to have acknowledged every journalist on whose work I relied in order to complete my own.

If a source is named in the text itself, it is not named below. If the source is very clearly part of the public record, like a presidential speech, I also did not name it. My goal here is to be transparent and hopefully illuminating, but not necessarily exhaustive. If any journalist is not fully credited for his or her work, the mistake is entirely accidental and will be corrected in subsequent editions of this book, should such editions be demanded by the reading public.

I reserve the right to correct any omission or mistake in my sourcing by purchasing the offended party a beer.

PROLOGUE: "GET THE HELL OUT OF HERE NOW"

I conducted an interview with President Trump on the afternoon of February 19, 2019, in the Oval Office. Sitting in were press secretary Sarah Huckabee Sanders and presidential adviser Kellyanne Conway.

PREFACE: THE END OF SOMETHING

This chapter was based almost exclusively on my conversations with a former high-ranking Department of Commerce official, who was able to confirm the details of Penny Pritzker's election night party from the notes they took that evening. Washington is the sort of place, I should say, where people take notes at parties. The individual was also able to provide me with a copy of the letter Pritzker wrote to her successor, Wilbur Ross.

The American Federation of Government Employees connected me with several employees of federal agencies; their accounts of life in the Trump administration are also included in this and other chapters.

INTRODUCTION: THE BEST PEOPLE

My understanding of how a presidential cabinet functions was based in good part on Mary Louise Hinsdale's 1911 *A History of the President's Cabinet.* I can't say it is a lost classic, but it has all the information one might hope for. Andrew Rudalevige, the Bowdoin professor, supplied the necessary context. As for Trump's first cabinet meeting, recordings are available online. Viewer discretion is advised.

I interviewed Joel Clement, the Department of Interior whistleblower, in the summer of 2018. His account is represented here, as well as in subsequent chapters.

Jared Kushner's tangled finances were the subject of a *Financial Times* article: "The crises engulfing Jared Kushner" (Edward Luce, 03/01/18).

For reporting on Steve Mnuchin's missing $100 million, see "Mnuchin Calls Failure to Disclose $100M in Assets an 'Oversight'" (Peter Schroeder, *The Hill*, 01/19/17). For reporting on Steve Mnuchin's career as a Hollywood producer, see "39 Movies Treasury Secretary Steve Mnuchin Executive Produced, from *Lego Batman* to *CHIPS*" (Phil Hornshaw, The Wrap, 03/24/17).

For Sonny Perdue's colorful political history, see "5 Sketchy Facts about Trump's Pick for USDA Chief" (Tom Philpott, *Mother Jones*, 01/23/17).

The estimate of a cabinet worth $4.5 million comes from *Forbes* ("Here's What Each Member of Trump's $4.5 Billion Cabinet Is Worth," Chase Peterson-Withorn, 12/22/16). Others pegged the cabinet's total worth at a lower figure.

My reporting on Reince Priebus's time as White House chief of staff comes from several West Wing sources, all of whom were consistently critical of his tenure. I asked Priebus on several occasions to offer his own recollections for this book. Those entreaties went unanswered.

The poll about Trump's best people was conducted by Monmouth University. ("Poll: Most Americans Think Trump Doesn't 'Hire the Best People,'" Caitlin Oprysko, Politico, 08/20/18).

CHAPTER 1: THE ACCIDENTAL VICTOR

I attended CPAC in 2018 and, having somehow survived, wrote about it for *Newsweek*. Some of that reporting appears here.

Clinton's six-point lead over Trump on October 18 is based on the results of a Quinnipiac poll.

John DiIulio is an unusual, brilliant, fascinating character, and I only wish I could have spoken to him for this book. Alas, he was unavailable, so I had to make do with *Bring Back the Bureaucrats*, his seminal 2014 study on federal government. DiIulio also summarized his ideas in a 2014 op-ed for the *Washington Post*, which the headline more or less gives away: "Want Better, Smaller Government? Hire Another Million Federal Bureaucrats" (08/29/14).

The history of Trump's promise to "drain the swamp" comes from reporting I did for *Newsweek*.

I interviewed presidential historian Elaine Kamarck at her wonderfully decorated Brookings office on November 20, 2018.

CHAPTER 2: "I WIPE MY ASS WITH THEIR THING"

Politico's Katie Glueck reported on the influence of the Heritage Foundation on Trump's transition, while her colleagues Andrew Restuccia and Nancy Cook expertly covered the political machinations taking place in Trump Tower throughout November.

Francis Romero of *Time* wrote about the history of presidential transitions in 2008.

I spoke to several high-ranking members of the transition who were sympathetic to Governor Christie and others who were extremely critical of him. I have done my best to delineate the tension between these views, which reflects fissures at work in the late fall and winter of 2016.

Scott Amey of the Project on Government Oversight and Max Stier of the Partnership for Public Service both spoke to me on the record in the summer of 2016.

My colleague Hunter Walker of Yahoo News related the "fucking phone" incident from election night, though it was also told to me by one high-ranking campaign official who was by Trump's side most of that night.

Philip Rucker and Karen Tumulty of the *Washington Post* reported on President-elect Trump's disdain for John Bolton's mustache: "Donald Trump Is Holding a Government Casting Call. He's Seeking 'the Look'" (12/22/16).

Christie made his comments on the presidential transition in Trenton on December 6, 2017. He called the transition "brutally unprofessional" in an ABC interview four months later. A number of high-ranking transition and campaign officials offered detailed accounts of his comportment during the campaign and after. Those accounts clashed strikingly with his own portrayal of his work. There is good reason to believe that his self-regard as Trump's transition manager was not warranted.

Bannon made his comments about Christie "not making the plane" to Charlie Rose during a *60 Minutes* interview that aired in September 2017.

For an account of Rich Bagger's meeting with lobbyists, see Isaac Arnsdorf in Politico: "K Street Huddles with Trump Transition" (11/03/16).

In response to my questions about the Christie-led transition, Bill Palatucci sent the following statement: "The transition team led by Gov. Christie was professional, comprehensive and ready on election day to advise the President-elect on all matters, including foreign and domestic policy, personnel, ethics, and government structure."

For the Obama official's critical comments on the Trump transition, see "Trump marginalizes D.C. transition staff" (Nancy Cook and Andrew Restuccia, Politico, 12/06/16).

CHAPTER 3: THE STRONGEST MEN OF THE PARTY

James Pfiffner's *White House Staff Versus the Cabinet: Centripetal and Centrifugal Forces* is among the smartest things on the American presidency that I have read. I am indebted enormously to him for his insight, and for the many excellent historical details he includes. Those details pepper this chapter.

Richard Hofstadter's *Anti-Intellectualism in American Life* included examples of how the *Saturday Evening Post* covered the New Deal.

William Safire's *Political Dictionary*, a slyly delightful history of American politics, provides the fullest account I know of the "eight millionaires and a plumber" quip about the Eisenhower administration.

David Halberstam's *The Best and the Brightest* was not just a source, but an inspiration throughout.

Marc Tracy was the *New York Times* reporter who spotted Steve Bannon reading Halberstam's book in an airport terminal ("Steve Bannon's Book Club," 02/04/17).

Shirley Anne Warshaw's *Guide to the White House Staff* includes Richard Nixon's ornery approach to domestic policy. Her *Powersharing: White House-Cabinet Relations in the Modern Presidency* related Jimmy Carter's management struggles.

Pat Buchanan's complaint about Reagan comes from historian Gil Troy, author of *Morning in America: How Ronald Reagan Invented the 1980s*.

For a good backgrounder on the Clinton-Trump similarities, see "How Trump Can Fix His Troubled White House" (David A. Graham, *Atlantic*, 03/21/17). Bill Galston's comments come from his interview with UVA's Miller Center, whose presidential oral histories are a priceless resource.

I consulted Fred I. Greenstein's *The Presidential Difference* for Dick Cheney's role in the Bush administration.

Robert Reich's quote comes from Chris Whipple's *The Gatekeepers: How the White House Chiefs of Staff Define Every Presidency*.

Most of the other chronicles of presidential cabinets come from research in the archives of the *New York Times*.

The "slutburger" quip comes from Gawker.

Recordings and transcripts of Trump cabinet nominees' hearings are easily accessed by anyone with an Internet connection. At least one of the recollections I include is from an individual who was seated at that table. Other recollections in the section come from high-ranking veterans of the Trump transition and campaign.

Coral Davenport and David E. Sanger of the *New York Times* reported on Rick Perry's confusion about what the Department of Energy did: "'Learning Curve' as Rick Perry Pursues a Job He Initially Misunderstood" (01/18/17).

Sam Levin of the *Guardian* conducted a thorough investigation into Steve Mnuchin's sordid history as a bottom-feeding banker: "Inside Trump Treasury Nominee's Past Life as 'Foreclosure King' of California" (12/02/16).

America Bridge 21st Century, the progressive opposition research firm, conducted the research on lobbyists in the Trump administration: "Trump's Corrupt White House" (06/02/17).

CHAPTER 4: FREE COMMERCIALS

I spoke at length with Walt Schaub, White House officials, and others about ethics, for a *Newsweek* cover story in the autumn of 2017: "Trump Is Leading the Most Corrupt Administration in U.S. History, One of First-Class Kleptocrats" (11/02/17). That same story included aspects of my extensive conversations with White House officials.

Christopher Hale of Catholics in Alliance for the Common Good was the young conservative commentator who criticized Trump for turning the White House into QVC on Fox News.

Shaub called Trump's United States a "laughingstock" in a July 17, 2017, story by Eric Lipton and Nicholas Fandos of the *New York Times*: "Departing Ethics Chief: U.S. Is 'Close to a Laughingstock.'"

My conversation with Norm Eisen was for the same *Newsweek* article that included Shaub's comments.

Statistics about the number of lobbyists in the new Trump administration come from research conducted by American Bridge 21st Century, a liberal Super PAC.

CHAPTER 5: ALLIGATORS AND LILY PADS

The Center for Responsive Politics has an excellent history of lobbying, as well as a database of members of Congress who have gone through the notorious revolving door. I used that database extensively. In particular, Anna Massoglia, a researcher there, proved an extremely reliable guide to the complexities of K Street.

See also Lee Drutman's essay in *The Atlantic*, "How Corporate Lobbyists Conquered American Democracy" (04/20/15). Drutman is also the author of *The Business of America is Lobbying: How Corporations Became Politicized and Politics Became More Corporate*, which was published the same year. Merriam-Webster's website contains a helpful article on the etymology of "lobbying" in the English language. It references the *Oxford English Dictionary*, which suggests that the term, as we know it today, originated in 1777.

My figures on the number of Heritage alumni in the Trump administration come directly from Heritage, whose Matthew Atwood kindly tracked down the statistics.

In 1987, Senator Robert Byrd gave a remarkable history of lobbying in a floor speech that had all the hallmarks of a Byrd soliloquy: erudition, wit, and grace.

I also relied on Kathryn Allamong Jacob's *King of the Lobby: The Life and Times of Sam Ward, Man-About-Washington in the Gilded Age* (Johns Hopkins University Press, 2010).

Michael Crowley's profile of Jack Abramoff in the *New York Times*

Magazine, "A Lobbyist in Full" (05/01/05), is an excellent introduction to the town Jack built.

Abramoff's lobbying on the behalf of Congo's president was reported on by Byron Tau of the *Wall Street Journal* ("Jack Abramoff Sought Meeting with Trump for Congo's Leader," 06/23/17).

Eric Lichtblau of the *New York Times* wrote about Obama aides' affinity for Caribou Coffee: "Across from White House, Coffee with Lobbyists" (06/24/10).

Rebecca Ballhaus of the *Wall Street Journal* reported on the granting of ethics waivers in the Trump administration: "Ethics Office to Release Two Dozen More Trump Waivers" (06/02/17).

Information on private funding of the inauguration comes from a U.S. Government Accountability Office: "Presidential Transition: Information on Ethics, Funding, and Agency Services" (09/07/17).

CHAPTER 6: "KIND OF A ROUGH START"

This chapter contains material from background interviews with senior White House officials who spent significant time in the Oval Office during the first weeks and months of the Trump administration.

On the number of federal jobs added by Reagan: "Why Reagan's Vaunted 'Starve the Beast' Plan Failed" (Robin Bravender, E&E News, 03/07/17).

On the shrinkage of the federal government under Clinton, I cite John Kamensky's summary of the efforts of the National Partnership for Reinventing Government, which he wrote in 1999.

On the growth of the federal workforce under Bush and Obama: "Federal Bureaucracy Grew 70% More Under Bush than Obama" (Chris Edwards, Foundation for Economic Education, 02/16/16).

Outgoing EPA administrator Gina McCarthy made her comments

about the transition to Politico: "Obama Officials Alarmed at Slow Pace of Agency-Level Transition" (Sarah Wheaton, 12/08/16).

A senior commerce official provided me with details of that department's more or less successful transition process. I also spoke to individuals who spent significant time at both Treasury and HUD. These were all background conversations, as was the episode from the CFPB transition included in this chapter.

Mother Jones reported on the career of Brian Klippenstein: "A Guy Who Exists Purely to Troll the Humane Society Was Just Hired by Donald Trump" (Tom Philpott, 12/13/16).

On the lack of political appointees in the new administration, see Jonathan Bernstein in *Bloomberg View*: "The Empty Trump Administration" (01/18/17).

McConnell made his "rough start" comment to *USA Today*'s Mary Troyan: "McConnell Blames Democrats for Bumps in Trump Transition" (01/18/17).

Trump told Patrick Healy of the *New York Times* about his government of "relationships" during the presidential primary: "'President Trump?' Here's How He Says It Would Look" (05/04/16).

Arden Farhi and Jacqueline Alemany of CBS News reported on the plight of Trump's beachhead teams: "Trump Loyalists Reshuffled at Key Agencies" (11/09/16).

For transition leaks, see "Transition Team's Request on Gender Equality Rattles State Dept." (Mark Landler, *New York Times*, 12/22/16) and "Trump Transition Team for Energy Department Seeks Names of Employees Involved in Climate Meetings" (Steven Mufson and Juliet Eilperin, *Washington Post*, 12/09/16).

The *Washington Post*'s "Behind the Chaos: Office That Vets Trump Appointees Plagued by Inexperience" (03/30/18) was a masterwork of investigative journalism by Robert O'Harrow Jr., and Shawn Boburg.

On length of Senate confirmation process, see Michelle Cheng,

"Trump Still Hasn't Filled Top Jobs, and He Has (Mostly) Himself to Blame" (FiveThirtyEight, 07/03/17).

I interviewed a number of West Wing staffers from that time. They were uniformly critical of the RNC crowd. The interviews were conducted on background.

Aaron Blake of the *Washington Post* reported on Representative Kelly's conspiratorial musings: "GOP Congressman Offers Strange Obama Conspiracy Theory—and Even Stranger Explanations" (03/11/17).

Politico (Alex Caton and Grace Watkins, 01/09/17) and CNN (Andrew Kaczynski, Chris Massie, Nathan McDermott, 01/12/17) reported on Monica Crowley's history of plagiarism.

Scott Higham and Lenny Bernstein of the *Washington Post* (10/16/17), as well as Bill Whitaker of *60 Minutes* (10/15/17), reported on Tom Marino allegedly profiting from the opioid crisis in his Pennsylvania district.

NRDC published a highly useful primer on Kathleen Hartnett White: "Trump's Pick to Head Council on Environmental Quality: 'Carbon Dioxide Is Harmless'" (10/12/17).

My understanding of Don McGahn's role in the White House comes from a trained lawyer who was able to closely observe him at work.

For an explanation of the Chevron deference, see "Kavanaugh and the 'Chevron Doctrine,'" by Michael McConnell, writing for the Hoover Institution's website (06/30/18).

Amanda Reilly of E&E News, a superb outlet on environmental matters, reported on Kavanaugh's speech at Notre Dame: "Would Kavanaugh Limit the Chevron Doctrine?" (06/10/18).

Ben Terris of the *Washington Post* wrote about Brett Talley's career as a horror novelist: "Meet the Ghost Hunter and Horror Novelist Who Writes Sen. Rob Portman's Speeches" (12/08/14).

CHAPTER 7: THE SHITSHOW STRATEGY

My chronicle of the federal government in the second half of the twentieth century comes, in good part, from research in the presidential archives of Johnson, Carter, Ford, Nixon, and Reagan. I also used the archives of the *New York Times* and the *Washington Post.*

For the number of regulations issued by Obama in 2016, see a *Forbes* blog post by Clyde Wayne Crew Jr., a conservative policy scholar: "Obama's Legacy: 2016 Ends with a Record-Shattering Regulatory Rulebook" (12/30/16).

Paul Conklin's account of the Johnson presidency comes from *Big Daddy from the Pedernales: Lyndon Baines Johnson* (Twayne Publishers, 1986).

James K. Galbraith's comment on Milton Friedman is from "How Milton Friedman Changed Economics, Policy and Markets" (Greg Ip and Mark Whitehouse, *Wall Street Journal,* 11/17/06).

On Gerald Ford's deregulatory policies, see Andrew Downer Crain's "Ford, Carter, and Deregulation in the 1970s" (*Journal on Telecommunications and High Technology Law*, 2007) as well as *Gerald Ford and the Challenges of the 1970s* by Yanek Mieczkowski (University of Kentucky Press, 2005).

For Jimmy Carter's unlikely legacy as a deregulator, see William L. Anderson, writing for the libertarian Mises Institute: "Rethinking Carter" (10/25/00).

For my account of how Trump used the CRA to enact regulatory rollback, I was able to talk to White House officials involved in that effort. I also used as reference Michael Grunwald's "Trump's Secret Weapon Against Obama's Legacy" (Politico, 04/10/17).

Carrie Levine reported extremely thoroughly on the Trump transition's reliance on corporate largesse in "Donald Trump's Inauguration Fueled by Tobacco, Oil and Drug Company Money" (Center for Public Integrity, 01/31/17).

For the quote from the National Mining Association representative, see "U.S. Coal Miners Applaud Republican Axing of Stream Protections" (Timothy Gardner, Reuters, 02/02/17).

Don Young's quote comes from the *Washington Post*: "Trump Administration Moves to End a Ban on Alaska Hunting Practices That Many Say Are Cruel" (Darryl Fears, 05/22/17).

The rest of this chapter relies on extensive background interviews.

CHAPTER 8: BETTER PEOPLE

This chapter relies on multiple background interviews with several former and current Trump administration officials.

CHAPTER 9: TURBULENCE

Dan Diamond and Rachana Pradhan reported on their own work in an engrossing *Politico Magazine* story, "How We Found Tom Price's Private Jets" (10/04/17). Their reporting is the basis for statistics about Price's flights cited subsequently in this chapter.

Greg Bluestein and Tamar Hallerman of the *Atlanta Journal-Constitution* profiled Price when he was nominated to head HHS: "Tom Price: The Georgia lawmaker Who Will Lead Trump's Health Policy" (12/03/16). I relied on the newspaper's archives in other portions of this chapter when discussing Price's rise in Georgia politics.

For the malevolent influence of Newt Gingrich on American politics, see Steve Kornacki's *The Red and the Blue: The 1990s and the Birth of Political Tribalism* (Ecco, 2018).

Dan Libit of Politico explained in an interview with Price why he had to shave his mustache (06/20/08).

Price's suspect stock deals were detailed by PBS: "HHS Pick Tom

Price Made 'Brazen' Stock Trades While His Committee Was Under Scrutiny" (Marisa Taylor and Christina Jewett, Kaiser Health News, 02/08/17).

Price's lack of influence on Capitol Hill was well known by mid-2017. For reference, see "Price Was Never a Player on Obamacare Repeal" (Adam Cancryn, Politico, 09/29/17).

The video of Tom Price at Bullfeathers was posted to Twitter by Yashar Ali, a writer for *New York* magazine and HuffPost.

Katie Rogers and Eric Lipton of the *New York Times* chronicled Price's newsletters in "Another Fantastic Week': Tom Price's Celebratory Travelogues" (09/29/17).

CHAPTER 10: FELLOW TRAVELERS

Some of the reporting in this chapter comes from a cover story I wrote for *Newsweek* in November 2017.

Travel-related scandals from the George H. W. Bush and Clinton administrations come from widespread newspaper accounts from that time.

The staff of former U.S. Representative Henry Waxman kindly found the letter he sent to then-OMB head Rob Portman.

My accounts of the VA under David Shulkin come from background reporting. The *Washington Post* reported on his travel-related scandal: "Veterans Affairs Chief Shulkin, Staff Misled Ethics Officials about European Trip, Report Finds" (Lisa Rein, 02/14/18).

ProPublica reported on the Mar-a-Lago influence at the VA: "The Shadow Rulers of the VA" (Isaac Arnsdorf, 08/07/18).

Steve Mnuchin's visit to Kentucky was covered by the Louisville *Courier-Journal*: "GOP Tax Reform Will Spur Wage Increases, Sen. McConnell and Treasury Secretary Mnuchin Say" (Grace Schneider, 08/21/17). The subsequent drama played out on Instagram and, later, in investigations by the Treasury Department's inspector general.

Tim Geithner's frugal travel arrangements were covered in 2009 by CNN: "Geithner Leads by Example...in Coach" (Lesa Jensen, 03/28/09).

Ryan Zinke's flight to Montana was covered by Matthew Daly of the Associated Press: "Interior Officials Approved $12K Zinke Charter Flight Without Complete Information, Watchdog Says" (04/16/18).

For reporting on Elaine Chao's investments, see "Elaine Chao, Champion of Trump's Infrastructure Plan, Chose to Keep Stock in a Building Company" (Tom Scheck, APM Reports, 09/29/17).

My reporting on how the White House handled cabinet members' travel-related scandals was conducted via background interviews with past and present members of the Trump administration, all of them sufficiently senior to have known exactly how things unraveled and who labored to put them back together again.

CHAPTER 11: THE POSSUM

I reported on Pruitt's policies and scandals for both *Newsweek* and Yahoo News, and some of that reporting has found its way into this chapter.

Accounts of the EPA transition, as well as accounts of the EPA under Pruitt, come from background reporting.

Robin Bravender's terrific profile of Pruitt in E&E News, "From 'The Possum' to EPA Boss," served as a guidepost to his background. So did reporting by the *Tulsa World*, which recognized Pruitt as a public menace long before anyone else did. In particular, I relied on reporting by Ziva Branstetter and Cary Aspinwall.

CapitolBeatOK's Patrick B. McGuigan reported on Pruitt's legal practice, as well as on his early political career.

I interviewed Tyler Laughlin, a former Pruitt aide, for *Newsweek*.

Conversations with Nancy MacLean, the Duke professor who authored *Democracy in Chains: The Deep History of the Radical Right's Stealth Plan for America*, informed my understanding of Pruitt's ties to the Koch network.

I discussed Pruitt's religious beliefs with Randall Balmer of Dartmouth and Julie Ingersoll of the University of North Florida, both of whom are experts of the first order in evangelical Christianity and its political implications.

The career of Dr. Nancy Beck was detailed in Eric Lipton's "Why Has the E.P.A. Shifted on Toxic Chemicals? An Industry Insider Helps Call the Shots" (*New York Times*, 10/21/17).

The Environmental Integrity Project detailed Pruitt's spending abuses during his first six months in office. I also drew on the work of the Environmental Defense Fund, whose policy experts and lawyers have time and again proved indispensable explainers of what Pruitt was doing, and why.

The story of LBJ's "rattlesnake" comes from David Halberstam's *The Best and the Brightest*.

Lisa Friedman, Marina Affo, and Derek Kravitz of the *New York Times* reported on EPA's brain drain: "E.P.A. Officials, Disheartened by Agency's Direction, Are Leaving in Droves" (12/22/17).

I interviewed Michael Cox for Yahoo News: "The Climate Change 'Resistance' Movement Inside the Trump Administration" (12/06/18). His resignation letter was widely shared on social media and in press reports.

Maxwell Tani of the Daily Beast broke the story of Pruitt's arrangement with Fox News: "'Fox & Friends' Fed Interview Script to Trump's EPA Chief, Emails Show" (11/27/18).

I am indebted to Eric Lipton and Lisa Friedman of the *New York Times* for their reporting on Pruitt's travel abroad, as well as his attempts to keep those travels secret.

A former EPA employee sent me an image of "A Year of Great Achievements for Coal, Gas, and Oil Billionaires," the poster mocking Pruitt that was installed—quite briefly, one imagines—at EPA headquarters.

Juliet Eilperin and Brady Dennis of the *Washington Post* reported on Nino Perrotta's career. So did Lisa Friedman and Coral Davenport of the *New York Times*.

I attended—and reported from—Pruitt's testimony before a Senate committee in the summer of 2018. Some of the reporting about his abuses comes from that hearing.

BuzzFeed reporters Zahra Hirji and Jason Leopold sued for the list of threats made against Pruitt, including the doctored *Newsweek* cover story ("Here Are the Actual Threats Made Against EPA Chief Scott Pruitt," 05/07/18).

The Associated Press reported on Pruitt's condominium lease: "EPA Chief Paid $50 a Night for DC Condo Linked to Lobbyist" (Michael Biesecker and Jonathan Lemire, 03/30/18).

For a detailed record of Pruitt's abuses—including using his influence to benefit his daughter McKenna—see "For Pruitt Aides, the Boss's Personal Life Was Part of the Job," by Eric Lipton, Steve Eder, Lisa Friedman, and Hiroko Tabuchi (*New York Times*, 06/15/18).

I reported on the extent of Pruitt's regulatory rollback for *Newsweek*.

I spoke to Betsy Sutherland, a former EPA scientist, for *Newsweek*.

My background reporting on Kevin Chmielewski's turn as a whistleblower indicated that EPA press secretary Jahan Wilcox attempted to discredit Chmielewski by planting stories in the conservative press. At the same time, it became clear that some close to Trump regarded Chmielewski with skepticism, even if they had no love for Pruitt.

The Environmental Defense Fund analyzed Pruitt's record as Oklahoma's attorney general in suing the EPA. I had included the unflattering results of that analysis in my previous reporting on Pruitt.

On Andrew Wheeler's use and abuse of social media, see "EPA Chief Andrew Wheeler Engaged with Racist, Conspiratorial Posts on Social Media" (Alexander C. Kaufman, HuffPost, 10/09/18).

CHAPTER 12: THE COWBOY

I reported on Zinke's time at the Department of the Interior for Yahoo News, and some of the sections in the chapter are based on that reporting. I also discussed Zinke's time as a department chief with several past and present members of the Trump administration.

Zinke's unusual press strategy was covered by Elaina Plott of the *Atlantic*, "A Pruitt Aide's Attack on Zinke Angers the White House" (05/03/18).

For coverage of Zinke's first day at Interior, see "The Interior Secretary, and the Horse He Rode in On" (Matthew Haag, *New York Times*, 03/02/17).

The process of Zinke's selection as Interior's chief was covered by Amy Harder, then of the *Wall Street Journal* ("Donald Trump Jr. Played a Key Role in Interior Pick," 12/15/16).

For previous instances of corruption at Interior, see Ron Chernow's *Grant*, Doris Kearns Goodwin's *The Bully Pulpit* and Laton McCartney's *The Teapot Dome Scandal: How Big Oil Bought the Harding White House and Tried to Steal the Country*. I also relied on the public record, including Senate history and, in the case of James Watt, court records, as well as the archives of the *New York Times* and *Washington Post*.

The *Washington Post* reported on Zinke's resignation letter ("Interior Secretary Zinke Resigns Amid Investigations," Juliet Eilperin, Josh Dawsey, and Darryl Fears, 12/15/18).

For Zinke's exaggerations regarding his military service, see "Interior Nominee Promotes Navy SEAL Career, While Playing Down 'Bad Judgment'" (Christopher Drew and Sean D. Naylor, *New York Times*, 01/16/17). Bailey's letter critical of Zinke appeared in the *Montana Post* and remains the most viewed article on that site.

David Bernhardt was profiled by Juliet Eilperin of the *Washington Post* ("'The Man Behind the Curtain': Interior's No. 2 Helps Drive Trump's Agenda," 11/18/18). Some of the other information on Zinke's political appointees comes from "Department of Influence," an excellent resource from the Western Values Project.

Ben Lefebvre of Politico reported on Zinke's travel to the Virgin Islands: "Interior Reimbursed for Zinke Virgin Island Fund-raiser, but Contributions Unaccounted For" (12/19/17). I also relied on a report by Interior's inspector general Mary Kendall, which detailed Zinke's various travel-related indiscretions.

Celeste Katz, with whom I worked at *Newsweek*, caught Zinke in his lies regarding the use of a firefighting helicopter over Nevada.

In addition, see David Choi's "Interior Secretary Ryan Zinke Reportedly Spent $6,250 on a Government Helicopter Ride so He Could Go Horseback Riding with Mike Pence" (Business Insider, 12/07/17).

I reported on Zinke's push to shrink Utah's two national monuments for Yahoo News. Aspects of that reporting are included here. Juliet Eilperin of the *Washington Post* reported on leaked Interior emails showing a desire to downplay the environmental effects of making those monuments smaller.

I reported on BLM's leasing strategy for Yahoo News.

For an account of the encounter outside of Zinke's house, see "Interior Secretary Ryan Zinke Called Police on His Neighbors Monday Night in a Kerfuffle Outside His Capitol Hill Home" (Juliet Eilperin, Darryl Fears, and Lisa Rein, *Washington Post*, 11/06/18).

CHAPTER 13: ATTENDANT LORDS

This chapter includes background material from interviews conducted with former high-ranking staffers at HUD and Treasury.

Rachel Calnek-Sugin, Chris Hays, and Arya Sundaram wrote about Mnuchin, Ross, and Carson at Yale in an admirably thorough article for the *New Journal*, a Yale student publication, in "Yale Men in the Cabinet" (02/16/17).

Carson's deceptions were legion, and were accordingly cited by many publications. I relied here on reporting by Kyle Cheney of Politico, who broke the story of Carson's fictional West Point scholarship, Reid J. Epstein of the *Wall Street Journal*, and CNN's Scott Glover and Mae Reston.

Alec MacGillis of ProPublica conducted an extensive, excellent review of HUD under Ben Carson: "Is Anybody Home at HUD?" (08/22/17).

Ben Carson's comments on public housing come from "Don't Make Housing for the Poor Too Cozy, Carson Warns" (Yamiche Alcindor, *New York Times*, 05/03/17).

The story of B. J. Carson and the Baltimore "listening tour" can be found in "'Using His Position for Private Gain': Ben Carson Was Warned He Might Run Afoul of Ethics Rules by Enlisting His Son," by Juliet Eilperin and Jack Gillum (*Washington Post*, 01/31/18).

In November, Cleve R. Wootson Jr., of the *Washington Post* reported on the Detroit charter school that no longer wants to be graced with Carson's name.

I spoke to several high-ranking Trump administration officials about Wilbur Ross's loss of influence.

Jonathan Swan of Axios also had colorful reporting on Ross in "The Decline and Fall of Wilbur Ross" (01/21/18).

NPR had an excellent time line of Ross and the citizenship

question: "How the 2020 Census Citizenship Question Ended Up in Court" (Hansi Lo Wang, 11/04/18).

For an explanation of why the citizenship question is so important, please see Michael Li and Eric Petry's "The Impact of *Evenwel*: How Using Voters Instead of People Would Dramatically Change Redistricting," published by the Brennan Center at the New York University School of Law (12/07/15).

For the "douche in fiduciary" comment, see "Trump's Fundraiser Eyes the Deal of a Lifetime" (Max Abelson and Zachary Mider, *Bloomberg Businessweek*, 08/31/16).

For responses to Mnuchin's tax plan rollout, see "Treasury Defends Tax Plan Cost with One-Page Analysis" (Alan Rappeport and Jim Tankersley, *New York Times*, 12/11/17).

I had previously reported on Steve Mnuchin's turn as Trump's main defender in *Newsweek*; some of that reporting can be found here. I also spoke to several administration officials, both past and current, about his role in the administration.

CHAPTER 14: ADVANCING GOD'S KINGDOM

I wrote about Betsy DeVos in a *Newsweek* feature article: "Betsy DeVos Is Coming for Your Public Schools" (01/10/17). This chapter is partly based on reporting for that endeavor.

For Bill Bennett's opinions on schooling, see Edward B. Fiske's "Reagan's Man for Education," in the *New York Times* (12/22/85).

The *Detroit Free Press* reported extensively on the backstory of Betsy DeVos. This chapter relies on that newspaper's archives.

To gain an understanding of Calvinism, I spoke to Randall Balmer of Dartmouth and Julie Ingersoll of the University of North Florida.

Philanthropy magazine interviewed DeVos for its spring 2013 issue: "Interview with Betsy DeVos, the Reformer."

Mitchell Robinson, a professor at Michigan State, highlighted GLEP's deceptive advertisements: "Hey, Great Lakes Education Project: Got Integrity?" (10/28/15).

Kate Zernike wrote of Detroit's educational morass in "How Trump's Education Nominee Bent Detroit to Her Will on Charter Schools" (*New York Times*, 12/12/16). Erin Einhorn of Chalkbeat covered Detroit's results on the NAEP exam: "Detroit Schools Ranked Worst on National Exam—Again. But Is There Hope That Things Can Improve?" (04/10/18).

Erica L. Green of the *New York Times* wrote several excellent articles on DeVos, her nominees, and her policies, including: "2 Education Dept. Picks Raise Fears on Civil Rights Enforcement" (04/04/17); "Some Hires by Betsy DeVos Are a Stark Departure From Her Reputation" (06/02/17); "Education Department Unwinds Unit Investigating Fraud at For-Profits" (05/13/18), with Danielle Ivory and Steve Eder); "Proposed Rules Would Reduce Sexual Misconduct Inquiries, Education Dept. Estimates" (09/19/18).

Annie Waldman of ProPublica wrote a detailed profile of Candice Jackson: "DeVos Pick to Head Civil Rights Office Once Said She Faced Discrimination for Being White" (04/14/17).

Jonathan Oosting of the *Detroit News* wrote about DeVos's comments at a Republican summit: "DeVos on Mackinac: 'Washington Knows Best' Is Over" (09/22/17).

Michael Stratford of Inside Higher Ed wrote about the Obamas' debt, "Obamas' Own Student Debt Topped $40,000 Each" (08/27/13).

On the career of Robert Eitel, see "Betsy DeVos's Hiring of For-Profit College Official Raises Impartiality Issues" (Patricia Cohen, *New York Times*, 03/17/17).

On the career of Julian Schmoke, see "Trump Administration Selects Former DeVry Official to Lead College Enforcement Unit" (Michael Stratford, Politico, 08/30/17).

Diana Ali, a policy analyst for the National Association of Student Personnel Administrators wrote an excellent primer on Obama's student loan rules: "What You Need to Know about Borrower Defense to Repayment" (08/09/18).

Emily Wilkins of Bloomberg Government clearly explained delays in DeVos's own rulemaking process: "Student Loan, Gainful Employment Rules Delayed, Official Says" (10/02/18).

CONCLUSION: SOME PEOPLE

I reported on the Trump job fair for Yahoo News. For the most part, I chose to simply listen to the conversations around me. This proved far more instructive than asking questions that, it became very quickly apparent, the job seekers did not want to answer.

Dan Friedman of *Mother Jones* reported on Matthew Whitaker's association with World Patent Marketing: "The Acting Attorney General Helped an Alleged Scam Company Hawk Bizarre Products" (11/14/18).

Rick Perlstein's *The Invisible Bridge: The Fall of Nixon and the Rise of Reagan* contains a superb account of how Ronald Reagan's "Time for Choosing" speech did far more for him than it did for Barry Goldwater.

See also "President Ronald Reagan's Economic Policies: How Reagan Ended the 1980s Recession" (Kimberly Amadeo, The Balance, 01/12/19).

INDEX